SUPERVISORY MANAGEMENT:
TOOLS AND TECHNIQUES

The West Series in Management

Consulting Editors:
Don Hellriegel
and
John W. Slocum, Jr.

SUPERVISORY MANAGEMENT: TOOLS AND TECHNIQUES

Edited by M. Gene Newport

WEST PUBLISHING CO.
St. Paul • New York • Boston
Los Angeles • San Francisco

COPYRIGHT © 1976 BY WEST PUBLISHING CO.

All rights reserved
Printed in the United States of America

Library of Congress Cataloging in Publication Data

Main entry under title:

    Supervisory management.

    Includes index.

    1. Supervision of employees—Addresses, essays,
lectures. I. Newport, Marvin Gene.
HF5549.S95   658.3'02   76-10379
ISBN 0-8299-0116-7

60,705

Preface

DURING World War II, supervisors were called on to play a critical role in maintaining a "butter and guns" economy. Since many were unprepared to meet the pressures and responsibilities of supervisory positions, concentrated training programs were developed to increase their human and technical skills. These programs, coupled with the motivation to launch a successful war effort, helped supervisors meet the challenges of the times. In general, some "muddled" through, others performed satisfactorily, and many were recognized for outstanding performance.

A shortage of managers following World War II caused the emphasis on development and training to shift to upper and middle management ranks. In the process, supervisory training programs were continued, but received less attention relative to the importance attached to developing people at other levels of management. Unfortunately, this trend was to continue for approximately twenty years. During the same period of time, union growth, technological advancements, legislation, the addition of staff groups, and other changes combined to increase the responsibilities of the supervisor's job. Yet, with few exceptions, the organizational status and authority granted to supervisors did not keep pace with their responsibilities.

Happily, the last ten years have seen a renewed interest in supervisory education and development. Many colleges and universities now offer courses and programs specifically designed to prepare people for supervisory positions. Without question, programs originally developed around the needs of persons entering the middle management ranks are inadequate for this purpose. Similarly, materials that focus on the foreman's position in manufacturing enterprises are inappropriate, since they overlook the supervisory role in hospitals, governmental agencies, retail stores, utilities, and a host of other nonmanufacturing organizations.

At present, more organizations are also developing in-house training programs to help supervisors meet their total responsibilities. Programs that deal exclusively with technical responsibilities are still important, but they are no longer adequate by themselves. Supervisors need more knowledge and skill in planning, organizing, coordinating, and controlling. They must be able to motivate, communicate, and lead. They need current knowledge and practical guidelines to meet their responsibilities in labor relations and affirmative action. Finally, they must understand their role as members of the management team and must see the value of continued personal development.

Seventeen authors have combined their teaching, consulting, and managerial experience to satisfy the major need outlined above: the need for a current, readable, and practical book written exclusively for the supervisors of today and tomorrow. The result is this book, which can be used in various settings: Credit or noncredit courses offered by colleges and universities; special seminars and conferences; personal development programs; or in-house programs conducted by all types of organizations.

To students, the book provides an important first exposure to the nature of supervision and management. To practicing supervisors, it offers concepts and practical guidelines essential to an understanding and satisfaction of job responsibilities. In either case, the readers' knowledge will be updated, analytical skills will be sharpened, and attitudes will be evaluated.

Editing this book has been a joy and privilege. The authors were conscientious in meeting deadlines, accepting editorial suggestions, and sharing their time. All are true professionals in their respective fields and I extend my sincere thanks to each of them. In addition, I thank my wife, Sandy, and our children for their support of my efforts. Finally, Mrs. Jan Tidwell deserves special recognition for her patience and skill in typing the final manuscript.

M. G. N.
Birmingham, Alabama
April, 1976

Contents

The Supervisory Role

*Keith Davis**

Chapter	1. *To provide an understanding of the supervisory role.*
Objectives	2. *To show that supervision can be taught and learned.*
	3. *To clarify the supervisor's unique organizational location.*
	4. *To emphasize the key role of supervision in organizations.*
	5. *To show the importance of technical, human, and conceptual skills in supervision.*
	6. *To stress the importance of two-way communication.*
	7. *To compare positive leadership with negative leadership.*
	8. *To discuss the wide variety of roles performed by supervision.*

PORTER VANCE is a supervisor in an office. The day started in a typical way. Three employees came to work late, and one employee called in sick. At 10:00 A.M. the photocopying machine broke down, causing the office to be late on a report that was due that afternoon. Vance walked toward the desk of one of his key employees to discuss what could be done about the late report. Vance was not sure how to approach this employee, because for the last two or three weeks the employee had been in an unpleasant mood. Vance did not know whether the cause was something he, Vance, had done, a problem at home, or something else, but he was worried because two or three near arguments with the employee had developed recently. As Vance approached, the employee turned aside from a pile of work and said in a loud, gruff voice, "Get off my back. I have enough problems already."

*Keith Davis is Professor of Management, College of Business Administration, Arizona State University.

The experiences of Porter Vance are typical, because supervisors are on the front lines of every organization. They are the ones who help solve daily operating problems. Their jobs are interesting ones filled with challenges and feelings of accomplishment, but also with problems and disappointments.

Understanding the Supervisor's Role
What Is a Supervisor?

Supervision may occur at various levels of an organization, but normally on the management level nearest to the workers. Viewed in this way, *supervisors are management representatives who direct the work of operating employees.* They perform management activities such as planning, organizing, staffing, directing, and controlling. Almost without exception they operate face to face with their people to accomplish the work that needs to be done. They are where the action is, surrounded by both problems and opportunities. If an organization's work is to be done at all, they are the ones directly involved in getting it done. Their world is one of action, not idle talk or theory.

The Supervisor's Unique Organizational Location

It is sometimes assumed that supervisors occupy a position like that of other members of management, but actually their position is somewhat different, as illustrated by the following chain of command in an organization. The president manages a top management family of vice presidents. The vice presidents manage a middle-management family, and department heads have a management family consisting of supervisors. The supervisors, on the other hand, head a nonmanagement family of workers. Therefore, they must work on a daily basis with managers above them and nonmanagers below them in the organization.

The supervisory job is further complicated, because there often is a union representing employees. Consequently, a supervisor must understand the union's way of life, its leaders, and how to talk with them. In addition there are personnel representatives, engineers, inspectors, and others that supervisors must deal with on a weekly or daily basis. Together, all of these individuals and groups make a complex situation that is difficult to supervise. As the saying goes, supervisors must wear many different hats as they talk with these various groups. Each has a different outlook and way of thinking, so supervisors need to vary their approaches to fit such differences.

Supervisors Are Made, Not Born

Many years ago we thought that supervisors needed to be "natural-born leaders." Unless people were born with the right set of personal characteristics, there was little chance for them to be successful supervisors. Potential supervisors were supposed to have strength of character, dominance, and other apparently desirable personal traits. The trait approach sounded reasonable in theory, but the problem was that it did not prove effective in practice. Successful supervisors exhibited a wide variety of personal traits, so it was impossible to identify any one or two traits that caused effective supervision.

We finally came to realize that success comes to supervisors not because of certain personal traits, but because of certain behavior that is appropriate in supervisory situations. Behavior is the key to supervision, not traits. This means that supervisors are made, not born. Supervision can be taught and learned, so there are plentiful opportunities for many types of people to become successful supervisors. This understanding resulted in an increase in supervisory training programs and improvements in the quality of supervision as supervisors learned more about their role. In short, training combined with on-the-line experience was found to provide the very best supervisory development.

Investment in Human Resources

The supervisor's principal responsibility is to assure that the organization's investment in human, technical, and economic resources is properly used. Supervisors, therefore, are the ones who help the organization gain a return on its investments. This responsibility applies whether the organization is profit making or not, because all organizations seek high outputs in relation to inputs. To do otherwise would be to waste society's resources, and in these times of scarce resources, waste is not acceptable.

The supervisor's responsibility for investments in human resources is particularly important. Engineers can determine how to use an organization's technical equipment, and economists can determine uses for economic resources. However, supervisors can make the most effective use of human resources, because they are the ones in direct, daily contact with employees.

Human resources also have a special characteristic. When properly nurtured, people can grow and develop to become more effective and more capable. It is a primary responsibility of supervisors to help their people grow so that they can become more capable persons. In this manner everyone benefits. Employee growth helps the organization, the employees, the society in which we live, and the supervisor. The organization is helped, because employees are able through growth to perform better work. The employees benefit, because they are more fulfilled as persons and can advance in the organization. Society especially benefits because better people make a better society. Finally, supervisors benefit because their employees are doing better work and are more satisfied with their jobs. As a result, human growth is perhaps the most beneficial of all the conditions that supervisors influence.

Key Persons in the Organizational System

Supervisors are key persons in the organizational system. They represent management to the workers, and they also represent workers to management. Workers know management primarily through their supervisors. Likewise, higher management knows the workers primarily through supervisors. They are an essential element, because they sit astride the chains of authority and communication, and can block almost anything going upward or downward. They make decisions, control work, communicate, lead, and generally play an active part in accomplishing organizational objectives.

Supervisors also bear major pressures of all types, both upward and downward. Workers communicate their expectations to supervisors and expect these ideas to move upward in the system, so that they can get more of what they want. Customers also bring pressures on supervisors for better products and services. In a downward direction, management has specific goals that it wants accomplished, and it brings substantial pressure to see that work is done as planned. Management has cost standards, legal restrictions, and other controls that put pressures on supervisors. They also receive pressure from various staff groups who help apply management standards. The result is that supervisors are placed under considerable stress unless they have learned to plan and organize effectively.

A Supportive Role

Essentially, supervisors perform a supportive role for their people. They try to supply the psychological, technical, and economic support necessary to get the job done. By providing such support, supervisors make the workers' jobs easier, more satisfying, and more effective. If better training is needed, supervisors help the employees get it. If more security is needed, supervisors try to provide it. They move right down the list of employees' job needs, trying to support all of them. As such, the supportive role is a substantial reversal of the old-fashioned role in which supervisors told employees what to do and they meekly followed. Instead, supportive behavior helps develop cooperation and teamwork in the organization, and supervisors are seen as useful and desirable members of the team because they help groups reach their work goals.

Psychological support for one's group is especially important. Supervisors can provide psychological support because of their face-to-face contact with employees and their control of the immediate work situation. Psychological support is provided through building job satisfaction, improving motivation, providing security for employees, and other similar actions. Such actions require supervisors who are willing to listen to their employees and learn their needs.

Keystone in the Organizational Arch

Perhaps the concept that best represents the supervisory role as one bearing pressures from both sides is that portraying supervisors as the keystone in the organizational arch. An arch is held together by the keystone that connects both sides and makes it possible for each to perform effectively. The keystone takes the pressure from both sides and uses that pressure to build a stronger arch. The sides can be held together only by the keystone, which strengthens, not weakens, the arch. This keystone position is the important role of supervisors in all organizations.

A related way of viewing the supervisor is as a linking pin connecting workers with the larger organization so that it may operate as a single entity. If it were not for this linking pin, the organization would be in shambles. Parts would be separated and heading off in their own directions. There would be no unity toward common objectives. From these illustrations it is evident that supervisors are crucial links in organizational systems.

Characteristics of the Supervisory Role

The supervisory role includes a large number of different activities. Supervisors need to have the flexibility and versatility to perform all of these activities, and most of them must be performed well if supervisors are to be effective. We will now discuss various characteristics of the supervisory role, and most of them will be developed further in subsequent chapters.

Leader

Supervisors are first of all leaders. This is their central role. The organization depends upon them to exercise face-to-face leadership in the front lines. Leadership expands and releases the potential that is in people. It creates motivated, willing followers. Top management and staff people can make beautiful plans outlining what should be done, but plans cannot succeed until supervisory leadership at the point of performance releases the powers in people. Thus, leadership is the ultimate act that brings to success all of the potential in an organization and its people.

Leaders need a balanced combination of three types of skills in order to perform effectively. The three are technical, human, and conceptual skills. Technical skill refers to a person's knowledge about various types of equipment and methods. Examples are skills learned by toolmakers, accountants, engineers, and nurses. At the supervisory level technical skill is not as important as it is at the operating level, but supervisors do need some skill of this type in order to be able to communicate with their people and understand their problems. Supervisors who are know-nothings about the technical activities of their departments will have difficulty getting their jobs done.

The leadership role of supervisors particularly requires human skill. It is the ability to interact effectively with people and to build teamwork, and no organization can do without it. Without human skill a team cannot be built, and people cannot be motivated. All supervisors who intend to hold their jobs must be able to work effectively with people.

Finally, supervisors need conceptual skill, because they deal with plans, complex relationships, and other abstractions. They need to be able to relate items A, B, and C in some reasonable pattern in order to understand what is happening in their department. Conceptual skill deals with ideas, human skill with people, and technical skill with things.

Decision Maker

Decision making requires the choice of one alternative compared with another, and it is the ever-present stock in trade that supervisors use day after day. Decision making requires a special type of courage. It is easy to study problems once and then to study them again, but it takes courage to decide what to do about them. Decisions require one to take responsibility and to initiate action. These actions invoke risk, because the decision could be wrong, thereby costing the organization money, discouraging employees, or driving away customers.

For supervisors the goal is not to be right all of the time, because that is impossible. A more modest and realistic goal is to be right most of the time, and that is the level of competence that higher management expects of supervisors. An even more important goal is to improve the percentage of right decisions as one gains more supervisory experience. Growth in competence occurs when a supervisor can move from 90 percent right decisions to 92 percent next year and perhaps 93 percent the year after that.

As a matter of fact, the term "right decisions" is somewhat inaccurate to describe what actually happens with supervisory decisions. In real situations, one can differentiate "right" decisions into "good" and "better" decisions.

Planner

Consider the situation of a supervisor by the name of Mabel Morris. Morris is a whiz with people, and she is an expert in the technical side of her office operation. She is a hard worker, arriving before her employees and leaving after they have departed for the day. By many standards Morris is an effective supervisor. Unfortunately, there is one problem, a small item but a significant one in any supervisor's collection of skills. Morris is a poor planner, or perhaps more accurately, she does not plan at all. Her employees try to make up for her deficiencies because they like her, but they cannot do the whole job. The result is that Morris's department is constantly out of schedule with other departments, because it cannot meet its commitments on time. The people in her department are not sure who should do what, or when they should do it. The situation generally is one of confusion, because Morris does not plan.

Planning is essential for total supervisory success. If it is not done well, then other activities are likely to be deficient because they depend upon accurate planning. Planning is something distinctly different from forecasting. The act of forecasting requires a prediction of the future, but planning organizes knowledge and resources to cause the future. For example, I forecast the weather, and then I plan a hike into the woods based on my forecast of the weather. The future action is based on the plan. Similarly, a supervisor forecasts work requirements for the next week and then plans how the department will get the work done.

A key supervisory planning activity is to set meaningful goals for subordinates. Group members need to feel that they have something worthwhile to do. Without goals, people go off in different directions and begin to lose sight of what the organization is trying to accomplish. The difficulty will continue as long as there is no common understanding of the goals involved.

Organizer

Modern work environments are complex. Organization is the grand strategy to bring order out of chaos when groups work together. Organizing sets the relationships between people, work, and resources. The necessity of organizing—and the havoc of disorganization—are illustrated by disorganizing a short sentence "riirggnagesnotztlsuse." In this form it is nonsense. The parts are not in any meaningful relationship, in the same way that a department can be a jumble of people and resources when it is disorganized. If we reorganize the sentence somewhat, it is workable, but difficult: "organizinggetsresults." By the slight change of converting to a capital "O" and adding two spaces, we achieve a useful, organized sentence: "Organizing gets results."

It is rather easy to see that organizing achieves a degree of order in work situations, but there is another part of organizing not so evident. Effective organizing is a useful way to bring security and psychological support to one's employees. It does so by helping employees know where they stand and to whom they should go for assistance. When people feel that the organization is set up to serve their job needs, then they tend to feel psychologically supported.

A key part of the organizing job is delegating work to people. When employees accept a delegation, they then become their supervisor's "delegate" or representative. If they do not accept, then delegation has been merely attempted, so delegation also requires behavioral skills to encourage people to accept the responsibilities that are delegated to them. The great advantage of delegation is that it permits supervisors to extend their influence beyond the limits of their own personal time, energy, and knowledge.

Inadequate delegation is a primary cause of supervisory failure. Some supervisors feel that delegation is giving away something, so they psychologically cannot bring themselves to do it for fear that it will weaken them. Others are such perfectionists that they have no confidence in letting others do work for which they are responsible. However, all supervisors need to realize that delegation is the act that makes supervision possible. If there is no delegation to others, there is no one to be supervised.

Sometimes supervisors have to learn the hard way that delegation is a desirable activity. One supervisor had difficulty delegating special reports to his people. He always felt that he could do a better job than they could, so he would not risk delegating a report to them. On one occasion he decided to prove to himself that he could not depend on others to prepare good reports. He assigned a special report to one of his women clerks, but he also worked privately at night on the same report. In this manner he could compare his report with hers to show that he could do better reports than his employees. When her report was received, he had to admit to himself that it was a better report. Having proved his point—but in the opposite of his expectations—he became more free with delegation in the future.

Motivator

An important part of the supervisory job that nearly all supervisors recognize is that of motivator. Motivation is concerned with the human side of supervision rather than the technical side. The basic strategy is to understand peoples' needs and then to relate those needs to the tasks that the organization is trying to accomplish.

The importance of relating human needs to motivational problems is illustrated by a comparison of machine malfunction and operator malfunction. When a machine malfunctions, people recognize that it needs something. Assume that a machine will not grind a piece of metal to a close enough tolerance. Perhaps it needs oil. Or maybe a nut is loose. First the operator tries to find the trouble. Then the supervisor is called. Finally a maintenance mechanic is called, or an engineer, and so on until the cause of the problem is found and the machine is put back into working order. All of the people who tried to find the cause of the machine breakdown did so (or should have done so) in an analytical manner based upon their knowledge of the machine's operations and needs. It would have been wasteful to begin haphazardly to tighten nuts and oil gears hoping that the trouble would be corrected. Such action might aggravate the malfunction.

Now suppose that the machine operator malfunctions. Perhaps the operator is not doing an adequate quality of work. The supervisor may feel like taking immediate action without analyzing the situation, but this approach would be no better than haphazard machine repair. Like the machine, the operator is malfunctioning because of particular needs. In the illustration just given, perhaps the operator lacks training, or has a conflict with another worker that is upsetting the operator psychologically. When the appropriate problem can be found and corrected, the operator is likely to perform satisfactory work.

Coordinator and Controller

It is necessary for supervisors to coordinate and control the complex environment of their departments. Can you imagine, for example, a football play that is not coordinated? People move in the wrong directions or they are in certain places at the wrong times, or both. The result is confusion and a broken play that often causes a loss for the team. The same situation exists with a work environment. The supervisor plays the role of quarterback and is responsible for assuring that all parts of the organization are working together smoothly.

Control and coordination are closely related to planning, because without plans coordination and control are almost impossible. Consider again the members of a football team. They spend many hours planning their different plays, and then additional hours in practice to be sure that they know how to carry out the plans. Without plans the team would be no more effective than the children's teams that develop spontaneously on playgrounds. They are fun, but they cannot compete with well-planned and coordinated teams. The same situation exists in a supervisor's department. If the supervisor is to be effective, it is essential to develop coordination and control based on sound plans.

Communicator

The importance of communication is made evident by imagining a situation in which supervisors are unable to communicate with their people in any way. The result would be a complete loss of the organization's ability to function. Work could not be done, because people would not know what was needed. Similarly, supervisors would not know what to do, because they would have no feedback from the work situation. The organization would be brought to a complete standstill. Organizations do not face this extreme condition, but many organizations do have such poor communication that there is interference with work performance.

Supervisory plans and ideas, no matter how outstanding they are, become useless unless they can be communicated to employees. Everything that a supervisor does eventually must pass through the bottleneck of communication if it is to reach those involved. Leadership, decision making, planning, organizing, motivating, and all the other supervisory activities require communication before they can take effect. Day-after-day, minute-after-minute, supervisors face a necessity to develop sound communication.

Effective supervisory communication needs to be two-way, upward as well as downward in the organization. The supervisor needs to be an effective receiver of messages as well as sender of them. As a matter of fact, studies show that supervisors usually spend even more of their time listening (receiving inputs) than they do talking (issuing outputs). Consider the process of making a decision. The quality of decisions will depend on the quality of information that supervisors have, and this information is secured by improving inputs from all parts of the organization. Unless supervisors learn from their employees the needs that exist at the work place, the supervisors cannot make effective decisions. Similarly, unless supervisors learn what higher management wants done, they cannot make effective decisions. The only way that supervisors can prepare themselves for decision making is to improve their inputs through listening to those both above and below them.

Supervisors are doubly responsible for building communication. First, they are responsible for developing their own proficient communication, as has been discussed. Second, they are responsible for encouraging their subordinates to be effective communicators among themselves and upward to the supervisor and others. In the successful department both the employees and the supervisor are effective communicators. They make up a single team and a single understanding unit that must know what is happening in order to get their jobs done.

From this discussion it is evident that supervisory communication has two broad purposes. First, it provides people the information and understanding they need to do their jobs. But just being able to work together is not enough. People also need suitable attitudes and motivation for working as a team; therefore, the second purpose of supervisory communication is to provide the attitudes for motivation, cooperation, teamwork, and job satisfaction. The accomplishment of both communication goals is required before a supervisor can be successful.

Reward Administrator

Another important supervisory activity is that of reward administrator. Supervisors acting as representatives of management provide employees with a proper mix of the rewards available in the organization. There are financial rewards as well as psychological-social ones, such as recognition. Even financial rewards often have overtones of psychological and social value. For example, a raise in pay provides more money, but it also may provide an employee with more status or a greater feeling of accomplishment. Thus, it is impossible for supervisors to separate completely the financial value and the psychological value of rewards.

Supervisors always are interested in getting maximum results from their budget, so they sometimes ask, "Which is more important to employees, financial rewards or psychological-social rewards?" This question is meaningless, because both are important. A more realistic question is how to integrate the two types of rewards so that employees have an effective mix of both.

Supervisors actually administer both rewards and punishments. If a supervisor emphasizes rewards, either financial or psychological-social, then the supervisor is practicing positive leadership. If penalties are emphasized, then the supervisor is applying negative leadership. Most supervisors apply some of both, but the approach that tends to dominate sets the climate in a department.

Negative approaches, such as threats and penalties, do accomplish acceptable performance in many situations, but their human costs are so high that they are not a wise alternative. Negative supervisors act domineering and superior with people. To get work done they hold over their personnel such penalties as loss of job, reprimand in the presence of others, and abusive communications. They display authority with the false assumption that it frightens employees into productivity. These people are really bosses more than supervisors.

Positive supervisors offer encouragement to employees. They give employees motivation to come to work in the morning, because the work is rewarding and satisfying to them. Some of the most important rewards do not cost any budget anything. One of these is recognition. Studies show that workers seek and appreciate it. It is a regular source of feelings of worth and fulfillment. When it is offered genuinely, based on actual achievements, it can be a powerful motivator. Another reward that should not cost any budget is a genuine interest in employees as persons. Employees want to know that they are considered important by supervisors, that supervisors do care, and that supervisors are interested in their problems.

Even the most competent supervisor will at times fall back upon negative approaches, because positive approaches are not always available. However, the historical trend is clearly toward more and more positive approaches to supervision.

Counselor

Another supervisory activity is the counseling of employees. Counseling has the objective of reducing or removing emotional problems that employees have. As people work together, frictions and problems naturally develop, and it is a supervisory responsibility to reduce these difficulties through counseling. No more complex unit exists than a human being; therefore, it is impossible for a person to be in optimum emotional balance all of the time.

Supervisors need to understand that emotional upsets are not necessarily undesirable or "wrong." Nature gave people their emotions, and sometimes it is more disastrous to suppress an emotion such as anger than to go ahead and express it. But emotional upsets can cause workers to do things that are harmful to their own interests as well as those of the organization. For example, one employee may quit an organization because of some trifling conflict that has been exaggerated until it seems large. In such instances, supervisory counseling may be helpful in retaining employees, thereby helping them as well as the organization. The important point is to channel human emotions along constructive lines rather than destructive ones. Emotions cannot be ignored with the hope that they will go away. They require supervisory efforts just like other parts of the supervisor's job.

When supervisors are working with emotional problems, they are not necessarily seeking the 90–95 percent success rate that is often required in other supervisory actions, such as living within the budget. If only 20 or 25 percent of the employees can be helped, then that is 20 or 25 percent more than would have been helped without counseling, so success has been achieved. However, emotional problems are extremely complex, and supervisors should not expect that they can be easily solved. In many instances, therefore, supervisors will send employees to others such as personnel specialists for counseling.

Trainer

Another activity of the supervisory role is training. Often this activity consumes a substantial portion of a supervisor's time. Training is rewarding both to the supervisor and to employees. If supervisors can develop competent, well-trained employees, then their jobs become easier, because employees can do their work without constant supervision. Employees also are helped. Their self-image and feeling of accomplishment are improved. By becoming better trained they also are more likely to take pride in performing high-quality work. Eventually, training should help them gain wage increases and promotions, because of their added qualifications.

Change Agent

A significant activity of supervisors is to administer change in their departments. With the fast technological and social progress that is being achieved in the world, change has become a necessary way of life in most organizations. As a representative of management at the work place, supervisors are in the center of the many difficulties caused by change. They need to understand change and how it affects people and organizations. Essentially, their objective is to introduce change with a minimum of upset and in such a way that the organization benefits in the long run. As the saying goes, "Reduce the harm and expand the benefit."

Group participation is an effective way to build support for change. Participation helps employees become involved so that they better understand the change, and it increases their commitment to the change. It assures them that management is not trying to put something over on them by deciding on a change and then imposing it by what is derisively called the "bulldozer" method of change. One special benefit of participation is that it may improve a proposed change by adding contributions from those who will work under it. Participation helps to amend poor plans, and almost always it broadens the supervisor's understanding about the change.

Employee resistance to change is not necessarily bad. In some instances resistance uncovers difficulties connected with the change that were not originally evident to the supervisor. Another benefit is that resistance may cause the supervisor to examine more carefully the negative side effects that accompany change, in the same way that they accompany powerful antibiotic drugs. In other instances resistance causes supervisors to clarify their reasons for introducing change and to define more precisely the desirable results that they expect from change. Resistance also may identify pockets of low job satisfaction and poor motivation in the organization, so that supervisors can take corrective action. Resistance can pinpoint weaknesses in communication, because they frequently arise from inadequate communication about change. And finally, resistance to change can cause supervisors to give more attention to building effective human relations in their departments, because they see that it is necessary to reduce resistance to change.

Other Activities

Our discussion certainly has not covered all of the activities that make up the supervisory job, but it has described some of the primary ones. There are others, such as handling grievances, maintaining discipline, providing suggestions for improvements, and creative thinking. The important point is that supervisors have a multitude of different duties requiring a wide variety of skills. Supervision is not an activity of one, two, or three skills, but of many skills often quite different from one another. It requires persons who are versatile and capable of understanding complex relationships. They are like jugglers, having to keep many events going at the same time as they work back and forth from one to the other.

A Favorable Organizational Climate

We can sum up the supervisory role by saying that most of what supervisors do is covered by the idea of building a favorable climate for job performance and for the personal growth and satisfaction of employees. The supervisory role exists to carry out organizational objectives, but also to accomplish objectives in such a way that people are rewarded.

A sound climate is a long-run proposition. Supervisors need to take an assets approach to climate, meaning that they take the long-run view of climate as an organizational asset. Unwise supervision, such as threatening and putting pressure on people, may temporarily increase production, but it may so alter the organizational climate that the department is in worse condition eventually. The far more effective way is to build a positive climate favorable to performance and personal growth in the beginning.

Summary

Supervisors are management representatives who direct the work of operating employees. Their world is one of action, not theory. They are made, not born, meaning that supervisory ability results from training and experience rather than inherited traits. Their principal responsibility is to assure that the organization's investment in human, technical, and economic resources is properly used. They do this by building an organizational climate that encourages production and employee growth. An effective climate is built by supervisors performing a supportive role for their people.

The supervisory role may be compared with the keystone in an arch. It absorbs the pressures from both sides of the organization, using them to build a stronger organization. In this way supervisors become linking pins between management and employees. The characteristics of this role require performance of a wide variety of duties, such as leader, decision maker, organizer, motivator, coordinator and controller, communicator, reward administrator, counselor, trainer, change agent, and others.

Questions for Discussion

1. Two machine shop supervisors were having lunch together, and one of them commented, "I've always found that the best way to handle people is to get tough with them. Keep them scared. Threaten them. If they are frightened that they will lose their job, they will work hard." You are the other supervisor. How would you respond?

2. A younger supervisor had an opportunity to attend a training program on "Effective Supervision," and he went to an older supervisor for advice about whether he should take the course. The older supervisor commented, "I suppose it won't hurt you, but it's not going to do you any good. Supervision is learned by experience." What do you think of the older supervisor's remarks?

3. Martha Mendoza was thinking about seeking a promotion to supervisor in her organization. She asked a fellow employee about this idea,

and her employee friend replied, "I wouldn't do it. You'll be just another worker with a glorified title. You'll be a pencil pusher and paper shuffler all day long, taking orders from everybody and having less freedom than we have now." What do you think about the comments of Mendoza's friend?

4. Consider the case of Porter Vance at the beginning of this chapter. If you were Vance, how would you respond to your employee?

5. Explain the idea of the supervisor as keystone in the organizational arch.

6. Distinguish between technical, human, and conceptual skills for supervisors.

7. It is said, "Supervisors are doubly responsible for building communication." What does that mean?

8. Compare positive and negative leadership.

Case Incidents

1. George Plencner, supervisor in the records office, had an employee with a miserable tardiness record. The employee had been tardy seven times in the preceding month. Plencner told the employee that if he did not achieve a better record, he might be disciplined, but the poor record continued.

Plencner's fellow supervisors with whom he discussed the case were in disagreement about what he should do. One said that the best approach was to give the employee three days off without pay to show him that Plencner meant what he said. Another said that Plencner should try to transfer the employee to a different job, because maybe he was bored with his present job. A third said that Plencner should show an interest in the employee and try in every way that he could to show that he really cared about the employee's problems. He should try to find what the employee's problems are and then help the employee to overcome them.

a. Comment on the proposals made. Which one is likely to be the best and why?

b. What name or term would you apply to the approach suggested by the third supervisor?

2. Marlene Kraus supervises an assembly line in a television factory. Kraus instructed one employee to go to the tool room to secure some tools. The employee replied, "I can't do that. It is not part of my job, and I am busy with my duties here." Kraus replied, "Perhaps there is some misunderstanding about what your job is. Let's sit down and talk about it."

On another occasion Kraus had an employee request the afternoon off for personal reasons, and the conversation developed as follows:

Kraus: "We can't give you time off because we have a heavy workload today."

Employee: "But I have to take off."

Kraus: "If you do leave, you are going to have a one-day suspension waiting for you tomorrow when you return. Now get back to work."

a. Which of Kraus's approaches to employees was the better one? Why?

b. In each instance what kind of leadership and reward administration did Kraus apply? Discuss.

Working With the Management Team

*Ferrel E. Underwood**

Chapter ***Objectives***	1. *To direct attention to the management-team approach as a highly useful technique.* 2. *To discuss types of management teams.* 3. *To develop an understanding of the team-management process.* 4. *To illustrate the role and requirements of supervisors as members of the management team.* 5. *To emphasize the advantages of teamwork to supervisors.*

As OUR SOCIETY depends more and more on institutions to satisfy its endless demand for goods and services, the need for dealing with the challenges created by the changing nature of organizations becomes more acute. A complicated pattern of factors makes it difficult to identify the adjustments in management approaches that are required to cope with the new order of things.

As organizations of all types struggle to adjust to the pressures of change, management often discovers that it is ill-equipped to respond with a minimum of internal tension and conflict. Thus, the top management of an organization experiencing rapid growth may suddenly find itself under an avalanche of hastily developed procedures and hurried appointments of personnel to responsible positions. At some point, however, someone finally gets around to noticing an underlying weakness that threatens to destroy the organization. Often, outside con-

*Ferrel E. Underwood is Deputy Regional Vice President-Operations, Alabama Region, State Farm Insurance Companies.

sultants are called in for assistance and the organization learns to its dismay that management theorists have been offering the same helpful advice for some time.

Without question, teamwork in management is not without critics. Some express concern that teamwork will lead to excessive conformity and further erode the principles of individual action. Additionally, the concept departs from many of the traditional principles of autocratic and classical management theory which are, unfortunately, still being followed in many institutions. In this chapter we discuss the nature of the management-team concept, its role in organizational design, and its implications so that supervisors will be able to assess its possible contributions to the achievement of both personal and organizational goals. At the same time, the discussion will clearly indicate other advantages of management teamwork, as well as the behavioral patterns that are required to make it successful.

Nature of the Management Team

As an organizational way of life, managerial teamwork is a post-World War II development; however, its roots are found in the human relations movement which began with the Hawthorne experiments conducted by F. J. Roethlisberger and William J. Dixon in 1927. For example, these researchers discovered that groups within an organization can defeat the benefits of rational organization set forth in the bureaucratic principles of Max Weber. As a result, organizations came to be described as social systems, and worker relationships were recognized as being more important to productivity than formal organizational structure.

For several years, much behavioral research has shown that participative management techniques can have a favorable effect on operating results. Although primarily concerned with relationships between the supervisor and subordinates, this research can also be applied to groups consisting entirely of management personnel. In other words, the principles of supportive roles, group decision making, and participative leadership are equally adaptable to management teams within departments or across departmental lines. For example, the head of a division divided into three sections can combine with the section chiefs to function as a team in meeting the responsibilities of the division. If the division manager is absent because of business trips, vacation, illness, temporary assignments, or other reasons, the team can carry on with little loss of effectiveness. Similarly, when the top executive of a region is unable to attend a staff meeting, the department heads can provide a continuity of operations in matters that do not require the executive's personal attention. In addition, if team management is practiced throughout an organization, supervisors among the different departments can make many important contributions.

Definition of a Management Team

A management team is a group of managerial personnel, each having the responsibility for directing a given group, as well as the authority necessary to work with members of other groups. Through the processes of delegation, communication, and leadership, along with the individual's sense of responsibility and initiative, a climate for teamwork is established and maintained. A bond of cohesiveness motivates group members to work together as a unit and continued success cultivates a team spirit that perpetuates itself. In short, the force that binds team members together is a common desire to achieve organizational and personal goals. Petty jealousies are laid to rest in favor of the benefits of group interaction, which, in turn, pay individual dividends in the form of recognition from top management.

A football squad serves as an example of the management-team concept in action. It is not unusual for a major university to have a coaching staff of more than fifteen people. Each coach has specific responsibilities, and each must coordinate assignments with all other coaches. When success comes to the team in the form of consistent winning seasons, some of the coaches are invariably sought by other schools. Yet, these coaches gained their reputations primarily because of group success rather than individual accomplishments. At the same time, we should recognize that an association with winners can lead to promotions for some group members who go on to fail in their new positions. In such cases, it is often discovered that group successes covered up individual weaknesses.

Every Team Needs a Leader

The primary role of the leader is to build constructive relationships among team members, provide the cohesiveness that gives the group staying power, exercise broad visibility, maintain group spirit during change and direct members toward objectives. Without the influence of a leader, employees tend to be more concerned with their own interests and inevitably drift into behavior patterns designed to further their own individual goals. They lack the sense of oneness necessary for effective group effort and display attitudes in opposition to the principles of managerial teamwork. In short, they become islands unto themselves and resist the team efforts of other organizational members.

As indicated, a team without a leader may achieve some degree of success in the short run. Eventually, however, the lack of coordination and direction becomes such a burden that team members lose their spirit of cooperation. Or, the group may select an informal leader who may not be primarily interested in furthering organizational goals and objectives. In addition, such leaders may not have the same sense of responsibility as those who have obtained their authority through formal appointment to a position.

The leader also determines the climate in which the managerial team operates. The atmosphere may be pleasant, comfortable, relaxed, and disciplined; or, it may be full of obvious tensions and signs of boredom. The successful leader spends considerable time improving the attitudes of team members toward their work environment. The leader does this by striving to create conditions that motivate members of the managerial team voluntarily to promote the welfare of the total organization as well as its individual members.

Types of Management Teams

Within any organizational system, there are various managerial teams. Supervisors find themselves with membership in two basic types of teams, each with its own behavioral patterns. Interdepartmental teams are similar to informal organizations where social relationships, authority, power, rank, status, and leadership are determined rather informally. Here, team members soon discover that social relationships are established not by formal authority, but by personal feelings and natural impulses. The second type of managerial team is the intradepartmental team where all functions, authority, and responsibilities are more clearly defined. Consequently, life in an intradepartmental team is more rigid and confining, because its patterns of behavior are structured to achieve efficiency and effectiveness. To illustrate, the following types of teams are found in a large service organization.

Total Office Management.   Here, all management personnel in the office compose an informal management team. Five levels of authority are represented, spread among four line departments and five staff functions. All department and staff heads report to a top executive, and the combined total of all groups is about seventy-five. Interviews with management personnel indicated a belief that the organization uses the team approach in carrying out its management functions. The organizational structure was considered to be clearly defined; a unity of purpose was present; and the level of cooperation was high. Most of the supervisors also felt a moral or ethical obligation to their colleagues in other departments and readily acknowledged the advantages of working together rather than separately.

Staff Team. The top formal team, excluding the three members of the Executive Office, is composed of all line and staff heads. The staff team is the main advisory body to the vice president on policy matters and is the point where all organizational groups within the office come together in the interests of the region and total company. Consequently, this team is extremely important, since the effectiveness of all top management decisions and policies depends on the attitudes and skills of these team members. For example, forced compliance can produce differences between attitudes and behavior, thereby diluting the intent of some messages. On the other hand, voluntary cooperation enhances the flow of communication that is so important to group performance.

Division Team. The operating division is led by a division manager with a section head in charge of each of three sections. The sections are further divided into units with each unit under the direction of a first-line supervisor. The manager, three section heads, and first line supervisors compose a formal management team responsible for technical, human, and conceptual contributions to divisional, regional, and company performance.

Section Team. Section heads and unit supervisors make up teams dedicated to carrying out the responsibilities of their respective sections. These teams are actually subgroups of the division team and, therefore, must work as teams by themselves in addition to being a part of the division team. Members of these section teams are in the unique position of being closest to the workers while also functioning as part of the total management group.

Framework of the Managerial Team

Conceptually, a management team must be highly sensitive to the increasing complexities of organizational life. Social, technological, economic, and political forces bring about change so quickly that reaction time for the team is often uncomfortably short. Twenty-five years ago, the American university was a comparatively simple operation, but a proliferation of activities has made life so complicated for academic administrators that reference to the "old university" and the "new university" is now quite common. As such fragmentation continues, the task of managing an academic institution grows more and more difficult. Many business organizations have now evolved from one-man leadership into global conglomerates that almost defy description. In these and other situations, management teamwork can be a useful technique for restoring the equilibrium that has been disturbed by growth and change. However, such teamwork does not happen by accident. Its building blocks are rooted in behavioral patterns that depart from the traditional principles of individualistic behavior.

Almost every organizational policy or philosophy must have top management support and team management is no exception. The management style must be open and participative, thereby demonstrating willingness to share organizational leadership and decision making. The management personnel of an organization normally will behave in direct correlation to the examples set by top executives. Therefore, top executives must show by personal example that they support the management-team concept. Personal differences may exist, but must be controlled outside the conference room. When the executives emerge from behind closed doors after having aired their differences, teamwork must go into action. If there is a lack of coordination and communication in the executive office, there will be disorder at all levels of management. As a result, the only force to bind individuals together will be their criticism of top management.

Knowledge of Company Policies and Goals

There is nothing more frustrating to team effort than insufficient knowledge about what the team is trying to accomplish. How can team members promote an affirmative action program if they do not know company policy on the subject? How can they improve productivity if they do not have the benefit of current policy statements to guide their actions? How can they live up to expectations if they do not know what is expected from them and their groups? Without such knowledge, supervisors operate in a vacuum. Similarly, unless they are able to see the "big picture," their contributions to team efforts are likely to be minimal.

Generally, there are several reasons why supervisors or other team members might not have all the information they need. First, there is the old problem of communication. When one considers the differences in knowledge, experience, attitudes, and cultural backgrounds that exist in groups, it is not surprising that communications barriers arise. Secondly, there may be a misguided sense of secrecy throughout the organization. Admittedly, some firms do have to be careful about information in their written communications. However, many "confidential" documents do not deserve to be labeled as such. Of course, there are other reasons for a lack of information among team members, but these suffice to illustrate the problem. Thus, if the full potential of the management team is to be realized, good communication is essential.

Common Purpose

Once supervisors are confident that top executives support and practice team management, and once they are armed with the necessary information, they are in a position to make a commitment. Thus, service teams must know that sales are expected to reach a certain level in order to produce a certain income. From this information, a division plan can be developed to maximize the team's contribution to the achievement of company goals. Expense ratios can be calculated, manpower requirements can be determined, training needs can be anticipated, and adjustments can be made to maintain the proper coordination with all other components of the system.

Being a member of a successful team is a very rewarding experience for most supervisors, especially if their total commitment has influenced the team's performance. Our previous example of an athletic team illustrates several factors involved in the team efforts of all organizations. The objective is to win. Although the criteria for determining whether victory has been achieved may differ, the same behavior emerges after victory. In athletic contests the numerical score provides the decision. Interviewing players after a victory of special significance usually elicits comments such as, "It was a team effort," "We were all committed to the same purpose," or "We had it all together today." In short, commitment to a common purpose can produce a team effort that is greater than the sum of each individual's contribution.

The Capacities of Team Members

There is no such thing as a permanent winning team in the middle management group of any organization. Internal and external changes take their toll over a period of time, requiring a constant search for the proper management mix for an effective team. Just being a member of an organization is challenge enough for many people, if we accept the thesis that a natural conflict exists between man and organization. Then, by asking people to be members of another group within the organization, we further complicate the behavioral aspects of team membership. Thus, one of the aims of the management-team concept is to convert potential conflict into a coordinated effort.

For the unfortunate supervisors who have been appointed to their positions without the necessary qualifications, organizational teamwork is a succession of miseries. If they lack the desire to manage others, and take the job for reasons of prestige and pay, they will have problems. If they are short on the analytical skills needed to diagnose problems, they will probably fail to meet their teamwork responsibilities. If they lack the ability to communicate downward, upward, or laterally, team effectiveness will be seriously affected. Like the proverbial chain, a management team is only as strong as its weakest member. Consequently, the leader of the team must have a penetrating insight into the complexities of managerial behavior if the weaker links are to be spotted and replaced for the sake of organizational effectiveness.

Team-Management Processes

It is necessary to recall that in fairly large organizations there are several management teams functioning simultaneously. Since no group operates in a vacuum, but as an integral part of the entire system, there must be a set of processes that link the groups. Although there are several processes vital to creating and maintaining a network of management teams, communication and delegation are vital.

Communication

Hardly a day goes by in any organization without some reference to the quality of communication, much of which is poor. "A breakdown in communications" is a phrase that has been used to rationalize many blunders in our society. The expression has almost become a rationale for incompetent performance and is supposed to soothe feelings and make everything right again. Although management groups continue to strive for a good communication record, there are certain social, educational, and technological forces at work that always serve to retard progress in this area.

For members of the management team, communication takes place under a variety of circumstances. Supervisors must communicate effectively with other team members in one-to-one situations as well as in group settings. They must understand what others are saying and must be able to get their points across to team members. Without good communication, no behavior will be modified, no change will be effected, and no goals will be achieved. In this respect, communication either links groups together in order to achieve a central purpose, or it fragments teams into individual units with each pursuing its own objectives.

Delegation

Without delegation, organizational effectiveness can be seriously retarded. Effective delegation is teamwork in action, but it cannot be left to chance. It happens by design. Attitudes toward delegation must be examined to determine individual feelings towards this important managerial technique. Among management personnel who view the act of delegation with disfavor, there will generally be found fears of inadequacy, defensiveness, jealousy, ignorance, or other undesirable traits. If the chief executive fails to delegate, the team will have static tendencies and its energy will remain dormant. In other words, a failure to delegate shows a lack of confidence in subordinates and, therefore, breeds a lack of confidence among team members.

It is one thing to voice support of delegation, but quite another to be a genuine practitioner. One common mistake made by all managers is that of delegating insignificant decisions while retaining those in which the consequences of error are greater. In this event the manager appears to lack confidence in team members while seeking the glory for decisions that have a high probability of success.

Another mistake in delegation is inconsistency. The team leader who moves back and forth between delegation and autocracy keeps the management group off balance and renders it ineffective. Considerable uncertainty, confusion, resentment, and frustration will characterize the feelings of team members and will indicate that delegation does not fit the leader's personality. This is not to imply that the degree of delegation is rigidly fixed and inflexible. It is at best a balancing act, but a clearly defined framework is necessary. Too little delegation will usually signal a concern for personal accomplishment, while too much can cause a loss of control and competition for power.

The Role of the Supervisor

Up to this point, our discussion has presented the team-management concept as an approach to better organizational performance. There has been no intent to imply that the management team works well in all organizations. There are numerous factors involved in a determination to use or reject the concept as a useful management approach.

If the leadership style of the chief executive is not compatible with the democratic or participative nature of the team approach, the traditional one-to-one relationship will probably be most appropriate. If there is an unusually high degree of risk involved because of supervisory immaturity, youth of the organization, or some crisis that seems to call for a more centralized leadership style, team management may be undesirable.

The remainder of this chapter focuses on the role of the supervisor in an organization that finds its climate conducive to the management-team concept. In the process, we will attempt to define the different behavioral patterns and attitudes that distinguish the team concept from the individual philosophy. Finally, the advantages for the supervisor who is an effective team member will be identified and discussed.

The Supervisor's Unique Position in the Hierarchy

There are certain distinguishing features that set supervisors apart from higher levels of management. The most unusual aspect of this situation is that supervisors wear two representative hats. They are the only members of management who represent both nonmanagement and management personnel. They are the last link in the chain of command and are responsible for motivating employees to perform at the highest possible level.

There are times when supervisors are not in agreement with certain team decisions that must be implemented in the best interest of other groups of which they are not members. However, they cannot pass the buck and make bad guys out of other team members. At the same time, they cannot make their people believe that they agree with all of the decisions that have to be implemented. People must have confidence in their supervisors, believing that they will represent their nonmanagement interests to higher management. For more on these and other points, review chapter 1, "The Supervisory Role."

Attitudes toward Group Effort

Although the importance of group effort to organizational performance seems obvious, management ranks still include supervisors who are highly resistant to the team concept. Many view team membership as forced conformity that causes individuals to lose their creativity and sense of identity. Others perceive a loss of opportunities to gain recognition for personal achievement, which they claim is already a problem in many organizations. Should the majority of managers in an organization hold such attitudes, the multiplying effect of team effort will probably never be experienced.

Supervisors who prefer to function as team members exhibit an altogether different outlook and are convinced that collective action is far superior to individual participation. They see strength in unity and experience a sense of belongingness from group interaction. Individual effort is channeled into group endeavors that make tremendous contributions to organizational success as well as personal welfare.

For those supervisors to whom the team approach has appeal, there are additional considerations that need to be weighed. First, they must recognize that teamwork does not relieve them of the responsibility for directing their own work groups. They remain accountable to higher management for the results of subordinates and should always remember that they are responsible for certain duties. In other words, they are primarily leaders of their own groups, and secondarily, members of management teams. Thus, again, they wear two hats. The balance between the two is not always easy to achieve. They are constantly attempting to develop their own groups, while at the same time devoting themselves to effective membership in other management teams. In this dual role they are required to be somewhat individualistic in supporting their own groups; on the other hand, they must also participate as members of the management team.

Supervisors must also be prepared to share duties, responsibilities, accomplishments, rewards, and penalties with other team members. Often, it is difficult to determine to whom most of the credit should be awarded for favorable results. By the same token, those most responsible for poor group performance are sometimes difficult to identify. In addition, there are some activities for which no one seems to be responsible. These must often be assumed voluntarily if team management is to succeed.

Skills of Interaction

A favorable attitude toward the management team concept will not guarantee that a supervisor's behavior will be of maximum benefit to the group. Furthermore, converting knowledge into effective action poses a special problem. Good intentions generally will not overcome personality traits that interfere with normal interpersonal relationships. As one supervisor puts it, "You don't *have* to like each other, but it sure does help." This same supervisor feels that mutual respect must exist among team members and will tend to offset some minor personality irritants. More specifically, technical competence and personal integrity are certain to be high on any list of personal characteristics that promote mutual respect among team members.

Since some teams include supervisors of staff functions working in close relationship with line-management personnel, interaction skills become even more important. Teamwork cannot become a reality unless problems between line and staff are minimized. Line managers are usually proud of their objective approach to "the real world." They are inclined to be highly achievement oriented and are at their best when getting things done through people.

It is not uncommon for line managers to have a jaundiced view of staff personnel, since there has been a constant erosion of line authority in some organizations. New staff departments have been created to specialize in various problem areas created by technological, governmental, economic, and social influences. Legal services have been expanded to deal with the growing legal requirements facing most organizations. The personnel department may be the fastest growing staff function in institutions today. Specialists are needed to cope with increased union demands, equal employment opportunity pressures, expanded governmental influence, and a host of other activities.

Staff supervisors are often characterized as thinkers rather than doers. Often, they do not have to be concerned with the ultimate consequences of their advice and are prone to rely heavily on observations, theory, and research as the foundations for their ideas. They sense the resentment of line managers, whom they perceive as being primarily concerned with maintaining complete control over their own worlds. In addition, staff supervisors feel that their credentials and specialized training are not appreciated, and that their efforts are often viewed as threats to authority.

In order for teamwork to thrive in any organization, line-staff relationships must focus on common objectives. The benefits of using the advice of staff supervisors to meet normal line responsibilities should be sufficient motivation for making management teams effective. However, interaction skills are vital if this important goal is to be accomplished. Finally, an ability to perceive and adapt to changing conditions will pay big dividends to team efforts. In this respect, the supervisor who exhibits diplomacy, tact, friendliness, and an interest in others will have a very strong base from which to develop good inter-personal relations.

Systems Orientation

An organization can be viewed as a goal-seeking system of inter-dependent decision centers tied together by a communication network and prescribed authority relationships. As such, a systems orientation can have a profound effect on organizational performance by attempting to make allowances for the consequences of an act on all parts of the system. In the insurance industry, for example, sales efforts must be coordinated with claim facilities. Otherwise, the tremendous influx of claims from increased sales will tax the claim department beyond its capacity, thereby causing bad publicity for poor claim service.

What are the implications of a systems approach for supervisors? An understanding of the balancing act that is required in coping with current and long-range problems will broaden the supervisors' understanding of their jobs, challenge some of their rigid attitudes, and improve their ability to learn from experience. Although supervisors are not directly involved with such complicated issues as financial ratios, working capital needs, legislative pressures, and debt structures, they can apply a systems orientation to their team relationships.

Supervisors who are well versed in the systems concept can avoid many of the problems that result from a more isolated and individualistic operation. Furthermore, they can enhance their own development for rewarding careers in the organization. As organizations continue their fragmentation into additional groups, supervisors face the career risk of becoming overspecialized. The systems concept will sharpen their ability to "*see* the big picture" so that managers will "*keep* them in the picture."

Personal Development

Supervisors who permit their jobs to grow faster than their own personal development cannot make significant contributions to team efforts. Far too many supervisors have allowed themselves to get caught in a web of inertia that has reduced their ability to help themselves or their teams. Of course, supervisors cannot bear all of the blame in this area. Organizational training programs are definitely lacking in preparing supervisors for teamwork in a world of change.

Although Alvin Toffler's book *Future Shock* may have overdramatized the effects of change, it did us a favor by focusing attention on the accelerating pace of change. Rapid change is far more disrupting than evolutionary change and, therefore, presents more serious challenges to the supervisor. What happens to our mental equilibrium during periods of adjustment to change determines the future stability and continuity of most organizations. Therefore, it is now appropriate to turn our attention to a few ingredients in the framework of change while relating each to the personal development of supervisors.

Technology. Technological developments have contributed greatly to a swift pace of change. Automation and sophisticated systems are now being substituted for many traditional supervisory roles. These developments have not only freed supervisors from some of their more menial chores, but also changed the way in which they spend the time available to them. Supervisors are now more concerned with planning, directing, motivating, and coordinating.

Secondly, technology has had the effect of changing organizational structures by further extending specialization into more and more staff groups. In turn, such specialization has made further inroads into the supervisors' authority, responsibility, and prestige. Thus they find themselves in a situation where their authority is being reduced while the need for technical knowledge is increasing. Needless to say, the impact can be quite severe unless supervisors take the initiative to acquire the additional skill and knowledge needed in their positions.

Changes in Societal Values. Most observers of the organizational scene are convinced that the values held by management should be in reasonable conformity with those of society at large. This is certainly a rational view when we consider that the values of new employees have been developed over a long period of time and are relatively difficult to change. It would be foolish for management to create problems with its work force by attempting to cast the new generation in an old organizational mold. As a result, changing life styles and the employment of people from different cultural backgrounds have produced a distinct change in management attitudes toward personal appearance and other behavioral patterns.

Scientific Decision Making. Supervisors who do not engage in a program of continuous personal development will be confused by such terms as probability theory, statistical analysis, regression and correlation analysis, and statistical decision theory. Although many supervisors are not directly involved in decisions requiring such sophisticated techniques, they must at least have an acquaintance with the basic approaches used in statistical decision-making. Although there will never be a complete substitute for intuitive judgment, statistical decision theories do increase the odds one way or the other. Consequently, some basic knowledge of the field in the early stages of a management career will help prevent managerial obsolescence.

Advantages of Teamwork to the Supervisor

Sooner or later any supervisor will have to choose the individual approach to management, the team concept, or some combination of the two. Although the philosophy and actions of top management are determining factors in choosing from among these alternatives, supervisors are still free to make certain adjustments. For example, they can give lip service to team management and then go on their own ways. Or, they can apply the team concept to unimportant assignments and revert back to the individual approach in more significant matters. To help you make a choice, it might be worthwhile to discuss a few of the advantages and disadvantages of each approach.

The Individual Approach to Supervision

The primary advantage of a style that emphasizes individual relationships is that the supervisor is able to retain a highly developed sense of independence. If the personality traits important to effective team management are not present, it may be impossible for some to change their supervisory style. Certainly, a depressed, silent, introverted supervisor will not have the degree of social adaptability necessary for group participation. It may be argued that such a person would be better off in a nonmanagement job, but the fact remains that many supervisors have these characteristics and will remain in their positions for some time.

Another advantage of the individual approach is that supervisors do not have to share success with anyone. "I did it on my own," or "I wish you'd leave me alone and let me run the department myself," are favorite expressions of these supervisors. In other words, a desire for privacy and a dislike for sharing credit for accomplishments characterize this approach to working with people. Finally, if the organization's product or service requires a high degree of technical skill, the supervisor may function better as an independent.

Membership in the Management Team

Supervisors who are committed to team management can look forward to a number of rewarding benefits. The most important are summarized below.

Career Progress.   In his book *The Crisis in Middle Management,* Emanuel Kay takes a hard look at the situation in which many middle managers in the thirty-five to forty-five age bracket find themselves. The crisis to which he refers is the growing evidence of discontent among middle management personnel. If his thesis is accurate, many middle managers have become ineffective because their continued career progress seems to be remote. Therefore, supervisors of today would be wise to take advantage of any approaches that might prevent such frustration as they advance through the management ranks.

To prevent the degrading status of obsolescence, supervisors must be perceptive to what is going on around them and how their careers are being affected. The qualities that have already been mentioned as being vital to good team performance are also the ones that lead to the most satisfying careers. Although there are undoubtedly many supervisors who will not progress beyond a certain point in an organization, far too many do not bother to develop the abilities that will prepare them for advancement. A commitment to the team concept will help in this respect.

Need Fulfillment.   Empirical studies have shown that persons reach the peak of effectiveness when the natural conflict between organizational and personal goals is reduced to a minimum. For the supervisor who seeks a high level of self-fulfillment from organizational life, membership in good management teams offers the best chance for integrating personal and organizational goals. In addition, team management offers an opportunity for increased job satisfaction through a form of job enlargement, since there is an exposure to areas under the direction of other team members. For example, the personnel manager or the data-processing supervisor who has functioned as a team member will be better equipped to assume a line position if the opportunity should arise.

Summary

This chapter has focused on teamwork as an approach that seeks to improve management's response to consumers and employees. However, since this process is relatively new in most organizations, its framework has not been fully recognized or defined. Therefore, this chapter has also sought to identify elements of the framework so that the supervisors can determine what they need to do in order to become more effective members of management teams. To be effective, supervisors will need a knowledge of company goals, a sense of common purpose, constructive attitudes toward group involvement, and a desire to cooperate with other team members. They cannot afford the luxury of extreme individualism.

For teamwork to work, good communication is also essential, since the transfer of information is vital to team efforts. Similarly, constructive relationships must be formed and maintained through the process of delegation, and supervisors must excel in interaction skills if they hope to minimize the adverse effects of tension and conflict among individuals. Finally, they must be able to visualize the organization as a system made up of several subsystems and must exhibit favorable attitudes toward personal development.

Bibliography

Argyris, C. *Personality and Organization.* New York: Harper, 1957.

Kay, Emanuel. *The Crisis in Middle Management.* New York: American Management Association, 1974.

"Developing Patterns in Management," in *Strengthening Management For The New Technology,* General Management Series No. 178. New York: American Management Association, Inc. 1955; and Part II in *Changing Patterns and Concepts in Management,* General Management Series No. 182, 1956.

Questions for Discussion

1. What are some of the personality traits a supervisor should have in order to function effectively as a member of a management team?

2. Why is personal development important to a management team member?

3. Explain two benefits which might accrue to a supervisor from team-management efforts.

4. What are some of the factors that must be present for the team-management concept to work?

5. Is team management appropriate in all organizations? Why or why not? What factors should be considered in making the determination?

6. What unique position do supervisors hold in the management structure and how does it effect their role in the organization?

Case Incidents

1. Wayne Vancil is the supervisor over Unit A in the production department of a large manufacturing company. Bob Archer holds the same position in Unit B. Both units are located under the same roof,

the two job descriptions are identical, and each supervisor has twenty people in his department. Because of a sudden flurry of terminations, transfers, and promotions, Wayne is suddenly confronted with the task of rebuilding his unit. Bob, on the other hand, has a fully staffed, stable, and well-trained group. While the two were having coffee together yesterday, Wayne asked Bob if he would be willing to transfer two of his trained people to Unit A. Bob replied in the negative.

a. What do you think about Bob's attitude?

b. Would Bob have anything to gain by being more receptive to the idea?

c. Under the team concept of management, what might have happened to balance the needs of the two departments?

2. Jack Stone is a Division Manager in a large corporation. The division is organized into three sections and the work of each is distinct. Jack, 57, has been in his position for fifteen years and probably won't go any higher. He has difficulty accepting change and prefers the status quo. However, he is known as a good "people" manager and his management style is rather democratic.

   The section supervisors in Jack's division are Ronald King, 24; Walt Heyer, 38; and George Allen, 50. Ronald was recently brought in from another plant and promoted over two older and more experienced candidates. He is well educated, ambitious, and looks like a good management prospect. Walt is congenial and highly respected for his character and integrity; however, his performance has been judged as only average. George is quiet, uneducated, immobile, defensive, and is known as a loner. Suddenly, Jack has a heart attack and is expected to be off for about three months.

a. Explain in detail how the three supervisors could carry on in Jack's absence.

b. What problems might they encounter?

c. What benefits would accrue to them if they were able, through teamwork, to be fully effective until Jack's return?

Supervisory Decision Making and Employee Participation

*W. Jack Duncan**

Chapter Objectives

1. *To differentiate between decisions and the decision-making process.*

2. *To itemize the steps in the decision-making process.*

3. *To examine different types of decisions and illustrate the importance of each.*

4. *To analyze real-world complications in supervisory decision making.*

5. *To discuss the advantages and disadvantages of group decision making and the pros and cons of employee participation in supervisory decisions.*

6. *To provide a checklist for more effective decision making.*

THIS CHAPTER deals with decision making and its relationship to employee participation. Decision making is applied problem solving. It is applied in that supervisors make decisions in an effort to accomplish goals. The goals pursued, in turn, are designed to contribute to the objectives of the organization.

Think for a moment about a typical day in the life of a supervisor, Jack Brown. Jack arrives at work and discovers the boss has left word for him to call immediately. Before the number can be dialed, an employee wants to talk about a problem that must be resolved before work can begin. As the supervisor puts down the telephone and listens to the tale of woe, the union steward rushes in and demands to know why the college student hired for the summer has not applied for a work permit from the union.

*W. Jack Duncan is Professor and Chairman, Department of Business Administration, School of Business, The University of Alabama in Birmingham.

The supervisor has a problem! In fact, several problems requiring some type of action have appeared and the day is less than an hour old. To further complicate matters, Jack's head is not yet clear because he was up until after midnight going over performance reports trying to allocate merit increases available to the work group.

Each issue discussed above is a situation requiring action—a problem. A decision must be made.

Decisions and Decision Making

A decision is an act of choice. It takes place when one alternative action is selected in preference to all others. On the other hand, decision making is a process, or series of events, leading to a choice and continuing after a choice is made.

Steps in Decision Making

To illustrate the nature of decisions and decision making, consider the illustration in Figure 3–1. Each stage in the process is important if we are to understand supervisory decision making. Therefore, let us briefly examine each phase.

Figure 3–1
The Decision-Making Process

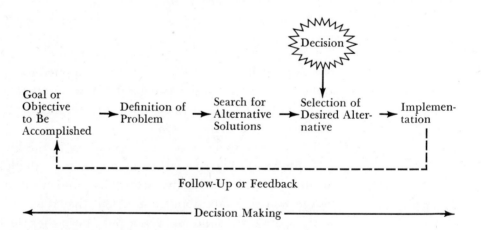

Establishment of the Goal. In making decisions, supervisors are concerned with an objective or a set of goals. This is their standard, their point of reference, when they select among alternative solutions to a problem. The goal may be productive efficiency, work-group satisfaction, industrial peace, or some other end considered desirable and supported by higher management.

Definition of the Problem. Before a problem can be solved, it must be accurately defined and analyzed. If, for example, supervisors are concerned about a reduction in the output of their units, care must be taken to analyze the problem thoroughly before taking corrective action. What has changed recently that could cause reductions in performance? Has there been a change in the incentive program? Are there rumors circulating about possible layoffs? Is the union contract up for renewal? These are but a few of the possible questions one might ask.

Search for Alternatives. Once the problem has been defined, possible solutions must be generated. It is unusual if only one course of action exists.

Let us assume that we know of rumors about possible layoffs. There are several things that might be done. The supervisor might allow the rumors to go unchecked. In this case, no action is the chosen alternative. Or, he or she may "level" with the group and tell them exactly what the situation is. It might also be advisable to have a member of the personnel department talk to the group. In other words, various alternatives are available to the supervisor.

Selection of the Alternative. After a proper evaluation, the supervisor must decide on the appropriate course of action. This is the point of decision. The choice is made with reference to the goal he is attempting to accomplish. The decision problem is to select the alternative that holds the greatest promise of accomplishing the objective.

Implementation. When the decision is made, the selected course of action must be put into practice. If the group leader decides to hold a meeting of employees to assure them that no plans are being made for layoffs, the conference must be scheduled and the time communicated to the work group.

Follow-Up. The supervisor should always be concerned with becoming a better decision maker. Therefore, it is important to monitor the results of a decision. This is a learning process whereby the supervisor reflects on the pros and cons of the selected course of action with respect to the goal being sought. Regardless of the outcome, lessons are always learned that can be useful in future decision making.

Thus, we see that decision making consists of several stages, only one of which constitutes the actual decision. We must recognize, however, that decision making does not stop with the evaluation or follow-up phase. Decisions have lasting effects on the person responsible for their implementation. Perhaps the most common effects are the anxiety and frustration that follow human choices.

When a supervisor chooses one act over others there are always certain aspects of the rejected alternatives that are favorable. Usually, we overcome frustrations by concentrating on the favorable aspects of the accepted course of action and suppressing the favorable features of rejected alternatives. Although this can be troublesome if taken too far, such reactions are basically functional in a psychological sense because they allow us to continue with some degree of sanity in accomplishing the complex tasks of supervision.[1]

Before looking in greater detail at the problem-solving process, we must examine some different ways of viewing decisions. This is the goal of the following section.

Basic Types of Decisions

There are numerous ways to look at supervisory decisions. Although we seldom classify them consciously in our minds, some awareness of each can aid in a more successful implementation of the decisions we make.

Means or Ends.   One of the most effective ways of emphasizing the importance of supervisory decisions is to look at the means-ends relationship they are designed to accomplish. This can be explained with the use of the following illustration.

Morgan Parker is a supervisor on the day shift in the Baker Machine Shop. At the present time he is interviewing several applicants referred by the personnel department for a job opening as a machinist's helper. In screening the applicants, Morgan is primarily concerned with hiring the helper who will be most effective in increasing the performance of the machinist to whom he will be assigned. The performance of the machinist is important to ensure the efficiency of the department. The department's efficiency contributes to the overall profitability of the firm. Thus, the means-ends relationship can be diagrammed as in Figure 3–2.

---

[1]In the technical management literature this phenomenon is known as cognitive dissonance. See Leon Festinger, *A Theory of Cognitive Dissonance* (Stanford, Calif.: Stanford University Press, 1957) and W. Jack Duncan, *Essentials of Management* (Hinsdale, Ill.: Dryden Press, 1975), pp. 100–102.

Figure 3–2
Decisions as Means-Ends Relationships

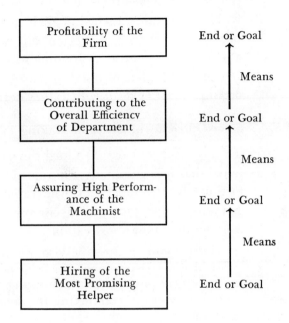

The logic of the means-ends relationship is important from the perspective of the firm. The selection of the proper helper is the immediate goal. The accomplishment of this goal, however, is the means to a higher level end—the machinist's proficiency. The machinist's proficiency, in turn, is the means to a more efficient department and ultimately to the profitability of the firm.

This view of supervisory decision making emphasizes the importance of seemingly routine actions on the accomplishment of organizational goals. In other words, the profitability of a firm, such as the Baker Machine Shop, is dependent on correct supervisory decisions.

Routine and Nonroutine Decisions.   Every supervisory job is a complex mixture of routine and nonroutine decisions. This terminology should not imply that one type is more or less important than the other.

Routine decisions are recurring and predictable. Production scheduling must be done at certain times, and everyone knows it. Schedules can be developed and plans made accordingly. This is also true of shift assignments and released time for vacations.

Nonroutine decisions are not recurring and cannot be easily predicted. Sometimes, without notice, a production line breaks down, an employee becomes ill and must be replaced, or your boss puts you in charge of implementing a new process that has not been used previously. Unlike making a schedule, it is impossible to predict exactly when this type of situation will occur, and when it does, little experience is available to guide you in deciding what to do. The point is simple—we can program, plan for, and anticipate routine decisions. Nonroutine decisions must be dealt with as they develop.

Some Outcomes of Decision Making

To this point we have examined the basic decision-making process and noted that it is essentially a means of systematic problem solving. Unfortunately, the supervisor who carefully follows the process is not guaranteed that successful decisions will always result. To illustrate, consider the following situation.

Lois Dodson is the supervisor of Steno Pool Number Three in the Engineering Department of a large petrochemical firm. In this capacity she is responsible for supervising ten senior typists and for assisting the group in completing the consistently heavy work load. The typists are all highly skilled employees because of the technical nature of the work. They are not unionized, but there have been rumors of organizing efforts by the local representative of the office workers' union.

In the past, vacation time has been scheduled on the basis of seniority. If more than one person applies for vacation time around Christmas, for example, the one with the longest service is given priority.

Recently, Lois received vacation requests from Janet Davis and Lawrence Beck for the week of December 25. Only one member of the group can leave on vacation at any given time and both of the applicants have equal time with the company.

Lois knows that Janet Davis's husband is a graduate student at the local university and Christmas is the only time they can travel to visit their families in a distant city. Lawrence Beck, on the other hand, plans to be married on December 23 and wants to combine the vacation with a honeymoon.

Sound familiar? Lois is confronted with a serious, although typical, supervisory decision. Let's see what can result.

First, Lois could decide to allow Lawrence Beck to go on vacation because of some criterion such as the alphabetical order of the applicants' last names. It is also possible that Janet might understand and yield to the decision. In this case a decision has been made and a satisfactory outcome has resulted.

On the other hand, Lois may decide in favor of Mr. Beck and Ms. Davis may be dissatisfied. The obvious charge could be that there is no policy for deciding on vacation time based on the alphabetical order of last names. Here, a decision has been made and conflict has resulted. Both of these possibilities could also be repeated with Ms. Davis going on vacation and Mr. Beck remaining at work.

There are, of course, other possibilities. Lois may decide that since both employees have the same seniority, there is no equitable way of resolving the issue and allow no one to leave during the Christmas week. Or, it may be possible to ask the two employees to come together, discuss the dilemma, and work out a compromise.

Obviously, in a decision of this nature, there is no absolute rule for action. What the supervisor does is a complex mixture of judgment, concern for justice, consideration of group performance, and numerous other factors. The important point is that a relatively routine issue can often become quite complex. To illustrate, look at Figure 3–3. Recognizing the complexity of the problem, the supervisor must look at the alternatives and select the one considered most appropriate. At times, reformulating the choices in the form of a decision tree like this can help in itemizing and examining alternatives.

The primary danger is to make complex decisions while assuming they are as simple as they appear. Through a more thorough and systematic analysis, the supervisor can at least anticipate possible outcomes and prevent, insofar as possible, the anxiety and frustration inherent in decision making. He or she can also prepare, in advance, methods of resolving conflicts that might result.

Decision Making: from Theory to Reality

To this point we have looked at decision making as a precise series of steps one follows in arriving at a desired goal. In reality, this is often impossible.

The supervisor often finds problem-solving situations more confusing than our discussion indicates. For example, problems develop from the very beginning of the process. Often the supervisor is not sure of the goal to be accomplished. Although upper management may devote considerable time to emphasizing the importance of profits, good labor relations, social responsibility, and so on, these objectives are difficult

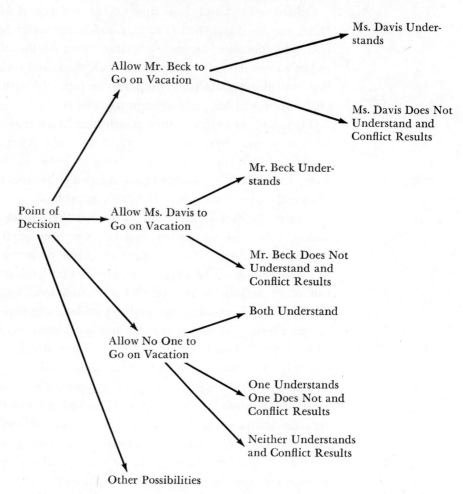

Figure 3-3
The Complexity of "Simple" Supervisory Decisions

to reformulate into precise guidelines for action. For example, will terminating an unsatisfactory employee increase the efficiency of the department and the profitability of the firm? On the surface the answer would appear to be yes. However, we must ask whether or not it would simultaneously result in unfavorable labor relations, reduced morale, and lower profits?

Another important complication is time. We would all probably agree that systematic problem solving is better than unsystematic behavior. It is also more time consuming. Thus, the practical issue becomes: How much effort can I devote to gathering and analyzing data without using an excessive amount of time? After all, the supervisor's days are far too short already!

The fact is that much of our decision-making behavior recognizes and allows for these realistic complications. We shall briefly look at how this is done.[2]

Goal Complexity

Few, if any, situations faced by a supervisor can be easily related to extremely clear and concise goals. This is true because of the very nature of organizational goals. Consider the problem with reference to Figure 3–4.

Figure 3–4
Influences on Supervisory Decision Making

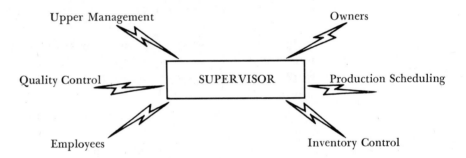

The supervisor here is pictured at the center of a network of relationships. All the individuals in this network are exerting certain influences on the decision maker with regard to their understanding of organizational goals. Upper management and owners are demanding profits, while employees are demanding higher wages. At the same time, production scheduling is insisting on a timetable to ensure that raw materials are available and efficiently utilized. Quality control is concerned with excessive waste, sales is concerned that a sufficient supply of finished products is available, and inventory control is upset over rising inventory costs. As a result, the logical means-ends relationship becomes less precise. Not only is it impossible to clearly "picture" the organizational goal, but the relationship among the various organizational interest groups is one of conflict. The efforts of the supervisor are thus directed toward compromising the various interest groups

[2]For a more detailed examination see James March and Herbert A. Simon, *Organizations* (New York: John Wiley, 1958).

rather than maximizing the interests of the owners. This is one reason why supervisory decision makers are often said to *satisfice;* that is, they try to achieve an outcome satisfactory to all the groups by minimizing conflict. This greatly complicates the maximization of performance. But, there is more to the problem.

Limited Knowledge

Supervisors also fail to maximize decisions because of the vast amounts of information necessary in even simple situations. In the case of Lois Dodson mentioned earlier, we itemized some of the options she might exercise, but were quick to admit that other alternatives were possible.

Decision makers generally have limited knowledge for one or more of the following reasons.

1. The problem is too complex to understand, or imagine, all possible courses of action.

2. The objective of some decisions makes complete knowledge unnecessary.

3. The cost and time necessary for gathering all information is prohibitive.

4. Search patterns limit the amount and quality of information generated.

Let us look briefly at each of these.

Problem Complexity.   There are very few problem situations where we are sure that we know all available courses of action. Even if we should be so lucky, we surely could not know the possible outcomes for each alternative. Yet, knowledge of both these items is necessary if we are to maximize the results of our decision making.

Objective of Decision Making.   Sometimes the task facing supervisors is not to generate alternatives but to analyze and select from among those presented to them. For example, a firm may have a centralized hiring policy where the supervisor reports job openings and the personnel department locates possible candidates. In one case personnel may send three applicants and ask the supervisor to make the final selection. Here, the decision maker may choose any of the three or reject all and ask for more applicants. In either event, the supervisor's job is to select among presented alternatives, not to generate new ones. Thus, the objective of decision making is an analysis of alternatives.

Information Cost and Time.   The acquisition of information, or generation of alternatives, consumes time and costs money, neither of which is plentiful in today's organizations. As a result, the supervisor may consciously decide to make a choice after a specific number of alternatives have been generated.

Search Patterns.   Not all supervisors search for alternatives in the same manner. Some, for example, will generate as many alternatives as possible. Others will make a decision on the basis of only one or a few available options. How supervisors search for information is related to a number of factors such as their personalities, past experiences, time commitments, etc.

Decision making is by its nature an individual activity. At times, however, groups are involved in the process. Probably the most common form of group decision making is the committee, but supervisors may involve others without the formality of a committee structure. Because of this, we must examine the pros and cons of group decision making and the related issue of employee participation.

Group Decision Making

Supervisors in all types of organizations are frequently faced with the question of whether or not to call on others for assistance in making important decisions. Although we joke about committees and say that no self-respecting supervisor would ever admit that committees are useful, the fact is that most organizations make extensive use of such groups. One survey, for example, found that almost all large firms studied acknowledged the use of committees in decision making.[3] Obviously, groups of this nature are objects of concern to supervisors.

Some Pros and Cons

If most organizations use committees, they must obviously have some advantages over individuals acting alone. The primary advantages usually include the following:

1. Groups expand the capabilities of individuals. This is particularly true when the groups are structured in certain ways.
2. Group decision making facilitates a sense of participation on the part of employees.
3. Representative groups reduce conflict when decisions under consideration have interdepartmental or interunit implications.

[3]See Rollie Tillman, Jr., "Problems in Review: Committee on Trial," *Harvard Business Review,* May-June, 1960, pp. 13–15.

Let us look in greater detail at each of the proposed advantages.

Expansion of Individual Capabilities.   All of us have, no doubt, experienced the mental stimulation that can be received from discussing things with others. Often, we think of numerous points that might not have been considered if someone had not made a certain statement.

Although we can be easily stimulated by group members with similar backgrounds and experience, we can also increase our creativity by interacting with others who view problems from a different perspective. For example, several foremen of production units may talk over a problem and examine numerous alternatives that would have never been considered by each foreman acting alone. Similarly, if a foreman is placed in a group with supervisors from other areas such as sales, finance, and personnel, more dimensions of the problem are likely to emerge.

Increase Participation.   Since we will deal with employee participation in the final section of this chapter, only a few comments will be made at this point. For our purposes, we can simply note that when people participate in problem solving they feel more a part of the solution. At least, they feel important because someone has asked their opinion. As a result, implementation of the proposed action should be easier.

Aiding in Interunit Cooperation.   Let us assume that production and sales are experiencing a typical conflict. The production department wants to schedule production runs over the year so as to avoid layoffs. Sales, however, recognizing that orders tend to cluster around certain months, wants production increased during such periods to ensure adequate inventory levels.

It is doubtful that either group would approve a solution dictated by the other. However, by working on a solution through representatives of both groups, they can develop a recommendation more satisfactory to each.

To this point, groups sound like good things. Lest we be misled, however, we must also note some possible disadvantages. A few of the more important are:

1. Groups are expensive and consume valuable time.

2. Some people are not secure in groups and may be inhibited by dominant personalities.

3. Groups make decisions that are too risky since no single individual is accountable for the outcome.

Expensive and Time Consuming.   Everyone in a supervisory position has probably experienced the frustration of attempting to obtain group agreement on some issue. The presentation and discussion of diverse opinions obviously takes longer than a single person's sitting down and making a choice. Also, it is usually difficult, if not impossible, to schedule a time when all concerned parties can attend meetings without disrupting normal operations.

When the group is assembled, each member's attention is also diverted from primary job duties. The person's pay, however, continues. As a result, group decision making becomes expensive in a monetary sense.

Inhibiting Effects on Individuals.   While a group setting stimulates some people, it frightens others. This can be a special problem where groups are composed of people from different levels of authority. For example, if supervisors and their bosses are members of the same problem-solving group, some supervisors may refrain from making suggestions for fear of their bosses' reaction.

Even where groups are carefully selected to ensure that only individuals of equal organizational status are represented, dominant personalities often emerge. Such people who become very stimulated by group discussions can sometimes discourage less dominant individuals from participating.

Groups Assume More Risk.   Some writers in the area argue that groups consistently make riskier decisions than individuals. The idea behind the argument is that when a group recommends a course of action, no single person is responsible for the outcome. Thus, the group feels more comfortable with risky actions. Research on the subject raises questions about this line of thought, since some studies have shown that groups tend to reach compromises that result in less risky recommendation.[4]

The point of this discussion is that groups offer advantages and disadvantages in the area of decision making. They are useful in building involvement and participation but can be expensive and time consuming. The practical issue for supervisors is that groups can assist in solving problems; however, the issue of participation raises additional points that supervisors should consider in the area of decision making.

[4]M. W. Belovicz, F. E. Finch, and Halsey Jones, "Do Groups Make Riskier Decisions Than Individuals?" *Academy of Management Proceedings,* December, 1968, pp. 73–85.

Employee Participation

Rensis Likert, former director of the Institute for Social Research at the University of Michigan, has worked extensively with the question of "how successful managers manage." On the basis of more than three hundred studies in all types of organizations, he developed a list of six characteristics possessed by good managers. These are:

1. The successful manager is technically competent in his or her job.
2. The successful manager formulates high-performance and challenging goals.
3. The successful manager supports subordinates by showing confidence and trust in them and by listening to what they have to contribute.
4. The successful manager builds effective work groups by involving subordinates in decisions affecting them.
5. The successful manager plans and organizes work so that the group knows what is going on.
6. The successful manager ensures that employees are well-trained.[5]

Three of these items (3, 4, and 5) relate directly to encouraging employee participation. Item four specifically notes that successful managers involve employees in the decisions that affect them.

The importance of participative management is becoming recognized by national governments as well as individual organizations. For example, in Sweden it is a law that all companies with one hundred or more employees must have worker representatives on their boards of directors. A similar system exists in West Germany.[6]

In this country, companies like Questor Corporation have involved employees in such basic decisions as workflow design with favorable effects on morale and reduced absenteeism.[7] In 1973, the Conference Board completed a survey of 147 organizations in an attempt to determine the extent of employee participation in decision making.[8] Although this survey used certain types of subcategories of organizations, several interesting results were obtained that are relevant for our purposes. First, it noted that more than 60 percent of the responding firms used participative-group methods of problem solving. However, most

[5]"How Successful Managers Manage," *Industry Week*, December 17, 1973, pp. 40–43.

[6]"When Workers Become Directors," *Business Week*, September 15, 1973, pp. 188–190 and 194–196.

[7]"Candid Management Gets Employee Participation," *Industry Week*, January 28, 1974, pp. 64–65.

[8]Harold F. Rush, "A Nonpartisan View of Participative Management," *Conference Board Record*, April, 1973, pp. 34–39.

restricted the participation to middle and upper management levels in the organization. Less than 10 percent involved lower levels of supervision and rank-and-file employees in participative problem solving. Thus, we see an interesting pattern in participative decision making as it exists in reality. It is used, but involvement is limited. Let us examine the topic in greater detail.

Some Advantages of Participation.   Advocates of participative decision making usually base their position on one or more of the following arguments, listed by Tannenbaum and Massarik:

1. Performance can be improved through higher rates of output and increases in the quality of the work. This is assumed to result from the feeling of greater involvement on the part of employees.

2. Because involvement increases, morale improves. The result is often less absenteeism and lower turnover rates.

3. Better company-union relations develop with a corresponding reduction in the number of grievances filed.

4. There is less resistance to change. Since employees feel a part of what is happening and have been included in decision making, there is less reason for them to resist the implementation of plans.

5. Improved decisions often result because more input has been obtained and a more critical analysis has been conducted.[9]

We see from this list that advocates of employee participation see many desirable effects resulting from the involvement of group members. Production is said to increase, morale is thought to improve, better union-management relations develop, individuals become less resistant to change, and better decisions result. If only this were true!

In some cases, no one would dispute the favorable effects resulting from participation. However, there is obviously another side to the coin or no one would be autocratic. Every successful manager would encourage and insist on participation. But this is not the case.

Some Disadvantages.   All supervisors do not encourage participation because there are certain disadvantages. A few of the more important are:

1. Urgent decisions require fast action. Obtaining inputs from even a few people takes time.

2. Threats to supervisory authority can result from participation. When you ask the opinions of others you have an obligation to con-

---

[9]Robert Tannenbaum and Fred Massarik, "Sharing Decision-Making with Subordinates," in Robert Dubin, ed., *Human Relations in Administration*, 3rd ed. (Englewood Cliffs, N.J.: Prentice-Hall, 1968), pp. 381–82.

sider suggestions seriously. Some supervisors may view this type of input as a threat to their position, since they assume that asking the opinions of others is a sign of weakness.

3. The supervisor cannot delegate responsibility. Regardless of how much you involve others in decision making, you alone are responsible for the action taken. Since you are responsible for the action taken, there is less incentive to give up control over decisions to be made.

4. Not all employees want to participate. Some choose not to be supervisors. They do not want to be bothered with decision making and may look upon it as not part of their job.

The choice between autocracy and democracy is not an easy one. For this reason, Le Forest Smith, General Director of the YMCA in Orange, New Jersey, suggests that the most effective supervisors are those who can accurately view a situation and decide "when to use group thinking and when to go solo."[10]

Concluding Guidelines and Summary

In Figure 3–5, we have attempted to develop a checklist of selected questions that should be asked throughout the decision-making process. These guidelines are presented merely as an initial check on the nature

Figure 3–5
Guidelines for Supervisory Decision Making

DECISION-MAKING PHASE	YES	NO	REQUIRED ACTION
I. Goal understanding			
A. Do I understand the primary goal of my work group?	☐	☐	If answer is "no" consult your immediate supervisor and ask for clarification.
B. Have I communicated group and organizational goals to my employees?	☐	☐	If answer is "no" devise most effective means of relating goals to the group immediately and inform them.
II. Problem definition			
A. Do I have a clear understanding of the problem demanding action?	☐	☐	If answer is "no" consider the issue in more detail before proceeding to next stage.
B. Does the problem have implications for work groups other than my own?	☐	☐	If answer is "yes" who else in the organization should be consulted about the problem?

[10]Le Forest C. Smith, "Can We Afford to Let Them Make the Decision?" *Administration,* April, 1973, p. 12.

Yes No

III. Search for alternatives

A. Have I generated all my relevant courses of action? ☐ ☐ If answer is "no" what other possibilities should be considered?

B. Can group members help in offering possible alternatives? ☐ ☐ If answer is "yes" approach members of the group and ask for their input.

C. Have I carefully considered the likely outcomes of each course of action? ☐ ☐ If answer is "no" devote time to anticipating the consequences of each known alternative.

D. Do I need specialized assistance in estimating possible outcomes? ☐ ☐ If answer is "yes" and if problem is of sufficient importance, request assistance.

IV. Selection of alternative

A. Do I need group assistance in making my choice? ☐ ☐ If answer is "yes" communicate with members of group and seek their opinions.

B. Are there any likely problems that will result from the selected course of action? ☐ ☐ If answer is "yes" calculate time available to prepare for problems and devote as much effort to the issue as possible.

C. Do I need to consult with my immediate supervisor before initiating action? ☐ ☐ If answer is "yes" schedule time to discuss proposed action with your boss.

V. Implementation

A. Can I expect resistance to the implementation of selected action in spite of previous efforts? ☐ ☐ If answer is "yes" time should be devoted to evaluating methods of reducing resistance.

B. Could the quality and/or speed of implementation be improved by encouraging employee participation? ☐ ☐ If answer is "yes" employee participation should be encouraged.

VI. Follow-up

A. Did I accomplish my goals and contribute to organizational objectives with my behavior? ☐ ☐ If answer is "no" or uncertain a period of objective review should be engaged in to determine what improvements might be made.

B. Should I obtain the reactions of employees on the decision made? ☐ ☐ In almost all cases, the answer to this is "yes" and a mechanism should be developed to acquire relevant information.

of supervisory decisions. Individual supervisors can easily expand this type of checklist for their own unique situations.

With this in mind let us briefly reflect on some of the topics we have discussed. We began by observing that a decision is applied problem solving. It is a single act of choice where one course of action is selected in preference to others. Thus, it is only one step in the entire process of decision making.

To illustrate the importance of supervisory decision making we looked at decisions as a means-ends relationship to show how all decisions are instrumental in accomplishing organizational goals. If work groups do not perform properly, organizations cannot make profits or accomplish other goals.

After discussing the process of decision making, real world complications were examined. Finally, group decision making and the importance of employee participation were considered as they relate to supervisory responsibilities.

Questions for Discussion

1. Explain the difference between decision making and a decision. How are they related?

2. List the steps in the decision-making process. Which step (s) do you consider most important? Why?

3. Explain the decision process in terms of a means-ends relationship. Illustrate the process with an actual organization with which you are familiar.

4. What do you consider the most important real-world complications in making effective and successful decisions?

5. Itemize the advantages and disadvantages of group decision making.

6. What are some of the advantages to be gained from involving employees in decision making? What are some important disadvantages?

Case Incidents

1. John Holley is a production supervisor in the Compton Steel Works. Recently, he was informed that the company had negotiated a new group insurance program with a large national firm. The contract was written to ensure that all employees covered under the old plan would have equivalent benefits with certain coverage expanded. There is also a provision for employees to take certain options at their own expense that were not previously available.

Because the old contract did not have optional provisions, company officials are concerned that employees may view the new program as a means of forcing them to pay for part of the benefits. All supervisors were asked to go over the provisions of the contract and ensure employees understand the program.

a. As a supervisor, how would you approach the orientation to ensure a minimum resistance to change?

b. Work through the process using the guidelines in Exhibit 3–1. List any factors you may not have considered in the absence of a systematic approach.

c. Should you request participation of selected employees prior to presenting the information? Why or why not? If you request suggestions, what types of things would you be asking from employees?

2. Beverly Baker is the supervisor of nurses in a large, comprehensive care hospital. Recently, she was informed by the Industrial Engineering Department that a series of studies was to be conducted on the effects of noise on patient comfort and employee performance.

The chief industrial engineer also requested that after the studies are completed he would like to discuss the results with her. In the meantime, she has been asked to develop a brief summary of her feelings with respect to noise levels in the hospital. She is free to present any item she desires regardless of whether it relates specifically to the nursing function.

Interestingly, Ms. Baker has already been thinking about the noise problem and has some rather specific ideas to present. She is not sure, however, that she has considered all aspects of the problem. Fortunately, the studies will not be completed for approximately sixty days.

a. Is this the type of problem that could be effectively analyzed by a group or committee? Why or why not?

b. If a committee is formed to assist in raising issues, what sorts of employees should be appointed to the team?

c. What problems might be anticipated if a committee is used? What problems might develop if Ms. Baker acts individually?

Planning
and
Control

*Dalton E. McFarland**

Dalton E. McFarland

Chapter
Objectives

1. *To describe the nature and function of supervisory planning and control.*

2. *To analyze the factors that inhibit effective planning and control.*

3. *To explain how the supervisor can improve planning activities and control procedures.*

4. *To review the human problems of planning and control.*

PLANNING AND CONTROL are managerial skills that earn for the supervisor the respect of subordinates. They will also improve the supervisor's standing with superiors. People like to work for organizations that are smoothly run and in which things get done in an orderly way. Planning and control therefore are vital to group solidarity and effective supervisory leadership.

Definitions

A working definition of the planning and control processes is essential:

Planning: Purposeful activity by which managers anticipate the future and determine the actions needed to attain desirable future conditions or results.

Control: A process by which managers govern activities so as to make sure that outcomes are achieved in accordance with desired standards.

*Dalton E. McFarland is University Professor and Professor of Business Administration, School of Business, The University of Alabama in Birmingham.

Planning and control go hand in glove. Changing the metaphor, most supervisors can achieve better planning and better control by realizing that they are two sides of the same coin. The most effective control is that built into the planning effort.

Problems of Planning

Planning poses difficulties because it is mainly concerned with controlling future outcomes. The future is often uncertain and difficult to predict, and unexpected events can throw the supervisor's work off base. Even the most careful plans cannot anticipate all the events that may occur. Nevertheless, judgments about the future must be made as carefully as possible so that the plans can be realistically tailored to changing needs. Though subject to a margin of error, estimates, forecasts, and opinions about future conditions must guide action in the present.

The effectiveness of supervisory planning depends heavily on the quality of planning that prevails in the rest of the organization. Unless planning skills are prevalent at all levels, planning in the supervisor's unit will suffer. The plans in one unit have to fit into the overall planning of other units and of the enterprise as a whole. Often the organization's information processing is weak, so that the supervisor finds it difficult to obtain needed data.

Planning is often inhibited by problems of cost. Planning takes time, money, and effort. Problem investigations, information searches, and analytical processes are costly. The organization must be willing to pay these administrative costs. Effective planning, however, is a good investment and is less costly to an organization than no planning at all.

Since it is costly, organizations need to avoid too much planning. Too many meetings and too much paperwork can discourage not only the planner but everyone else. Most organizations, however, have a tendency to plan too little. Underplanning is often justified on the grounds of the high cost of planning. The burden of current pressures is a convenient excuse. "I'm too busy taking care of today's pressures," is a familiar cry. In many organizations, pressures of the present do interfere with thought for the future. Yet planning is basically a tool of preventive action. Much of the pressure that is said to interfere with better planning can be planned out of the system.

Another difficulty with planning is that it is essentially a thinking process. Most people are more ready to take action now than to think about the possible actions of the future, and there are times when immediate action must take place with little or no time for planning. Thinking requires a supervisor to work problems through conceptually, and to imagine the consequences of various alternative plans. In planning, supervisors deal with abstractions and anticipations that seem vague compared to what is happening in the present. Thoughtful planning requires a disciplined, attentive mind. It is essentially a mental activity that considers the future compared to the present.

One of the greatest obstacles to better planning is the lack of clear objectives and a sharp definition of the problems toward which planning is being directed. Planning itself is needed to determine objectives, and to formulate problems in terms that show what actions to take.

Problems and objectives may not only be unclear. They may also be wrong. For example, a supervisor may believe that absenteeism among employees is too high. To notice the figures that show this condition is only the beginning. To give the situation a label such as "absenteeism" is not enough. One still has to define the problem exactly and correctly, and in operational terms. To define the problem as one of poor selection of employees, or as one calling for stronger discipline and punishment is typical but also inadequate. To define it as a problem of morale or motivation may be closer to the truth, but many elements may be involved simultaneously. The only way to sort out such difficulties is to discover all the significant elements of the problem. Only then can one plan the steps needed for corrective action. The answers depend heavily upon the definition of the problem.

Achieving Better Planning

The first step toward better planning is to understand that most excuses for poor planning or no planning are not really valid. The supervisor who determines to achieve better planning will come out on top of those who cannot or will not plan. This step reflects the need *to allocate time each day* to engage in planning activity.

By systematically setting aside an hour a day for planning, the supervisor will develop improved planning skills and overcome the causes of poor planning. This time allocation need not be rigid or routine, but it should become something of a daily habit.

In planning, the supervisor should (1) review the planning process itself, (2) review existing plans to see where changes are needed, and

(3) review operations to determine where whole new plans should be developed.

Reviewing the planning process itself will keep the machinery of planning well oiled. Is enough time being devoted to planning? Are the key people helping who should be? What things tend to interfere with the planning process? What resources or help from others is required? The process of planning itself has a developmental aspect of value to the supervisor. Often the processes by which a plan is developed and implemented are as valuable as the resulting plan, because the need for planning is a focal point around which supervisors are forced to organize the entire range of managerial capabilities within their units.

The review of existing plans is needed to see if the unit is on target. Are loopholes, bottlenecks, and deviations under surveillance? Should changes be made in parts of the plan? Are the plans timely, complete, and useful? Have some plans achieved their purpose and reached the point of being discarded?

Reviewing operations to see what new plans are needed may be the most important part of planning. It is also the hardest part, because it requires advanced, speculative, and imaginative thinking. What should the group be doing that it is not doing? What needs the most improvement? Is the group ready for changes that may occur? In planning, nothing can safely be taken for granted.

Being close to the scenes of action and operation, the supervisor is often the first to be aware of problems as they start to become serious. Worsening conditions can be prevented if the supervisor keeps others informed and proceeds to institute planning among all persons whose work may be affected.

Planning Offices

Many organizations today use planning directors who head centralized staff units charged with implementing planning activities. Such units are more often concerned with strategic goals and over-all, long-run strategies than with operating, day-to-day problems. Planning departments concentrate on forecasting, observing trends, analyzing data, and making recommendations. They can function best, however, with grass roots inputs from managers in the operating units. Supervisors therefore may be called upon to participate in planning work that goes beyond their immediate department.

It has been difficult for planning officers to communicate to supervisors and other managers the importance of strategic planning. Good coordination between high-level planners and grassroots managers is hard to establish and maintain. Supervisors often feel that staff planners are unrealistic, making undue demands on their time. Planning officials often deserve the cold shoulder of supervisors by being impatient, arrogant, excessively demanding. This results in a lack of cooperation with the planners, and translates into a lack of confidence in planning at grassroots levels.

Supervisors should avoid getting into serious arguments over planning wherever possible. They should also avoid buck passing and the "let George do it" philosophy, which is sheer abdication of responsibility. That supervisors may have to contribute to planning efforts under less than ideal conditions does not free them from planning responsibilities. Indeed, corporate planning officers and their staffs can be more a resource than a hindrance. Planning by doers supplemented by the planning support of staff specialists is a combination that is hard to beat.

In today's uncertain conditions, corporate planners are shifting from the old idea of a single forward plan to the development of multiple plans affording greater flexibility and capacity to meet rapid and severe changes. This effort occurs mainly at the top levels of an organization, but there is always an impact on the planning work of the supervisor.

Developing and Implementing Plans

Supervisors who know their jobs do not need to be told to plan, but in every organization the planning effort moves in cycles or phases, complete with deadlines. For example, the fiscal year may impose deadlines for an annual budget. The completion of one plan may reflect the need for another. As old plans lose value new ones are phased in. And separate plans must be related to each other in the overall strategies of the organization. Therefore, the supervisor's planning responsibility involves devising, using, and completing a number of plans simultaneously for a variety of purposes over varying spans of time. Planning is therefore a continuing, ever-present responsibility.

The following considerations are vital for supervisors who seek to achieve more effective planning:

1. Planning is preceded by policy determinations that should be reviewed and incorporated into the planning process.

2. Organizational resources need to be marshalled specifically for planning. These include time, manpower, relevant data, and financial resources.

3. Budgeting should be recognized as both a planning and control process. The costs of carrying out plans must be dealt with. A budget is one of the tangible expressions of the planning effort.

4. Time frames are important. Planning is related to various time spans: Short range, intermediate, and long range. Control addresses itself to the present, and evaluation reviews the impact and success of plans in the past.

5. Keep plans, budgets, and systems as simple as possible. Most planning involves a large number of people. Involve those who are affected.

6. Establish priorities among the various plans put into action.

7. Determine to make plans concrete by putting them in writing. This not only improves planning itself but also facilitates communication and persuasion on committed action. Incorporate reasoning in every plan.

8. Build in task assignments, authority delegations, and responsibilities for specific people. Specify the outcomes or results desired.

9. Maintain the plans by specific review and control processes. Make changes, set deadlines, and provide for continuous monitoring and evaluation.

10. Be alert for doubts and conflicts that arise during implementation stages, and be prepared to resolve them. Deal directly with the feelings and attitudes of those who disagree with an adopted plan.

Setting Priorities

There is usually a lot of difference between what people in an organization say is going on and what is actually happening. A leader energizes a group by keeping its members close to reality. Most supervisors have priorities in mind concerning problems to be solved or missions to accomplish. Since a group cannot do everything at once or perform in all areas equally well, priorities must somehow be set. It is the task of supervisors to communicate their views on the priorities they advocate, and the reasoning that supports those priorities.

No doubt some subordinates will be disappointed if their part of the work has received a lower priority than they feel it should. The supervisor combats the possibilities for low morale that ensue by indicating when priorities will shift and by stressing the logic of the selected priorities. To the extent that subordinates make a contribution to the selection of priorities, they themselves will come to know the timing of changes and the logic employed.

The concrete existence of a plan contains its own booby trap: Getting locked into the plan so completely that the need for change, speed, and flexibility is lost sight of. A plan is effective only if it does not forever become the sole end of all effort. As needs change, priorities must be shifted.

Only one plan of action on a given aim or problem can be put to work at a time. Dual plans would cause undue confusion. General plans, however, are supported by related specific plans, but these must be linked to the overall plan. A change in a supporting plan deserves careful thought, for it is likely to cause a change in other support plans of the general plan. Unity, continuity, and precision are the necessary features of any plan. Once established, a plan becomes effective until changed by mutual agreement or higher decision.

Supervisory Attributes for Planning

Fayol, the great management pioneer, formulated the requirements of the successful planner: skill in handling subordinates, considerable energy, moral courage, continuity of tenure, and professional competence and experience.

In working with subordinates, the supervisor sets the pace for the planning process. The supervisor's work demonstrates the usefulness of planning. If the supervisor does not believe in it or merely pays it lip service, so too will subordinates. Supervisors therefore need to be aware of the human factors at work in planning, both in themselves and others.

Planning is demanding on one's mental and physical energies. The need for planning competes with other needs, and so must become part of the supervisor's total approach to his work.

Moral courage is required to recognize and admit the wrong assumptions that may have affected planning, and to make changes as needed. It takes courage to admit mistakes. It also takes courage to be realistic in planning and to avoid raising false hopes or setting tasks impossible to fulfill. Timid supervisors are often tempted to make small plans when large plans are required, or to suppress or sabotage plans they dislike.

Continuity of tenure strengthens planning, for the supervisor thus gains a useful time perspective. Frequent changes in leadership mean that continuities are lost. Planning suffers because each new supervisor undergoes the start-up costs again. Also, the responsibility for carrying out plans becomes more uncertain. It is often difficult for the new supervisor to fulfill plans set by the person being followed.

Finally, professional competence born of experience and applied judgment is a vital factor in planning. Planning becomes the ultimate test of the effective supervisor. Where effective planning exists, "management by crisis" is at a minimum. Planning requires knowledge, and knowledge is power.

Problems of Control

Control is a frequently misunderstood concept in management. It is often equated with punishment, or disciplinary action. The definition of control cited at the beginning of this chapter emphasizes instead that control is managerial action that adjusts operations to desired, predetermined standards. Control is thus a condition resulting from a number of complex managerial actions. Basically, a condition of control exists when an operating unit or individual is "on target" or "on plan." Deviations are kept within an acceptable, preplanned range.

Conditions of control are best viewed as the product of a control system. A control system is composed of human inputs, such as the supervisor's careful observation of performance, and technical elements such as workflow procedures, records, dials, gauges and measuring devices. The human elements in control are the most difficult and unpredictable. The technical elements can be tested and refined by engineering methods and practical use patterns. Control systems are most effective when they are structured into plans.

As an example of a control system, consider the case in which a supervisor delegates to a subordinate the responsibility for coordinating vacation requests from members of the department. For control to be effective, the supervisor devises a system that includes a written delegation, together with applicable policy guidelines, a deadline for completion of the plan, and a request for periodic reports and a report of the final result. The supervisor includes an objective: To satisfy vacation time requests as far as possible without sacrificing operational effectiveness. These are technical elements. In addition, the supervisor recognizes that unexpected problems may arise, and remains available to resolve unexpected difficulties. By delegating in this way the supervisor avoids having to perform these duties personally without dodging ultimate responsibility. The supervisor is available for consultation, advice, and problem solving, and has established check points at the beginning, middle, and end of the process. It is important to monitor the progress of planned activities and to be informed of their completion. The human elements of the system are found in the personality and capabilities of the subordinate who does the work, the quality of the working relationships between supervisor and the subordinate, and the attitudes of group members toward their boss, the organization, and their work. Vacation planning may run into the emotions of persons trying to get vacation times that do not fit operational requirements, so feelings must be considered.

Any control system for any purpose should be as simple as possible, and it should be arranged to involve as low a cost as possible. It should also be practical, have acceptance by those affected, and be precise in its operation. Such criteria can be met only by considering the total system and the relation of its parts to the system and to each other.

The development of a control system is complicated and it takes time to make it effective. One reason for this is that skill and experience must be carefully developed. The group must learn to handle the technical elements—keep records, process information, establish checkpoints, audits, and inspections, improve forecasting, and judge historical trends.

Establishing and Maintaining Control

The supervisor faces two kinds of danger with respect to control, undercontrol and overcontrol. Undercontrol results from not caring about the need for control actions, laissez-faire attitudes, or overconfidence in the basic qualities of the operating system or of people. In effect, the supervisor ducks an important aspect of management responsibility. This neglect produces anxieties and errors on the part of subordinates who become uncertain and distrustful of their supervisor.

Overcontrol keeps the supervisor too busy with reports, excessive reviews, approvals. Instead of freeing the supervisor from routine details, it increases them. It subtracts from time better spent on planning, leading, and coordinating. Overcontrol also adds to clerical and labor costs.

The most effective means of control at the supervisor's disposal is to build control into the system and into every plan. Every procedure has a control aspect; every plan should include attention to the internal controls, standards and methods of evaluation. All too often, plans are filed or forgotten because they are difficult to carry out or because no one cares enough to perform the fine tuning that all plans require when they go into action. No plan is perfect, and its flaws may not appear until it is launched and put to the test.

Control by Exception

The fundamental nature of effective control is revealed in the principle of exceptional cases. Let us say that historically the scrap rate for raw material used in a department averages from 7 to 10 percent each month. The supervisor need not be disturbed by scrap rate reports that indicate monthly rates within this range. But if the figure jumps to 12 percent, and again to 14 percent, the supervisor faces a problem demanding immediate attention. It calls for examining the production system to discover and correct causes. Similarly, he will be interested in reports of 5 or 6 percent scrap rates to discover what is causing the improvement and whether it is a real or false change. Thus he uses simple reports to monitor conditions by dealing with exceptional cases.

The essence of control is based on probability statistics. This is most evident in the case of quality control for a machined part. What is required is (1) a goal that tells what is to be done, (2) a procedure that specifies how and when something is to be done, and who does it, (3) a standard of satisfactory performance, and (4) a checkup to see whether the work was done correctly. Steps 3 and 4 are essentially statistical problems. A standard is usually set in terms of a range of acceptable bounds known as tolerances. Parts machined within the range are accepted. Those falling above or below are not acceptable. Those below are likely to fail in use. Those above are being produced at too high a cost. The laws of probability hold that where large numbers of parts are involved, a certain predictable percentage will be off standards. Thus, selected check points can be established to monitor the process. Sampling procedures based on laws of probability permit reasonable control at reasonable cost.

Usually one cannot afford to measure or check all parts being mass produced in batches. If the sample items are rejected, the batch is suspected of not meeting standards. Further samples may be drawn before a decision is made.

Sampling is required not only to keep control costs low, but also because some tests destroy the part. For example, a test of tensile strength might require breaking or damaging the test part. Obviously a 100 percent testing is not feasible.

Much managerial control, of course, is not subject to statistically measurable control procedures. Nevertheless, sampling and probability apply to other types of controls. For example, a sales supervisor cannot possibly monitor all the activities of field salesmen. The supervisor can only watch for exceptions and monitor key behavior patterns and actions. The president of an organization cannot control everything that members of an organization do. As we look upward in the levels of an organization, we see that the focus of control changes from the specific to the general. The supervisor watches operational controls, objective measures, and a smaller number or range of problems. The president deals with broad categories, key objectives, long-range plans, and major policies. But both must be selective and hence are subject to the laws of probability and statistics.

In sum, two key activities form the center of supervisory control procedures: Monitoring, and feedback. By monitoring the behavior and effectiveness of subordinates, the supervisor keeps abreast of the situation. The supervisor's very presence is an element of control, but even further, it is the supervisor's task to notice what is going on and to bring undesired performance back to standards. Effective monitoring assures feedback, without which no learning takes place and control cannot be maintained. There are forces at work attempting to distort or eliminate proper feedback. For example, subordinates may not inform their bosses of mistakes or deviations. Effective monitoring is necessary, therefore, to assure effective and accurate feedback.

Human Aspects of Planning and Control

Planning and control are processes that help establish order and predictability within a system. Accordingly, they meet basic human needs. People want things to make sense, to know where they are going, and what their chances are for getting there.

At the same time, however, planning and control processes clash with other kinds of human characteristics. Planning implies changes for the organization and its people, and employees are often reluctant to accept even orderly, planned change. Furthermore, the need for control imposes limits on people that they may or may not be willing to accept.

Thus employees both favor and dislike planning and control. They do not want chaos or neglect of order, but neither do they want close supervision, loss of independence, or excessive controls. Therefore, the supervisor who thinks about planning and control must also consider finding a balance between these two extremes.

Many supervisors tend to neglect the human factor in planning, largely because they focus on the problems they are trying to solve, most of which concern immediate pressures. The physical aspects of the operation—tools, equipment, property, buildings, or raw materials, pose more definite problems than humans do. Also, the results expected of supervisors tend to be measured in costs of labor and materials, accident rates, inventories, and scrap counts. The human aspects of planning and control are hard to bring together in a concrete way for purposes of evaluation or measurement. Human factors pose problems because they do not provide clear criteria for evaluating planning and control.

Another cause of neglect of the human elements is that pressure for planning and control activities is often from the outside. The focus on environment and on the future places attention on demands from the outside and on the significance of forecasts, technological change, and style trends. These outside elements tend to be accepted as givens, and we forget that they can be influenced by people.

The supervisor's planning and control must take into account that people tend to resent close supervision and constant, obvious monitoring. They are often reluctant to help in planning because this changes the status quo. These problems can be overcome by relating specific goals to specific people, so that they can see how they are affected and how they will be rewarded. The supervisor must deal carefully with problems posed by human emotions and the difficulty of predicting or understanding human behavior. The best control is that which is built into the total situation. In both planning and control, the most demanding aspect for the supervisor is that of applying an effective management style to meet the needs of both the organization and subordinates.

Questions for
Discussion

1. In your own words, what is meant by the terms *planning* and *control?*

2. Why is it important to consider planning and control as parts of the same general area of supervisory responsibility?

3. What do you think are the most important obstacles to good planning, and why?

4. Where do most control efforts go wrong? How can such problems be prevented?

5. What steps can you take to improve planning and control in your own organization?

6. What are some of the human relations factors that need to be considered in effective planning and control?

Case Incidents

1. Fred Jones, a highly skilled lathe operator, has recently been transferred to your department from another division of the company where for eight years he served as subforeman.

After a month of satisfactory service as a lathe operator in your department, Jones develops a habit of arriving late for work. His piece-work performance is such that he can easily make up his lost time through superior performance. On several occasions he has said to his fellow employees that he was turning in a good day's work, so nobody had any kick coming regarding his lateness. No formal policy exists governing tardiness.

a. What is the human relations problem?

b. What is the control problem?

c. What additional information do you need as supervisor in this situation?

d. What actions would you take in the situation?

2. You are the supervisor of a shipping room where ten packers, fifteen mailers, five fork-lift truck operators, and three clerical people form your team. Expanding operations dictate that your team and all equipment will have to be relocated to another part of the building. Some of your equipment is old, out-of-date, and not in good repair. You have not been satisfied with the layout of your department. However, most of your subordinates have found ways of getting around the problems, and you have learned that they are disturbed over rumors of change. On May 1 you receive notice that in thirty days you must be ready to move your department.

a. What elements should go into your moving plan, and why?

b. What problems may arise in your work group, and how will you combat them?

c. Explain how you will establish effective controls to make sure your plans will work.

Management by Objectives

*Peter P. Schoderbek**

Chapter Objectives	1. *To introduce the reader to the widely employed system of management by objectives (MBO).*
	2. *To provide an understanding of the benefits of MBO.*
	3. *To explain the use of management by objectives as an appraisal tool.*
	4. *To outline and discuss the procedures for implementing MBO.*
	5. *To identify some of the difficulties associated with MBO.*
	6. *To present specific guidelines for writing objectives.*

IF PEOPLE were to ask, "What should an organization be accomplishing? How should it go about doing it? How does the organization know when accomplishments are met?" they would be focusing on one of the fundamental and primary tasks of management—planning. Of all managerial functions, planning is the most important, since organizing, directing, and controlling are all derived from the planning function. In this sense, planning includes all the managerial activities concerned with the direction in which an organization should be headed.

Of the various advances made in the field of management in recent years, the acceptance of the concept of accountability for results has been quite noteworthy. This results-oriented approach, often popularly known as management by objectives (MBO), aims to provide for systematic and orderly organizational growth by exacting performance standards with respect to specified goals. It demands both the identifi-

*Peter P. Schoderbek is Professor of Business Administration, College of Business Administration, The University of Iowa.

cation of job-related goals and the measurement of results against shared expectations of performance. It is a way of managing, and in its simplest form it can be described as a system in which managers with their subordinates agree on what is to be accomplished in the next time frame and how these accomplishments are to be measured. Subordinates enjoy wide latitude as to how they will bring about these results within organizational constraints. Then at the end of the time period, the actual results of subordinates are jointly reviewed against the previously agreed upon goals. An appraisal of the employees is then made and the process repeats itself.

The acceptance of MBO as a tool for planning is shown by its widespread use in industry. Perhaps the primary reason for its general adoption is the applicability of this technique to areas that transcend many other managerial functions. MBO is a system that aids planning, since it is concerned with the direction in which an organization is supposed to go. It provides for better organization, since it forces one to examine the structure of the organization, its authority lines, communication networks, and so forth. It also serves as a motivational tool, since it encourages people to set the goals they themselves wish to achieve. It serves as a vehicle for communication between the boss and subordinates and provides an opportunity for counseling when performance is under review. It aids in administering a fair wage and salary program that is tied to performance. Finally, it functions as a control tool of the highest order.

Benefits of Management by Objectives

In a study by Aplin and Schoderbek, the following responses were noted to the question: "What are the purposes of the (MBO) program as you see them and what is the rationale for the approach?"

That 64 percent of the respondents viewed MBO as an appraisal

RESPONSES	PERCENT OF RESPONDENTS*
To link evaluation to performance	64.1
To aid managers in planning	53.0
To motivate managers	24.2
To increase boss/subordinate interaction and feedback	22.7
To develop management potential	19.2
To link company objectives to department objectives	54.0

*Percents do not add up to 100 because of multiple responses.
N = 198

tool is not surprising since the system was first conceived as an objective approach to appraising managers. What is surprising, however, is that the additional benefits that have accrued from the use of this technique are even more important than the appraisal aspect. For example, the benefits cited below concern many of the problems that all managers encounter.

1. A major strength of any MBO system is that it forces one to examine and clarify the structural and functional aspects of an organization. Since MBO centers on key results areas, it entails an assessment of these aspects together with an identification of responsibility and authority. If a unit manager's goal is to achieve a predetermined volume of sales and a stated level of profitability, the authority of the position should be equal to its responsibilities. In other words, the authority should extend over those factors affecting goal attainment. When authority is shared, as it is in many instances, the exact nature of this sharing should also be duly noted for all parties.

This forced examination of organizational functions and structure is vitally important, since the principle of equality of authority and responsibility is so frequently violated. In organizations lacking basic job descriptions that spell out the responsibilities of the various roles and positions, one can hardly expect to find objectives clearly defined. Unless the key areas of responsibility are initially defined for an individual, there is little reason to expect predetermined results that are in line with organizational goals.

2. Another of the benefits of MBO is the identification of competent people by examining performance results. The best indicator of future performance is still past performance, and performance on lesser jobs can serve as evidence of leadership for higher ones. Most managers and top executives who have worked their way up through the organizational ranks have done so chiefly because they have satisfied their job requirements in an outstanding manner. Thus, the real test of any appraisal system is whether it allows competent individuals to rise while preventing the incompetent from doing so. MBO, which is results-oriented, serves admirably in this regard.

If an appraisal system can discriminate between good and bad performance, then the organization is in a position to reward employees on the basis of merit and to administer a sophisticated salary program. On the other hand, it is quite demoralizing to see employees rewarded who are unable to pull their own weight in the organization.

3. MBO also develops teamwork. Overall performance demands that

departmental objectives, as well as those of individuals, be directed toward the objectives of the whole organization. Objectives should be set by the boss and the subordinate manager. By taking part in the goal-setting process, subordinate managers commit themselves to the attainment of stated objectives. Thus while attaining their own objectives, they are at the same time attaining the objectives of the organization. This dual attainment is one of the more significant benefits of MBO, and lies behind some of the currently popular motivation theories. It assumes, of course, that the objectives actually spell out an individual's contribution to organizational goals and that these goals are challenging and meaningful to the individual.

The accomplishment of objectives also contributes to a sense of achievement on the part of subordinates who are largely in control of their own fate. MBO allows people to experience a powerful human desire—the desire to achieve and the desire to excel largely on one's own.

4. MBO also supplies the means for a person to exercise self-control rather than to be controlled. Most control systems lack critical control points that show progress being achieved, but MBO lets managers provide the control they need.

The implications of the self-control permitted by MBO are obvious. If subordinates are committed to objectives representing their jobs, and are to be judged according to the results accomplished, then there is less need for supervisors to dictate what the subordinates should or should not do. It is precisely this factor that enables many supervisors to get along with little direction or control from above. Such an approach recognizes an individual's strengths, weaknesses, and responsibilities. Managers fulfill objectives because their tasks and not their bosses demand it. Management can thus ensure results by transforming organizational objectives into personal goals.

MBO clarifies the direction in which an organization is headed, not only for managers at the top of the organization, but for supervisory levels as well. As shown in Figure 5–1, the system shows supervisors how their efforts tie into overall organizational objectives; it not only fosters commitment on their part, but also serves as a communication tool which is often lacking at this level.

Management by Objectives as an Appraisal Tool

Management by objectives enables one to evaluate the contributions of employees toward the realization of organizational goals. To grasp

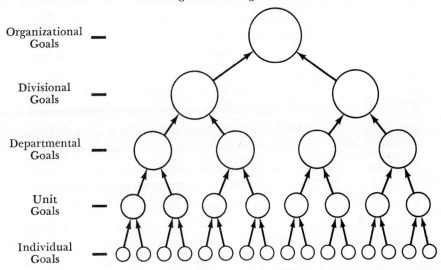

Figure 5–1
The Integration of Organizational Goals

Organizational Goals —

Divisional Goals —

Departmental Goals —

Unit Goals —

Individual Goals —

the significance of this, perhaps one should look at some of the factors that current appraisal systems consider in order to note their limitations.

When discussing appraisal systems, one is usually concerned with measuring a person's performance on the job. Although appraisal systems go under many different names (some call them performance reviews, progress evaluations, or merit ratings), they all deal with the application of established standards for measuring the work to be done by a person.

The following pitfalls are associated with many appraisal systems and are encountered all too often.

1. Rating the person for personality traits. For years managers were led to believe that there were certain desirable traits that they should look for when hiring and rating employees. Even though empirical studies have provided little or no support for this theory, the belief that some personality traits are related to satisfactory job performance still persists to some degree.

Unfortunately, the fact that many organizations still use personality traits in their appraisal systems does not indicate their usefulness, but rather denotes the slow rate of progress in getting organizations to accept more effective methods. One need only look at some of the systems used by various governmental agencies to find such traits as initiative, industry, loyalty, cooperativeness, and innovativeness included in appraisal forms. These qualities are not only difficult to measure, but are often not even defined. Thus, implicit in this approach is the unwarranted assumption that a given trait under consideration is clearly understood by all the parties concerned. Similarly, it is assumed that a uniform standard is at hand for determining various degrees of each trait.

Traits such as cooperativeness and initiative, which are found on many appraisal forms, are indeed difficult to describe and even more difficult to measure quantitatively. On the other hand, while loyalty may be a desirable attribute among employees, there is no evidence whatsoever that loyal personnel are more productive than others. Thus, the essential point here is that appraisal systems should measure personal performance and not the personality traits of individuals.

2. Failure to specify from the start the components of satisfactory job performance. Many employees have complained that they simply were never told what was required of them and were never informed that their performance was other than satisfactory. When the results of a job appraisal are communicated to such employees, it often comes as a complete surprise when they learn that their work left much to be desired.

A manager recently confided to the author that he was somewhat confused because he received a $1,200 raise this year, whereas last year he did not receive any, although there was no change in his performance. He has no idea of what to expect for the coming year and is still at a loss to know when he is performing satisfactorily or when he is not. There are other instances where people who thought they were burning up the rungs of the ladder learned later that they were not climbing up the right ladder. The essential point here is that employees have the right to know the basis on which their performance is to be evaluated and the specific measures for doing so.

Procedures of Management by Objectives

There can be little doubt that both government and industry are experiencing rapid change and that to meet today's challenges an organization must keep aware of all the factors linked to success. Management simply cannot operate forever on a crisis basis, reacting to events as they occur; it must seize responsibility for making things happen. And the places where it should be making things happen are none other than the areas on which survival itself rests.

Identifying Key Results Areas

All organizations must ask the same basic question, "What are the areas of operation in which results must be obtained to stay in business?" This holds true for nonprofit organizations as well as for those geared to profit. For most private establishments one of the key areas is profitability. Without the achievement of profit, it is doubtful that any firm would be around long enough to satisfy other objectives. But, as most managers must realize, profitability is not the only objective. They must also concern themselves with the quality of service, with financial resources, productivity, growth, and especially with managerial development.

The key results areas should constitute the core of organizational concern. Firms do have multiple and interlocking objectives, not just a single goal. Emphasis on only one objective can put the realization of others in jeopardy. To stress profit, for example, by cutting costs through a lowering of quality could well endanger sales. Likewise, to neglect the development of managers while concentrating on growth could easily be self-defeating in the long run.

These key results areas should be identified along with the major responsibilities typically spelled out in job descriptions. These descriptions are an invaluable aid to managers inasmuch as they not only describe the formal reporting structure, but also mark out the areas of responsibility. They are, however, no substitute for objectives, since they do not indicate the level of performance expected for each area of responsibility. Thus, a job description may state that a supervisor is responsible for costs, but it does not and cannot specify the level of costs.

A particular level of performance will necessarily vary with the type, size, and location of operations as well as with a host of other factors. Job descriptions can identify what employees are responsible for; they cannot indicate levels of performance, nor can they spell out how this responsibility should be met. This latter point is worth underlining since management by objectives is results-oriented, not activity-oriented. Thus, different people may achieve the same results by different means.

Many managers do not make use of job descriptions after their first week on the job, and these are often filed away and forgotten. Too often they do the tasks with which they are familiar and ignore those that are unfamiliar, difficult, or uncomfortable, even though their superior may consider the latter to be important. In fact, studies dealing with superior-subordinate perception show differences upward of 50 percent regarding the identification of vital tasks as well as their priority rankings.

Even with conscious efforts to keep job descriptions up-to-date, the way people perceive their jobs is related to:

- their technical abilities, which change over time
- the importance of the job as influenced by internal or external factors, or both
- the availability of staff assistance permitting delegation of authority
- the perception of the managerial role by other managers with whom one interacts.

Thus, while recognizing that job descriptions do serve many useful purposes in organizations, one must also be aware of the dynamic nature of many jobs as well as the variables affecting individual employees. Because job descriptions do not and cannot include specific performance standards, they cannot serve in lieu of MBO. They can, however, serve as starting points for MBO since they spell out areas of responsibility for each employee.

To summarize, the first step in the MBO process is to review the responsibilities in either the job description or the management by objectives work sheet from the preceding year. Any changes that may have taken place should be discussed with the supervisor, and if significant changes are warranted, they should be discussed with the personnel manager.

> ☑   Identify Key Results Areas

Setting Objectives for Key Results Areas

Once the key responsibility areas have been identified, the next step is to establish objectives in each of these areas. It is quite possible to have more than one objective in an area. For example, in the area of profitability, one objective might be set for labor costs, another for material costs, and yet another for volume.

Objectives need not be new or innovative in the sense that brand new goals are always needed. An objective to maintain costs at a predetermined level is a very legitimate one. To put it more simply, the normal work output should also be included in the objectives. Too often objectives focus on novel projects or endeavors that somehow never get off the ground because the normal daily output is not specified. This does not mean that innovations and radically new ideas are not wanted or sought, but that these should not be pursued at the expense of day-to-day operations.

Objectives should reflect the manager's overall contribution to the organization. Although objectives should attempt to reflect the total job picture, they seldom can because of the many routine areas in which one does not wish to set objectives. Such areas could include functions like the following: Attendance at weekly meetings, the drawing up of monthly budgets, weekly scheduling, and other routine functions.

In the absence of any job description outlining areas of responsibility, one way of writing objectives is to ask, "What product or service constitutes the work unit's normal output?" This ought to provide some guidelines for determining just where one's efforts are to be expended. Or one can look at the normal output of the work unit and ask, "Where can performance be improved?" In this case the objective or objectives will take the form "to reduce" costs, labor turnover, etc., or "to increase" sales volume, product turnover, etc.

Each of the major responsibility areas should have at least one objective. If one should happen to experience difficulty determining whether a particular area is one of major importance, his superiors ought to be able to help. One can sometimes gauge the importance of an activity by the amount of one's time generally allocated to it. This is, of course, no guarantee that priorities will be correctly assessed, nor is it proof that it is results-oriented. What such an analysis may bring to light is that a relatively insignificant area may actually be consuming a disproportionate part of one's time.

When setting objectives one need not specifically indicate why the objective is necessary. It can be reasonably assumed that those involved in formulating objectives know why they are necessary. Otherwise they would never have been singled out.

To review, the setting of objectives is the most critical step in the MBO process, since without clearcut objectives all subsequent activity is meaningless. Each objective, to be specific, should also include a stated completion point or target date.

This step appears to be relatively simple, but it is the backbone of MBO, since all subsequent analysis and measurement will be done against stated objectives. The beginner may experience considerable difficulty and frustration when first setting objectives. However, later efforts should be easier and more satisfying as well as more successful. Once managers gain experience with MBO, they will be very reluctant to switch to any other method.

> ☑   Identify Key Results Areas
>
> ☑   Set Objectives for Key Results Areas

Establishing Priorities

Few managers, at one time or another, have not thought that the work they were doing had top priority, only to be informed by a superior that other tasks ranked higher. This problem, no doubt, exists because different levels of management see organizational objectives differently. Yet with a simple ranking of priorities, many of these problems can be overcome or eliminated completely. Just as we try to specify the things we wish to accomplish, so too should we strive to be specific in the ordering of objectives. This can be done by a simple weighting procedure that uses the following categories.

Priority 1.   This means that an objective is essential to the job performed by a given person. These are the events that managers will make happen through their efforts. These are primary in the sense that without them a noticeable and sizeable gap would result in organizational performance. These top-priority objectives revolve around the essential parts of one's job. If they are omitted, there simply would not be enough left in the person's job around which to build a job description.

Priority 2.   This type of objective, although important, is not as essential as the Priority 1 type. Increases in volume may not be as important as maintaining profit ratios, or a decrease in costs may or may not be more important than an increase in volume. The priority of an objective is determined by superiors with their subordinate managers, although the former make the final determination. Too often, however, an individual manager fails to train subordinate managers in such priority determination.

Priority 3.   An objective of this type enjoys the least importance. This is not to say that its accomplishment is unimportant. It simply indicates a lower ranking than that given to the others, even though accomplishment may still be necessary for an overall satisfaction of job responsibilities.

In short, the use of the above scheme for ranking priorities leaves little doubt in the mind of subordinates as to the relative importance of various objectives.

> ☑   Identify Key Results Areas
>
> ☑   Set Objectives for Key Results Areas
>
> ☑   Establish Priorities

Establishing Performance Standards

Accepting the premise that it is better to measure than not to measure, one now proceeds to set up a measurement instrument that is reliable and clear. To measure means to bring together similar units and thus to determine the extent, capacity, quantity, or degree of likeness among them. In the absence of a quantitative measure, managers must set up standards of a subjective or qualitative nature.

Measurement is an integral part of control, which implies comparison with a standard. It is because of this comparison against a predetermined standard that control is termed the other side of the coin of planning. One must control against a plan. So, too, with performance; there must be something to compare it with. In the absence of standards, there is no clear way of knowing whether or not objectives are being achieved. In the absence of a standard it is very difficult to determine an equitable wage and salary structure, since the relative value of work done by employees cannot be assessed.

Objective units of measurement are, of course, preferable to subjective ones. The latter, however, are preferable to none at all, even though they are inferior by nature. But this is no excuse for formulating subjective measures that are not even capable of being put into operation. The following objective developed by one manager lacked an operational definition and so, for all practical purposes, was meaningless:

> Each manager is responsible for maintaining the morale of subordinates, providing comprehensive objectives, sound training, adequate discipline, and decisive leadership.

How can one determine the performance level of this manager? How is morale to be measured? What does adequate discipline mean? When is training sound and leadership decisive? Without a further definition of these concepts, measurement is bound to be arbitrary, haphazard, and unreliable.

Standards should be chosen that are relevant to the tasks at hand, since standards are the means by which the accomplishment of objectives is to be measured. The standards should also leave little room for subjectivity and should serve as indicators of satisfactory or unsatisfactory performance on the job. Once measurement scales are identified, some point must then be chosen to indicate the level of expected performance.

One must exercise deliberate caution when comparing one department with another, since differing performance standards may be in operation. Some of the service functions such as personnel management, public relations, and management development obviously cannot be subjected to unit cost standards at particular performance levels. In such cases, however, budgeted costs can be used to determine an overall level of performance.

Whenever quantitative measures are difficult to establish, it may be impossible to use ratios, percentages, and other relative measures. In such cases, it may be necessary to judge the performance level only by the end result and not by a number of exact standards. Again, though it is obviously difficult to evaluate the service departments of organizations, it is possible to get some indication of their performance level by the end result and not by a number of exact standards. It is also possible to get some indication of performance of these departments by the number of complaints. The fact remains that some measurement must be made of results if performance is to be evaluated. If the result cannot be described or measured, it probably is not worthwhile dealing with it.

The more managers work with the management by objectives system, the more they discover that many factors can be quantified. In fact, there is hardly any objective which cannot be quantified to some extent when both superior and subordinate managers know what performance is expected of them.

☑	Identify Key Results Areas
☑	Set Objectives for Key Results Areas
☑	Establish Priorities
☑	Establish Performance Standards

Developing Action Plans

In organizations where MBO has been in operation for several years, it is generally not necessary to specify how results will be achieved so long as they are achieved within organizational constraints. What one should aim at is to give employees as much latitude as they need to accomplish their objectives. Otherwise, a close monitoring of the methods used to achieve goals might suggest a lack of confidence and can easily be resented. Yet, to set objectives without planning how they will be achieved is also futile.

Specifying the action steps by which objectives can be attained is an integral part of the MBO process. Spelling out the action steps provides not only for a check on the reasonableness of goals but also for an additional base for evaluating performance. If a goal is attainable, it should be supported by several action steps; in other words, there should be more than one way to accomplish the objective. How detailed the action steps should be will depend upon the ability and the experience of subordinates. Where an experienced subordinate agrees with the goal and says, "No need to worry about it. I'll get it done on time," one ought to let good enough along. Such employees should be given ample freedom to use their own initiative. It may still be helpful, however, to touch upon the key activities they plan to initiate to achieve their objectives.

Finally, it should be clear that persons are not to be evaluated against their action plans but rather against their objectives. MBO is results-oriented, not activity-oriented. Results speak louder than activities. In this respect, discussions centering on the development of objectives and the formulation of action plans provide excellent opportunities for clarifying authority problems, any training needed by subordinates, and possible problems to be encountered. Thus, it is the responsibility of each superior to establish a favorable climate for these all-important discussion sessions.

☑	Identify Key Results Areas
☑	Set Objectives for Key Results Areas
☑	Establish Priorities
☑	Establish Performance Standards
☑	Develop Action Plans

The five steps outlined above are illustrated in Figure 5–2 which presents a Performance Planning and Review Form that can be used in the goal-setting process. The first element on the worksheet concerns areas of responsibility. This should be of interest since each major area of responsibility must have an objective. Of course, the areas of responsibility listed on the worksheet should be the same as those identified in the job description. Typical areas might be supervision, profitability, staff development, policies, and operations. The priority of these areas of responsibility should also be noted as well as the steps to be taken in achieving stated objectives. When performance is reviewed, the actual results will be noted and a suitable rating given.

Reviewing Performance

It is usually recommended that performance be reviewed at least twice a year, with one of the two reviews coming at the end of the organization's annual operating period. Such periodic reviews not only ensure that objectives will be evaluated at least twice a year, but also provide for discussions of the accomplishment or nonaccomplishment of objectives with employees before a final written review.

While the year-end review is greatly simplified if objectives are adequately set at the beginning of the year, it is possible that the assumptions on which original objectives were based will change significantly, thus rendering these objectives inappropriate. The review session provides a good opportunity for discussing such changes, and lets employees point out those factors that may be preventing them from making satisfactory progress toward their goals. Logically, any factors affecting the subordinates' ability to meet their goals should have been identified when objectives were first set, but this is not always possible. However, if progress is reviewed twice annually, the year-end review should not produce any startling surprises for the employees.

When evaluating a subordinate's performance, one should also examine the methods used to achieve actual results. Obviously, a short-run cost reduction program at the expense of service may produce a desired result, but the consequences in terms of overall performance may be disastrous. To assist in this area, employees should be asked to provide all of the necessary information they believe will be of value in evaluations of their performance. A written evaluation should then be completed by the superior, because it becomes part of an employee's permanent record, and because it can serve as a constructive critique as well.

Figure 5–2
Suggested Form
For
Performance Planning and Review

Name:_____

Date of
Performance Planning:_____

Department:_____

Date of
Performance Review:_____

Supervisor:_____

Length of
Planning Period:_____

Performance Planning

RESULTS TO BE ACHIEVED A specific statement of the major goals the employee is expected to achieve in the period.	ACTION STEPS TO ACHIEVE OBJECTIVE	PRIORITY OF OBJECTIVE 1 = primary 2 = secondary 3 = least important
AREA OF RESPONSIBILITY: (Use key word (s)) OBJECTIVE:		1 2 3 (circle one)
AREA OF RESPONSIBILITY: OBJECTIVE:		1 2 3
AREA OF RESPONSIBILITY: OBJECTIVE:		1 2 3
AREA OF RESPONSIBILITY: OBJECTIVE:		1 2 3
AREA OF RESPONSIBILITY: OBJECTIVE:		1 2 3

Performance Review

ACTUAL ACHIEVEMENTS	LEVEL OF GOAL ACHIEVEMENT				Continuing Responsibilities
	exceeded	fully met	not fully met	unsatisfactory	(Responsibilities not covered in objectives, to be considered only when they have a *significant* effect on performance.)
					_____
					_____
					_____
					_____
					_____
					_____
					Unprogrammed Accomplishments
					_____
					_____
					_____
					_____
					_____
					_____

Overall Rating

☐ Consistently exceeds requirements of job.

☐ Fully meets the requirements of job.

☐ Does not fully meet requirements of job.

☐ Unsatisfactory performance.

SUGGESTED TRAINING _____

_____

_____

_____

INTERVIEW COMMENTS (Significant items discussed in the interview but not recorded elsewhere on this form)

_____

_____

_____

_____

_____

I certify that this report has been discussed with me. I understand that my signature does not necessarily indicate agreement. Please indicate any substantial disagreements with the evaluation.

_____   _____
Employee Signature   Date

_____   _____
Reviewer's Signature   Date

MANAGEMENT REVIEW (Optional comments by reviewer concerning goals/ performance review)

_____

_____

_____

EMPLOYEE REVIEW (Optional comments by employee concerning goals/ performance review)

_____

_____

_____

During the performance review, merit increases should not be discussed since to do so often diverts the conversation away from a consideration of objectives and toward salary. Also, until superiors have had an opportunity to discuss how well objectives were met, they do not have all of the information needed to make decisions about salary.

Although no clear and definite pattern can be found for the best time interval between evaluation and merit discussions, some managers feel that it should take place shortly after the evaluation. As a result, many organizations regard two weeks as the longest permissible time interval between the two meetings.

> ☑ Identify Key Results Areas
> ☑ Set Objectives for Key Results Areas
> ☑ Establish Priorities
> ☑ Establish Performance Standards
> ☑ Develop Action Plans
> ☑ Review Performance

Experiences with Management by Objectives

Many organizations have experienced remarkable success with management by objectives; others have gone overboard and believe that all managerial problems can be solved with MBO. One should always remember that MBO is but a management tool, albeit a powerful one. However, as with all tools, there are unavoidable limitations. Several of these are examined here.

Difficulties with the MBO System

1. Failure to clarify objectives for the entire unit or department before setting them for individuals.

The sum of the goals of the individuals within a department should be equal to, or greater than, the sum of the goals of the total department. When individuals meet their goals, but the goals do not tie in with those of the department, their meaningfulness to each individual is certain to be less.

2. Failure to adjust subordinate goals when previously agreed upon objectives have changed.

Changes in priorities or in major departmental goals should obviously be reflected in the goals of subordinates. Otherwise, evaluation will take place against a different set of standards than originally agreed upon. The entire MBO system will not be meaningful if such changes are not noted.

3. Failure to reward successful goal accomplishment or failure to take corrective action for nonaccomplishment. One organization that experienced less than the expected returns on MBO still gave a bonus to all managers in the department, regardless of the results attained. Such action must be approached with caution, but the lack of visible rewards for successful managers can certainly lead to motivational problems.

4. Failure to give direction on how a subordinate's goals can be met.

The amount of direction given by the superior in determining how goals will be accomplished is dependent upon the past performance of subordinates, their experience on the job, their level of ability, and other factors. A new employee on the job will require more direction than a seasoned one. The superior may be more familiar than the subordinate with the various ways to accomplish goals. Such experience should be shared with the subordinate, and the superior should not fail to outline the scope of authority accompanying the new employee's responsibilities.

5. Failure to set goals high enough to challenge the individual, or low enough to enable the subordinate to attain them.

When goals are set either too high or too low, subordinates will tend to drop out of the program. In the first instance, the job does not present any challenge and the subordinate may feel that the work is insignificant, routine, and not worthwhile. Anyone can do it. On the other hand, when goals are set too high, they are generally unattainable, and employees may become quite frustrated or may simply give up without making any serious attempt to realize them. Dissatisfaction sets in on all sides; objectives are not realized; and even attempts to realize them are abandoned.

6. Failure to get participation in goal setting.

This is quite likely to happen when managers simply ignore the goals proposed by subordinates and, instead, impose those which they deem suitable. Studies show that MBO is more effective when goals are jointly determined rather than imposed upon employees from above.

7. Failure to set the proper number of individual goals.

The setting of too many objectives for an individual serves no useful purpose. Typically, no employee should have more than five or six objectives, although these numbers are not sacred. Rules of thumb differ. One manager with over twenty major goals saw that they were unattainable within the time period under consideration. Therefore, this person concentrated on the less important ones in the hope that the largest number of them would be completed, regardless of their importance.

Guidelines for Writing Objectives

The following suggestions provide some useful guidelines for developing objectives. Not all of the suggestions mentioned here apply in all situations, but they should at least be considered and tested to see if they will work. It should also be remembered that these are merely guidelines to be used in the MBO process. They cannot replace the substance of objectives themselves. Finally, such procedures will not guarantee the success of an MBO program, but they are useful in getting started.

1. Since objectives are actions or events that are to be realized, it is convenient to begin describing them with the word *to,* followed by an action verb. Thus,

to implement current guidelines . . .
to increase sales . . .
to decrease labor turnover . . .
to maintain labor costs . . .
to develop and install a training program . . .

Nearly all objectives can be formulated in this manner.

2. If possible, try to identify present and future performance levels. An objective "to reduce turnover by 10 percent" is meaningless unless one knows what the present level is. Otherwise, one simply cannot know when the level has been reduced by 10 percent. This prescription applies to all objectives involving a quantifiable change. Thus, the objective quoted above could be formulated as:

To reduce turnover in Department A from
the present level of 30 percent to 20 percent . . .

3. A specific target date, as well as an interim date, should be included with each objective. This prescription is made to ensure that both the superior and the subordinate manager know when the objective is to be achieved. The excuse, "I could easily have gotten it done if you had only told me you wanted it by this date" simply will not be accepted. Thus, our previous objective could read:

To reduce turnover in Department A from
the present level of 30 percent to 20 percent by July 1.
A reduction of 5 percent is expected by March 1.

In this way one can monitor objectives as time goes on. At an early date one will have some idea of whether or not the objectives are likely to be attained. Instead of waiting until a situation is completely out of control, one will see the need for corrective action before things get out of hand and will be in a position to do something about it. This principle is used daily in other phases of a manager's operations. Similarly, in MBO one likes to know if subordinate managers are on schedule and if not, why not.

4. When writing objectives, avoid words and expressions which cannot be measured. The following list indicates such words. Ask yourself if they can be measured.

acceptable	efficient	realistic
adequate	good	regular
appropriate	innovative	sound
as soon as possible	orderly	timely
comprehensive	pertinent	tolerable
decisive	progressive	workable
effective	quality	

5. Personalize objectives as much as possible. People have differing abilities and experiences, and require a different amount of supervision. The performance expected of a young college graduate with no previous experience should obviously be less than that expected of an experienced and seasoned employee. A failure to consider the varying factors in a given situation can make expected performance levels unrealistic, maybe even impossible. It can also call forth undesirable behavior on the part of employees. For example, a person may try to meet a given objective at any cost, or, because of the unrealistic nature of the proposed goal, may simply shrug off all accountability for not meeting it. Therefore, one of the possible consequences of not taking specific situational factors into account is the development of negative attitudes on the part of the employees toward all future MBO programs.

6. Get the subordinate manager to participate in the goal-setting process. There is evidence to show that when people are personally involved in the planning process, they will not only commit themselves to objectives, but will also strive much more vigorously to bring them about. On the other hand, people are not particularly turned on when the boss provides them with their work assignments. In fact, studies show that management by objectives is less effective when managers set objectives for their employees. Thus, without participation, goals often take on the appearance of imposed quotas.

Many companies have taken the position that objectives should come from the top down, thereby insuring that overall organizational and departmental goals are met. Those who hold this view believe that the sum of the goals of departments must be equal to, or greater than, the sum of the goals of the unit immediately above. The top-down approach makes this clearly apparent. However, it should be noted here that any MBO program in which objectives are set only by those at the top will be less than successful. Successful MBO programs involve mutual goal setting and communication between superiors and subordinates. The basic reason for this stems from the fact that managers at all levels must do the actual planning required to accomplish the goals of their units. Consequently, they must be personally involved. What better way to bring about personal involvement in the results than to bring them into the goal-setting process.

7. When discussing objectives with the subordinate, you should follow a list of items to be covered so that little will be left to chance. Major points might well be these:

a. Do the objectives tie in with the key results areas of the department?

b. Are the objectives challenging, yet realistic? Can they be met with the resources available to the subordinate? Does the subordinate have the authority necessary to control the resources which affect the performance level?

c. Are there other objectives that the subordinate considers important enough to add to the worksheet? Should others be modified?

d. Is there agreement on the priorities assigned to the various objectives?

e. Are there target dates for each of the objectives?

f. Is there agreement on how results will be measured?

g. What can the manager do to help or advise the subordinate manager in achieving objectives?

8. Try to focus objectives on a few vital areas of responsibility rather than on many trivial ones. A part of any job involves repetitive tasks, and the manager's job is no different. In the MBO program these routine responsibilities are typically not specified, not because they are unimportant but because of the need to identify those which are vital. Routine responsibilities are more commonly included in job descriptions and should be managed by the exception principle; that is, situations will be noted only when performance deviates from expected standards. Obviously, this assumes that there is also mutual agreement on what these routine activities are as well as their expected level of

performance. To assure this, it is well to review routine duties about once a year and to put in writing any notable changes.

An MBO program that separates the few vital areas of responsibility from the many trivial ones permits the establishment of more creative and significant objectives, at least as far as the individual is concerned. It also avoids the danger that employees will tend to concentrate on the easier and more routine objectives, secure in the belief that they have completed many of those proposed, when in reality they may have missed the most important ones.

Summary

Many managers find it difficult to measure the results of a subordinate's performance when employing the traditional personality measures. Managers who have contributed their share to the success of an organization may remain unrewarded, because their contributions have never been identified or recorded. On the other hand, those who failed to perform satisfactorily remain untouched because their responsibilities were not clearly defined.

An effective alternative to the largely inadequate traditional approach to appraisal is management by objectives. This technique sets up definite performance standards that a manager is expected to meet within a given time period. The resultant statement of accountability tells managers what is expected of them and identifies the criteria by which their performance will be measured. Uncertainty is virtually eliminated, since performance will be measured against known and agreed upon objectives.

The use of management by objectives can provide for the continued professional growth of all managers. In government or industry, managers must not simply react to change; they must be agents of change. Management by objectives is one tried and tested vehicle for making desired change occur.

Questions for Discussion

1. Why has management by objectives replaced the trait approach to performance appraisal in many organizations?

2. Examine an appraisal form from a company that still uses the trait approach and discuss the difficulties with the form.

3. Talk to some friends who manage under MBO and note the problems that they have had in employing it.

4. How would the use of MBO differ between an autocratic boss and a participative one?

5. What dangers are inherent in the MBO system if it becomes a tool for discipline when objectives are not met?

6. Show how your household is in fact managed by objectives even though you may not be conscious of it.

7. Show why many governmental programs in such areas as drug abuse and welfare are seldom evaluated.

8. Why is it important to involve lower levels of supervision in setting objectives, since they are so far removed from the overall goals of top management?

Case Incidents

1. Wally Krebitz was a salesman for Associated Drug Company, a wholesale firm in Massachusetts. One day he was called into his district manager's office and told that he was being terminated. His boss said, "The sales in your territory are only half of what we expected of you, your order size is too small, and the number of new contacts isn't enough." Wally was bitter about the situation, since not once had his boss told him what was expected of him. In fact, Wally thought that he was doing an excellent job. Wally was then employed by a competitor and was very successful.

a. How would you explain Wally's failure?

b. What could the company have done to prevent this situation?

2. George Miller was foreman in the 38″ rolling mill of the Morris Sheet Metal Company. Although George consistently produced more tonnage than the other foremen, he was told that he could not be promoted because he was not popular with his men. George then decided if he was going to get promoted he had better ease up.

He started drinking beer with his crew, joined the bowling league, and became lax in his supervision over them. George became one of the boys, but at the same time his production was dropping. Management started putting pressure on him to get his production up and told him that he could not get promoted without production.

a. How could this incident have been prevented?

b. What was the underlying cause that led to this incident?

c. What should George do now?

Organization Structure, Coordination, And Job Design

*Bernard J. White**

Chapter Objectives

1. *To define what is meant by the term organizational structure and explain why structure is essential to any organization.*

2. *To identify (a) the major components of structure, (b) the various ways organizations divide up their work, and (c) the mechanisms of coordination employed by organizations.*

3. *To identify those aspects of structure which are likely to be "fixed" for the supervisor, and to explain how certain aspects can affect supervisory performance.*

4. *To identify those aspects of structure which supervisors can influence, and to explain how and why they might wish to do so.*

FOR MANY PEOPLE, the words *organization* and *structure* are nearly the same and, in some respects, this view is not far from the truth. For example, an "organization" chart is actually a picture of an organization's "structure." It is a fact that structure alone does not make an organization; however, *there is no organization without some degree of structure.* And, as we shall see, understanding an organization's structure can make a big difference in how, and how well, supervisors meet their responsibilities.

In this chapter, we will discuss briefly: (1) what we mean by the important concept of *structure;* (2) why organizations must have some degree of structure; (3) what the components of structure are; (4) how and why structure varies from organization to organization; and

---

*Bernard J. White is Assistant Professor of Organization Behavior/Industrial Relations, Graduate School of Business Administration, The University of Michigan.

most important, (5) what impact varying types of structure have on supervisory effectiveness. In this respect, the roles people are expected to play in an organization depend very much on the type of structure in which they find themselves. Finally, we will look in more detail at one very important component of structure, namely the design of jobs.

What Do We Mean by Structure?

Our earlier reference to the organization chart as a picture of an organization's structure is a good starting point. What does a chart show? It is a "map" of the formal reporting relationships in an organization. It gives you an idea of who has formal authority over whom, and in what areas. It shows who is responsible to whom, and it also suggests the paths along which communications should formally travel up, down, and across the organization. Thus, we may define structure as "the formal, prescribed set of relationships among the different jobs in an organization." During their first day on the job, supervisors are usually introduced to their bosses, their subordinates, and other supervisors. Through this process, they are told where they "fit" in the formal structure of the organization. Now, with our definition in mind, let's see why organizations need structure, and then look at the basic components of structure.

Why Structure?

Structure is absolutely basic to organizations for the simple reason that they are created by people to achieve goals and perform tasks that are too large or too complex for any one individual to accomplish. Therefore, structure is the means of assuring that all of the component jobs and subobjectives of any large undertaking are achieved in such a way that overall organizational goals are satisfied.

Basic Components of Organizational Structure

The absolutely basic components of structure, namely, division of labor and coordination, were present in simple, ancient organizations and are similarly present in the large, complex organizations of today's world. For our primitive ancestors, a division of labor may have meant little more than assigning each person to a post on a rock being pushed. Coordination was achieved by a shout to begin, or perhaps a series of quick kicks in strategic locations. Compare this picture with a division of labor in modern organizations like the Boeing Company with its assembly of "747" airliners. Here, a detailed division of labor involves thousands of specific jobs, with coordination achieved through massive computer scheduling programs and the efforts of hundreds of managers and supervisors. In either situation, however, it is important to note that a division of labor and coordination are present, as they must be in any cooperative effort.

Modern organizations achieve the necessary degrees of division of labor and coordination in a number of different ways. We will look next at some of these ways and, in so doing, begin to explore the meaning of labels like "centralized" versus "decentralized" organizations and "wide" versus "narrow" spans of control. We will also shed light on some interesting questions like, "Why do organizations have so many rules and procedures (other than to complicate your life with red tape)?" Or, "Why are we always setting up committees or teams to handle special problems?" Most important, we will always keep in mind the question, "How do all of these elements of structure affect the supervisor?" But first, some basics.

Division of Labor: How Organizations Divide up the Work

Management decisions on four important questions determine how an organization is structured, or more specifically, how the overall work of an organization is divided and allocated. The four questions are:

1. To what extent should the overall task of the organization (or a particular subunit) be divided and redivided into job specialties? (This is the question of job design.)

2. How should these jobs then be combined into groups reporting to a common supervisor? (This is the question of departmentalization.)

3. What is the appropriate size of each of these groups? (This is the question of span of control.)

4. How much authority should be given to the individual doing each job and to the supervisor of each group? (This is the question of delegation.)

Management's answers to each of these questions can vary; thus there is a wide range of possibilities in how an organization is ultimately structured. The extremes in each case are shown in Figure 6–1. Please study it carefully.

Several observations can be drawn from Figure 6–1. First, while decisions could be made separately by management on each of the four

Figure 6–1

Options in Division of Labor Decisions

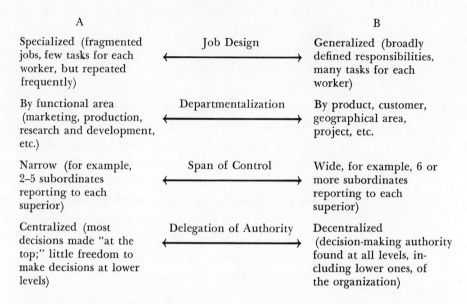

A		B
Specialized (fragmented jobs, few tasks for each worker, but repeated frequently)	Job Design ←————————→	Generalized (broadly defined responsibilities, many tasks for each worker)
By functional area (marketing, production, research and development, etc.)	Departmentalization ←————————→	By product, customer, geographical area, project, etc.
Narrow (for example, 2–5 subordinates reporting to each superior)	Span of Control ←————————→	Wide, for example, 6 or more subordinates reporting to each superior)
Centralized (most decisions made "at the top;" little freedom to make decisions at lower levels)	Delegation of Authority ←————————→	Decentralized (decision-making authority found at all levels, including lower ones, of the organization)

elements listed, they seldom are. Consequently, an organization departmentalized by function is also likely to have rather specialized jobs in each functional area with centralized decision making.[1] It would be an "A" type organization as shown by the heading on the left in Figure 6–1. On the other hand, an organization departmentalized by product is likely to have more generalized jobs with more decentralized decision-making authority. It would be a "B" type organization.

A second observation is that efforts to figure out where your particular organization falls in these categories will depend on how you define "your organization." For example, General Motors as a whole is departmentalized by product (Chevrolet, Buick, Cadillac, etc.), but within the particular divisions (Chevrolet division, for example), you will also find departmentalization by function. Therefore, (and this holds true for all four elements of division of labor), in any one large organization you may find examples of nearly all of the possibilities shown in Figure 6–1. The figure should, however, help you to classify how your particular unit is organized.

Once you have classified your unit, you are ready for the next and

---

[1]Span of control should not really be included in this generalization since factors like the type of work involved, the abilities of the superior, the skills of the subordinates, etc., determine the appropriate span.

most interesting observation concerning Figure 6–1. An "A" type organization is clearly going to be a very different place in which to do your job as a supervisor than a "B" type organization. Why? To answer the question, consider yourself from the perspective of the proverbial "man (or woman) in the middle." Supervisors are both superiors and subordinates.

They supervise the members of their work groups, but are subordinate to their own bosses. This fact has important implications in terms of how structure affects supervisors and how they can affect structure.

Division of Labor: Implications for the Supervisor

Given this "man in the middle" perspective, we can see that supervisors are doubly and directly affected by three of the four major elements of division of labor: Namely, job design, span of control, and delegation of authority. They are affected by the issue of departmentalization primarily as a function of whether they are in a staff department (serving other units of the organization) or a line department (directly involved in the production or distribution of the organization's goods and services). If they are members of the line, they will probably have plenty of authority to carry out their responsibilities. If in a staff department, they may frequently find that they are held responsible for more than their authority permits. Beyond this, you can gain a much better understanding of your own job and those of your people by trying to answer the following questions:

1. *Job design:* a. How specialized or general are my tasks?
   b. How specialized or general are the tasks of my subordinates?

2. *Span of Control:* a. How many people report to my boss?
   b. How many people do I have reporting to me?

3. *Delegation of Authority:* a. How much decision-making authority has my boss given me?
   b. How much freedom in solving problems and making decisions can I give to my people?

Your answers to these questions should immediately begin to point up a reality of organizational life. For the supervisor, many structural conditions are simply givens. In other words, they are factors over which supervisors have little or no control. Examples include: (1) The way their organizations are departmentalized; (2) the design of their own jobs (i.e., the extent of their responsibilities); (3) their boss's span of control as well as their own span of control; and (4) how much authority has been delegated to them. Now, the fact that these structural conditions cannot be easily changed should not imply that they do not affect the difficulty or ease with which supervisors do their jobs, or how relatively successful or unsuccessful they might be. Instead, it is implied that the only real alternative is to learn to operate within, and cope with, these conditions precisely because they are givens. Let's look at an example.

A supervisor, Bruce Todd, finds that he has twelve people reporting to him when he feels he can handle only eight comfortably. His boss has told him that in other groups doing the same kind of work supervisors seem able to deal with twelve subordinates; and, in any case, the company cannot afford to have spans of control less than twelve in this operation. What can Bruce do? His span of control is fixed. He needs some way to cope with the situation.

Obviously, Bruce can only make adjustments in those areas over which he has some control. However, from the list of structural factors and related questions developed above, there appear to be only two fairly controllable areas for him to consider. One is the design of his subordinates' jobs; the other is the extent to which he delegates authority to them. Thus, the question becomes, Can supervisors who are having trouble with a span of control that is too wide (an uncontrollable structural factor for them) solve the problem by either (1) making changes in the job designs of their people, or (2) changing their delegation practices (both of which are somewhat controllable structural factors)?

Although all supervisors must answer the question for themselves, the answer seems to be a very possible "yes." For example, by giving his people more freedom to solve their own problems within general guidelines he establishes, and by giving his help only when it is specifically requested, the supervisor in our example will probably be better able to cope with his wide span of control. In short, he can supervise each person "less closely."

The important point to recognize is that most structural factors affecting supervisors are fixed or given; supervisors can influence only a few. Thus, it is important in one's particular job situation to recognize those factors that fall into each category, and to learn to cope with the fixed ones by working with those that are not. Incidentally, we will very shortly have more to say about adjusting the job designs of your people. In addition to delegation, this is the other major factor over which supervisors have some degree of control.

Coordination: How Organizations "Get It Together"

To refresh your memory, the aspects of organizational structure discussed above are really ways in which management divides up the work that must be done. Management designs jobs, arranges jobs into departments, decides on spans of control, and assigns (delegates) authority down through the organization. But the important question still remains: Once all the work is allocated to various departments, work groups, and individuals, how does the organization achieve the second absolutely necessary component of organizational structure, namely, coordination among those departments, groups, and individuals?

There are several ways to achieve coordination. An awareness of them may make you more sympathetic toward what is usually viewed as "bureaucratic red tape," perhaps even making you willing (if not eager) to help make them work through your participation as a supervisor. The major mechanisms of coordination in organizations are: (1) The formal structure (hierarchy) itself; (2) various rules and established procedures; (3) informal communication; and (4) committees, teams, and task forces. We will briefly discuss these, mentioning in each case the role of supervisors and how they fit into the total coordination effort.

Structure (Hierarchy)

It was mentioned earlier that the supervisor has often been called the "person in the middle." This label hints at the way in which the formal structure or hierarchy is the most basic means of organizational coordination. Supervisors are the links, the coordinators, between subordinates and higher levels of management. They receive directives, policies, procedures, and information from above, and communicate, enact, and enforce them with those below. Similarly, they solicit and accept information, monitor performance, and identify problems below, and communicate these upward to the higher management of the organization.

The supervisor is in a key position in the hierarchy not only as a vertical (up and down) coordinator, but also in horizontal (across the organization) coordination. For example, look at the structure depicted in Figure 6–2. If the work group under the Supervisor: Operations is having difficulty getting adequate maintenance for their machinery, they have no formal access to the Plant Maintenance Department. Therefore, to resolve this problem, they go to their supervisor who can bridge the gap, or coordinate relations between the two departments by going directly to the Supervisor of Maintenance and requesting better service. Furthermore, if these two supervisors are unable to resolve the problem, the structure still accommodates coordination by providing them both access to their mutual superior at the next level. In such cases, Foreman B may have to resolve disputes between the two supervisors concerning (1) what constitutes adequate maintenance, (2) the intervals at which maintenance is to be performed, and (3) the times of day or night when maintenance will be done on various machines.

Figure 6–2
Partial Organization Chart

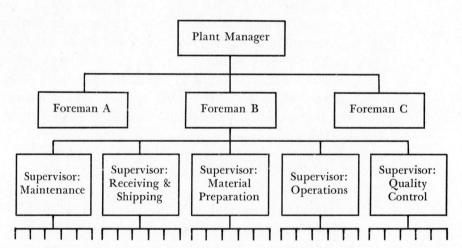

The important point to recognize is that the structure provides a means for coordinating tasks, communication flows, and decision making up, down, and across the organization. Accordingly, the absolutely critical coordinating role of supervisors in the structure should be quite evident. They represent the one and only link between their work groups and the rest of the organization.

Rules and Established Procedures

Our previous example of a coordination problem between an Operations and a Maintenance group in a manufacturing organization provides an excellent starting point for demonstrating the importance of rules and procedures in achieving coordination. If Foreman B in our example recognizes that the machinery in Operations is used in essentially the same way, at the same rate, day after day, he can avoid having to coordinate relations repeatedly between Operations and Maintenance by simply establishing a procedure. A procedure of this type might state that machine "a" will be serviced in a specified way at interval "b," machine "x" will be serviced at interval "y," and so on. The relationship between the two groups is thus automatically coordinated by the procedure. The Maintenance supervisor knows what is expected, and the Operations supervisor knows what to expect. The foreman needs only to monitor exceptions to the procedure.

Rules serve the same coordinating purpose as procedures. Working hours (starting and stopping times) are usually fixed and must be enforced strictly because operations, and the people who perform them, are dependent on each other and must be coordinated. Consequently, such rules attempt to ensure that all of the elements required to get a job done will be in place and operating at the same time.

Although many other examples might be cited, it should be clear that rules and procedures ideally help the supervisor and others in an organization to do their jobs by making coordination "automatic." Yet, ironically, these same rules and procedures sometimes seem to get in the way and are labeled as "red tape," nuisances, etc. How can we explain this paradox? There are probably two explanations. The first is that organizations seldom give the reasons for rules and procedures, and indeed the reasons are not always self-evident. Thus, they appear to be nuisances rather than helps. Secondly, certain rules and procedures are, in fact, nuisances. Their purpose may not have been well thought out in the first place, or perhaps they have outlived their original usefulness but remain "on the books."

Supervisors are held responsible for the enforcement of many rules and procedures among their subordinates. The preceding observations thus hold several important implications for supervisors. One is certainly the importance of recognizing why rules and procedures must be enforced if any organization's efforts are to be effectively coordinated. Next, when rules and procedures appear to be getting in the way instead of helping out, the supervisor should consider several possible reasons and remedies. Is the rule a good one, but not well understood by subordinates? Take time to explain it. Is the procedure not really needed, or perhaps outdated? Raise the question with your superior, and suggest the possibility of improving or dropping it. Is the purpose of the rule or procedure unclear to supervisors themselves? Ask your superior for an explanation, and be sure it makes sense to you.

In summary, rules and procedures are the "invisible coordinators" of organization. Ideally, they should serve the people of the organization by facilitating their work.

Informal Communications

We should make brief mention of another obvious and very important means of organizational coordination. This is the informal network of relationships, including the communications grapevine, that exists side by side with the formal structure. In our earlier example of a coordination problem between Maintenance and Operations, it is possible that a member of the Operations group might mention the problem to a close friend in the Maintenance group. As a result, the friend might initiate the needed maintenance and the supervisors would never become involved.

Such informal coordination occurs all the time in organizations. Its major advantages are its speed, and its handling of many coordination problems that would otherwise burden the hierarchy or result in an excessive number of rules and procedures. Its major disadvantages are its hiding from supervisors and higher level management fundamental coordination problems that require management decisions or the institution of a rule or procedure, and the possibility of a nonstandardized handling of problems that should be handled in a uniform way, or perhaps outright violations of approved practices.

The implication for supervisors is the need to be always sensitive to the informal coordination going on between their own people and those elsewhere in the organization. When prescribed methods are being violated, or when the informal should be formalized, supervisors can step in or call the situation to the attention of their superiors. In the same way, supervisors should monitor their own use of informal coordination, continuing to use it when appropriate, but being careful not to contradict formal rules and procedures in the process.

Committees, Teams, and Task Forces

Most supervisors would probably rate committees next to rules and procedures as "nuisances" imposed on them by higher levels of management. They are time consuming. They are bothersome. They are often indecisive and ineffective. But, if properly designed and judiciously used, committees, teams, and task forces can be effective means of achieving coordination between groups who must work together on a common problem, or make joint decisions based on information possessed by members of both groups.

Think again of the earlier example of necessary coordination between Operations and Maintenance groups. If the machinery in Operations is used only irregularly, then it may be difficult to establish a regular maintenance schedule, that is, a procedure for automatically providing maintenance. Perhaps a two- or three-person committee, composed of Operations and Maintenance workers, could be established by Foreman B. The committee could meet on a weekly basis, consider machine use, and schedule maintenance for the coming week.

The general point is that committees, teams, and task forces are established to deal with problems and decisions across groups. Such problems may need special attention, or perhaps they cannot be covered by a rule or procedure. As with rules and procedures, however, supervisors should support, and encourage their people to support, those committees genuinely needed for coordination. Similarly, they should attempt to improve or disband ineffective committees through discussions with and suggestions to their own superiors. Like all mechanisms of coordination, these groups should facilitate rather than inhibit work accomplishment.

Is There One Best Way to Organize?

Having examined the many different ways in which organizations can divide up and coordinate their work, it is now fair to ask the question: Is there one best way to organize? For years, many people (including those who studied and those who actually managed organizations) did in fact seek the "one best way" to organize. In other words, they looked for one best set of structural components and means of coordination to suit all organizations at all times. Today, managers and theorists alike recognize that such a search is futile. Organizations (and even subunits within large organizations) differ so greatly in their size, in the nature of the work they do, and in the types of people who make up their membership, that no one structure will suit them all.

Without question, organizations and their subunits differ greatly in the way they are departmentalized, in the size of their spans of control, in the degree of centralization and decentralization, in the design of their jobs, and in the mechanisms used to achieve coordination. Unfortunately, there are few simple rules to guide managers in their choice of a structure. Instead, a careful analysis of each unique situation is required. For this reason, and because the structure in which supervisors find themselves is to a large extent a given, the major objective of this chapter has been to enable supervisors to identify, understand, and cope with the structure of their organization as it affects them.

In the next, and final section of this chapter, we will examine one component of structure over which the supervisor can exercise considerable influence: Job design.

Job Design

Job design refers to three aspects of a person's work: (1) The number and type of tasks to be performed; (2) the amount of freedom or discretion an individual has in doing these tasks; and (3) the degree to which individuals participate in decisions affecting their jobs and their work groups. All three of these factors have a significant effect on how well people do their jobs and how satisfied they are with their work situation. These two conditions, the satisfaction and performance of subordinates, are obviously ones in which a supervisor is vitally interested.

Can a supervisor vary any of the elements of subordinates' job designs in order to improve their performance and increase their satisfaction? The answer seems to be a qualified "yes." It must be qualified because many of the elements of job design are fixed by things like the machinery being used, the flow of work, and established rules and procedures. Therefore, supervisors may not be able to influence the formal job design very much. However, they may well be able to "enrich" or improve the jobs of their subordinates in informal ways. For example, they may be able to train their more capable and experienced people to do a number of different jobs for which their work groups are responsible. With such training, subordinates may be allowed to rotate the performance of these jobs among themselves as they see fit. Perhaps they can even participate with the supervisor in deciding who will get what kinds of training. This type of program, initiated by the supervisor, will affect all three elements of job design: The number of tasks to be performed, the amount of freedom, and the degree of participation. As a result, this program may well improve the performance and satisfaction of some subordinates who desire more challenging and varied jobs. Others may be well satisfied with their jobs as presently designed. They, of course, need not be involved in such a program.

Two words of caution should be added here. First, in some organizations supervisors may not (because of the design of their own jobs) have the authority to take the actions described above to redesign the jobs of their people informally and of course, should not attempt to do so. The second caution recognizes that programs of informal job redesign should be discussed with the immediate superior, both for guidance and approval.

Given these cautions, we must still conclude that today's supervisors are faced with managing a better educated, more affluent, and independent work force. Consequently, they must at least be aware of the possible ways for making their subordinates' jobs more meaningful. The traditional design of jobs in U. S. industry—specialized and repetitive, with little freedom and scant participation in decisions affecting the work group—appears to be less and less satisfying to a growing number of workers. Formal programs of job redesign are slow and expensive. Informal job redesign for those workers who want and can handle it may be best accomplished through actions taken by their immediate supervisor.

Questions for Discussion

1. What is meant by the term *organization structure*? Discuss this statement: "There is no organization without some degree of structure."

2. What are the major ways in which organizations divide up and assign responsibility for doing their work? What choices are available to the organization in each of the ways you have identified?

3. Is there "one best way to organize"? Why or why not?

4. In what way does the hierarchy of the organization or the structure itself facilitate coordination?

5. It was stated in the chapter that rules and procedures, and committees, teams, and task forces are important means of achieving coordination within an organization. Yet, many people, including supervisors, complain that these things are "red tape," "a waste of time," etc. Discuss this discrepancy in views. What are the implications for a supervisor?

6. What is meant by the term "job design"? How can supervisors influence or change the design of the jobs of their people? Under what circumstances should they? How will the design of their own jobs affect the degree to which they can redesign the jobs of their subordinates?

Case Incidents

1. Brenda L. was upset. Six weeks ago she had been hired as the Head Nurse of the Med-Surg Unit of Small Town Hospital. She had gone through an orientation period for the first two weeks. During this time she was invited to lunch and coffee breaks with various hospital personnel and had found her unit staff most cooperative and helpful.

Brenda had told her unit staff that she stood ready to help them coordinate their activities with other units in the hospital. She encouraged suggestions from her staff and met with them on a formal basis once each week. Initially, the unit staff seemed receptive to her approach. After six weeks, however, attendance at the weekly staff meetings started to fall off and there was little discussion among those who were present. In addition, none of her staff members was coming to her with either suggestions or problems.

After some investigation, Brenda discovered that her staff viewed her as little more than a figure head. She was not the center of communication for her unit and she wondered what problems were being handled without her knowledge. In fact, she has just received a memo from the pharmacy requesting that she inform her staff of the procedure to be followed in requesting certain medications.

a. Is there an actual or potential coordination problem between Brenda's unit and other units of the hospital?

b. Since Brenda has the authority to coordinate the activities of her unit, what has gone wrong?

c. What can Brenda do to correct the situation at this point?

2. Bruce T. is the president and major stockholder of a corporation holding the local franchises for twenty units of a national hamburger chain. All units are located in a metropolitan area of approximately one million population. The personnel in each unit are trained as "specialists." For example, one person prepares french fries, another prepares milk shakes, another adds the onions, pickles, catsup, and mustard to each hamburger and so forth. In the past, Bruce felt that such specialization was essential if fast service was to be provided for all customers.

Recently, Bruce visited the owner of several franchise units in another state. The owner, Monty G., cross-trained all of his personnel on various jobs in each unit. As a result, operations were not disrupted when someone was ill or could not get to work. Since other unit personnel knew the job, they could "fill in," or any off-duty employee could be called in to help out. Bruce was impressed with the efficiency and morale of the employees he observed and decided to implement cross-training in his franchised units.

After returning to his office, Bruce called a meeting of all unit supervisors. He told them that he wanted them to start cross-training their employees immediately. In short, Bruce said, "I want all jobs redesigned to make all employees happier and more productive."

Some supervisors complained that their employees were not qualified for cross-training. Others stated that some of their employees were very satisfied because they had only one job and were very good at it. "Don't worry," said Bruce. "They will learn to swim when you throw them in the water."

a. Did Bruce approach job redesign in an appropriate manner? Why or why not?

b. What factors must be considered prior to an implementation of job design or job redesign?

c. Can Bruce do anything to salvage his plan at this point? If so, what? If not, what should he do next?

Supervisory Authority and Delegation

*Elmer H. Burack**

Chapter Objectives	1. *To help develop an understanding of one's outlook on authority-related issues and how it compares to current management practice and emerging research findings.*
	2. *To identify the forces, work systems, and considerations shaping authority practices and delegation.*
	3. *To specify the impact of change on supervisory authority and its subsequent effect on individual supervisors.*
	4. *To provide the understanding and guidelines for a more effective use and delegation of authority.*

IN BIBLICAL DAYS, it was said that even the meanest person invested with authority must be treated with the respect that would be accorded to the worthiest occupant of that office. (I Sam. 12:2). My, how things have changed! This chapter provides a capsule view of where authority practices have been, where they are going, and how you tie into these changes.

Today, supervisors are confronted with a complex blend of traditional challenges and a whole set of new issues brought on by vast changes in organizations and society. The following quotes from research studies and consulting assignments indicate the scope of these matters.

*Elmer H. Burack is Professor of Management, Stuart School of Management and Finance, Illinois Institute of Technology.

The Issues: What Are They Saying?

> *Workers:* The supervisor doesn't even know the answer
> to my questions.
> - I don't even bother going to him anymore—
>   he's of no help.
> - He doesn't do anything for us—why should
>   we support him?
> - She wants to be in on everything—I can't
>   even go to the washroom without clearance.

> *Supervisors:* I've been loyal to the company . . . but has the
> company been loyal to me?
> - I really wonder if I can do it—for years
>   all women did around here was straighten their
>   boss's desk or push pencils.
> - Nobody ever tells me what's going on.
> - Management listens more to the union steward
>   than to what I have to say.
> - A black guy's got to be better than most to make
>   supervisor—but then there's no place to go.

Most of us have used road maps while traveling. What follows is an attempt to provide a "roadmap" of what is coming up and the "sights" along the way.

Roadmap

Many of the session leaders in supervisory training programs assume that their audience is largely ignorant of their wise pronouncements. We avoid such a foolish assumption. Each section to follow is descriptively labeled and you can pursue the subject matter best suited to your needs (and perhaps patience). In order to further assist choice, the order of topic presentation is as follows:

1. How up-to-date are your views on authority and delegation?
2. The authority tradition
3. Authority—where does it come from?
4. Authority and training: The ability to deliver
5. Models of supervisory authority: Past and future
6. Guidelines
7. The authority story or, "What's left for me after everybody else slices up the authority pie?"
8. Supervisory authority obsolescence

How Up-to-Date Are Your Views on Authority and Delegation?
A Quiz and Commentary

The authority we assert in our relationships with work group members emerges over an extended period reflecting many organizational and personal considerations. Some actions are consciously adopted in response to specific situations. Others may have been unconsciously adopted because our manager was "bugging us" about a lack of employee discipline, lateness in getting out an important job, customer complaints, employee absenteeism, or maybe even a lawsuit.

Consequently, our ideas of what is proper spring from specific beliefs regarding the trustworthiness of employees and confidence in their ability to carry on if we are out-of-town or to handle an important phone call. Activity patterns such as the hourly patrol around the shop, dropping in unannounced at one of the sales offices, or making the "important" decisions, represent our ideas of what's proper, efficient and businesslike, and in fact what we do "do." However, as an old acquaintance once told me, "Elmer, when you start quoting yourself as the last word on a particular subject, you had better go back to the drawing board because you've probably grown out-of-touch with things." The lesson one can derive from this observation is simply that for all kinds of obvious reasons we grow accustomed to, and feel comfortable with, our ways of handling things. In the meantime, circumstances such as the context of work or the beliefs of our younger employees may change (and have changed) and require at times a major overhauling of personal attitudes and activity patterns.

One way to get at the potential need for personal change is to understand our own beliefs. Next, we examine these against the patterns of attitudes and behavior which behavioral experts believe are supportive of people and satisfying in work relationships. The likely result is an ability to maintain or improve work outputs as well as peoples' performance (reduced tardiness, absenteeism, or turnover). The following quiz was developed for these purposes.

Instructions: The following forms have been used to record how one feels about important aspects of supervisory authority and delegation. To permit self-scoring and analysis, it is important that you express how you really feel concerning these matters as opposed to any idea of how people are supposed to feel. Each item contains five possible responses: Agree (A); slightly agree (SA); undecided (?); slightly disagree (SD); disagree (D).

The response that most closely approximates how you really act or deal with the situation, or your attitude concerning the matter is the proper answer. At the end of the form you will find further instructions. However, work through the form before looking at the scoring information.

Figure 7–1
Supervisory Views on

Authority and Delegation

	A	SA	?	SD	D
1. Good supervisory practice requires that all group members be handled the same way in dealing with complaints, improvements, and training for example.	—	—	—	—	—
2. Departmental training requirements should be the sole responsibility of the department supervisor.	—	—	—	—	—
3. Respect for authority requires that a supervisor doesn't ask a "how to" question or encourage suggestions from group members.	—	—	—	—	—
4. Age and years of experience are often uncertain guides in predicting ability or job performance of workers.	—	—	—	—	—
5. Good worker performance depends largely on maintaining pressure for output and reprimanding undesired activity.	—	—	—	—	—
6. Women are largely incapable of assuming authority positions.	—	—	—	—	—
7. Willingness to listen to employees' suggestions or questions implies a need to respond to or act on the suggestions or questions.	—	—	—	—	—
8. Results are what count; consequently, supervisory behavior need not be a model of how to act.	—	—	—	—	—
9. The performance of black supervisors has proved to be inferior to that of whites.	—	—	—	—	—
10. "I've got to handle the details (as supervisor) if things are to go smoothly."	—	—	—	—	—
11. Two-way communication between supervisors and employees should be (and is) concerned primarily with directing subordinates and receiving feedback from them to indicate an understanding of instructions.	—	—	—	—	—

	A	SA	?	SD	D

12. A supervisor who says, "I don't know, but I'll get the answer for you," doesn't necessarily look bad to an employee.

13. A common cause of supervisory failure is a lack of technical know-how.

14. Training is a general responsibility of personnel/industrial relations; it's up to them to make sure it gets done.

15. On balance, supervisors should be facilitators and take care of employees' work needs, rather than being directors of their activities.

16. First line supervisors are closer to their employees than to management.

17. Technical ability is authority—it can effectively replace skills in handling people.

18. The actions of a supervisor must reflect jointly what his boss thinks is desired, as well as what the group members think is appropriate.

19. Staff activities, policies, and regulations have left little of importance for supervisors to do.

20. The needs of female employees in business for such things as achievement, job satisfaction, and money have been shown to be similar to male needs.

21. Possessing information gives one power— the supervisor should provide only that information which is required for the immediate situation.

22. High performance, in most cases, requires close supervision.

23. Supervisors should delegate only responsibility, not authority, to employees.

24. Listening to employees' suggestions, complaints, or questions is a necessary, often important, part of the supervisory job.

25. Authority is mostly a matter of personal leadership qualities and rights of the office.

Scoring: After completing the form, plot your answers on either or both of the two charts in Figure 7–2. The key questions are:

    a. Which pattern most closely fits your responses— the "traditional" or "current"?

    b. In what areas is there the most agreement? Disagreement?

Interpretation: A comparison of the "traditional" and "current" approaches as shown in Figure 7–2 indicates that some significant changes have taken place in the area of recommended supervisory practices. For example, the traditional view was that blacks and women were incapable of assuming important areas of authority or responsibility. Also, in the traditional view it was assumed that the needs of "minority groups" differed substantially from those of the "majority" and, thus, required quite different supervisory styles. However, research and experiences with programs such as those of the National Alliance of Businessmen deny the validity of these traditional assumptions.

Delegation is another highly controversial area. The traditional view held that supervisors should be aloof and maintain an arm's length relationship with work group members. However, modern management practices have turned more towards participative approaches that permit employees to play an enlarged role, if they are qualified.

Exceptions: There are always exceptions for situations that reflect specific conditions or circumstances:

Training. Where employee groups lack adequate training, an obvious and greater reliance is placed on the consultation and direction provided by supervisors. Unfortunately, these situations may become self-fulfilling and the circle is never broken because we fail to provide adequate training for workers.

Company or department size. Large size by its very nature may force a more detailed division and control of tasks. Yet, newer approaches to job design permit improved handling of these situations.

Dangerous operating conditions. Where distinct hazards exist regarding accidents or possible loss of life, a high degree of authority may have to remain with the supervisor as (a) the person most knowledgeable about the situations which might arise; and (b) as the person who may need to make quick decisions.

On balance, then, this supervisory attitude form can be used as a device to provide insights into one's beliefs. At the same time, it can raise questions concerning the validity of some of these outlooks in the light of current behavioral research and management practices.

The Authority Tradition

The authority tradition has undergone considerable changes. However, before proceeding to these changes and the factors responsible

Figure 7–2
**Supervisory Outlook on Authority and Delegation:
Traditional Assumptions and Current Outlook**

Question Number

	1	2	3	4	5	6	7	8	9	10	11	12	13	14	15	16	17	18	19	20	21	22	23	24	25

Traditional

Agree

Mildly Agree

?

Mildly Disagree

Disagree

Current Outlooks

Agree

Mildly Agree

?

Mildly Disagree

Disagree

for them, a brief review of the central features of the authority tradition will prove helpful. Basically, its central elements include:

Hierarchical Authority

1. The chain of command within an organization includes people at successively higher levels of authority who possess the right to direct those below them. As such, the chain of command provides a logical pattern of work activities and responsibilities which assures efficiency and minimizes duplication.

2. Authority is more general as one goes up in an organization and more specific and detailed as one goes down.

3. Supervisors, serving at the lower rungs of the chain of command, have a more limited scope of authority relative to higher levels in the hierarchy.

4. Supervisors are at the point of coordination between individuals and work groups on the one hand and higher management levels on the other.

Authority Structure

1. This structure joins all organizational participants into an integrated whole focused on securing the central goals of an organization.

2. Through an allocation of authority and responsibilities, the structure includes all primary activities considered necessary for securing the central goals. Assignment of duties is by task, territory, subject matter, product, or service.

Specialization

1. As one proceeds down the authority hierarchy, tasks become increasingly differentiated and specialized.

2. The boundaries of an individual's supervisory responsibilities are frequently established by the "logic" of:

    a. expertness in a segment of work—an assembly operation on a production line, or procedures in an intensive care unit in a hospital.

    b. limits in walking or traveling time—urban sales territories versus those in rural areas.

    c. confines of a building—a shop for welding, storage, or order filling, or the receiving dock for a food store.

    d. subject matter, product, or service—life insurance versus auto insurance—tooth paste versus mouth wash—textbooks for universities versus those for company training programs.

3. Supervisors are typically the central representatives of management charged with, and directly involved in, institutional performance relative to products (as in manufacturing) or service (as in merchandising, health care delivery, insurance, and banking).

Unity of Direction

Generally, the activities of an individual should be directed by only one supervisor in order to facilitate control, avoid conflicting orders or directions, and facilitate the assessment of individual performance.

Span of Control

Realistic limits exist on the abilities of a supervisor to control the activities of subordinates, to provide requested assistance, or to administer and coordinate the activities of individual group members. General experience suggests that a span of control involving more than twenty is not workable.

Commensurate Authority and Responsibility

When the responsibility for some aspect of work performance is assigned, it should be accompanied by appropriate authority.

Change in the Authority Tradition

As mentioned earlier, the authority tradition has sustained many modifications in recent years. We are now at the point where it is no longer useful to discuss either "authority principles" or general guidelines. Let's see what developments have accounted for an erosion of the "principles" and where we stand today regarding supervisory authority and responsibilities.

Two general developments have taken place that have affected the scope and content of supervisory authority. In one development, the overall scope of supervisory authority has been increasingly confined. For a considerable length of time, unions and staff departments such as personnel and industrial relations have become increasingly involved in what were once viewed as supervisory responsibilities. Also, the substitution of rules and policies regarding various work-related activities (employment, hours, working conditions, hiring, firing, wage and salary administration, union relations, and the like), have blocked out large areas of responsibilities that resided with supervisors in past years.

Some of these developments are the inevitable consequence of growth in institutional size, the increasing complexity of business and work, and the need for specialized abilities, as in the administration of fringe benefits and training. However, despite the appearance to the contrary, the task of supervision has retained numerous key authority elements and some new ones have been added. More on this in just a moment.

The second major development affecting supervisory authority reflects a shift in work content resulting from a vast series of social, economic, and technological changes. Two incidents will help to illustrate the extent to which change has influenced the supervisor's world of work.

In a southern sewing plant, the techniques of sewing and the basic work machinery (the sewing machine) were long established. In fact, the production of sewing machines was one of the first mass production industries in the United States, dating back to the 1890s. Also, the needle trades have reflected the heavy hand of industrial engineers and powerful unions to the point that work processing has been studied and analyzed in great detail.

In this plant, the tradition was to promote supervisors out of the employee groups. Candidates were often considered to be "super workers" who had constantly exceeded production standards with good quality.

One of the important product lines for this company was toweling of "flat goods." These tended to be low-profit, high-volume items, and competition was very strong. Supervisors, possessing only a work-related background, were at a disadvantage in proposing cost or methods improvements. Also, competitors were "automating" various sewing operations, and it became apparent that a different type of supervisor was going to be needed.

Instead of an individual supervising large groups of machine operators, the emphasis shifted to large equipment groupings with only a few operators. A practical background in mechanical and electronic repairs became a necessity to keep these lines going. The mastery of sewing was now handled by the equipment and supervisors focused more attention on maintaining the production flow, a challenging task, but quite different from their previous work activity.

In the field of architecture, an ability to express forms, or the thoughtful, creative filling of living spaces was once considered the highest expression of architectural art. Even in the commercial area, architectural designers assumed considerable latitude in expressing themselves for commercial undertakings.

However, over time the realization of design became an exceedingly complex matter, often involving a high level of interaction between designer, engineer, and, more recently, systems expert. Construction has moved from individual to team-oriented projects. Now, the project or group leader must be able to bring together the collective knowledge and experience of several people and focus them on specific problems and projects. This project orientation and its accompanying need for the mastery of business and management concepts have brought about changes in the focus of architectural education, whether in formal educational programs or continuing career development.

These two incidents help to illustrate the widespread changes taking place in the authority tradition. On the one hand, authority may indeed have been reduced in response to a variety of institutional and technical changes. Conversely, other changes have taken place that indicate a very significant and meaningful role for supervision. In turn, these changes require a thoughtful use and delegation of authority if satisfactory performance and meaningful employee involvement are to be forthcoming.

Authority: Where Does it Come From?

Supervisory time is often taken up with the demands, questions, and crises of the moment, with little opportunity to think about the source of authority. And besides, "What difference does it make?" Some answers to this question will be forthcoming shortly. However, a short answer might go along the following lines:

> A knowledge of the sources of authority expands our understanding of how others view our job; it permits a realistic assessment of the boundaries of our job and its potential for self-fulfillment as well as a basis for judging the match (or mismatch) between responsibilities and authority; and, finally, it provides a foundation for job design which must consider authority, responsibilities, work relationships, and job activities.

Some supervisors (the uninitiated) would probably say that their authority must come from their job description. "After all, the description says I'm responsible for such and such; therefore, I must have the authority that goes with it." At this, experienced supervisors start to shake their heads and mutter, "Boy, he doesn't have his head on straight. Everybody knows that one thing (responsibility) has nothing to do with the other (authority)."

Now, let's get more specific. Initially, the authority accorded to any position can only be understood when it is viewed in the context of work and the meaning attached to the work role by society. Thus, the work to be accomplished in a particular organization determines the workflow, procedures, methods, and the technology of work accomplishment.

For an office supervisor, procedures and methods may be quite valuable and in direct response to the need for customer credit checks or the assignment of tasks to keep things going. Here, the technology of work accomplishment may be nothing more than a ball point pen backed up by experience, patience, and an ability to help "bail out" office personnel when they get in trouble or need assistance. For this job, authority is assigned to the position of Office Supervisor by virtue of past history within the organization, and is defined formally or informally by some manager, boss, officer, or the president.

The authority of the job is further reinforced through the "hardware" and privileges that communicate to all organization members and visitors that "I'm a supervisor." A telephone, private office, white helmet, freedom to take coffee breaks, a signal "beeper," and other symbols of the job help to reinforce the authority assigned to a supervisory position. Figure 7–3 serves to summarize these points while bringing out other notions regarding the sources of supervisory authority.

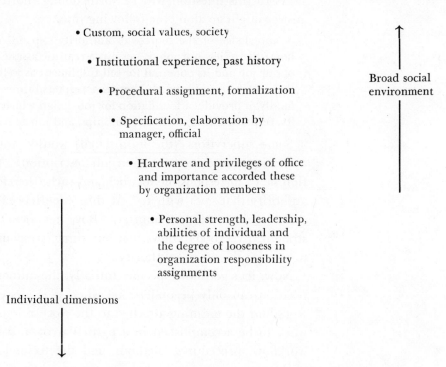

Figure 7–3
Factors Shaping Authority

• Custom, social values, society

• Institutional experience, past history

• Procedural assignment, formalization

• Specification, elaboration by
  manager, official

• Hardware and privileges of office
  and importance accorded these
  by organization members

• Personal strength, leadership,
  abilities of individual and
  the degree of looseness in
  organization responsibility
  assignments

Broad social
environment

Individual dimensions

In Figure 7–3, it is suggested that broad social or environmental considerations establish the foundation for definitions of authority. If Aunt Martha quotes her doctor as saying, "You should never gulp your food down," she has been persuaded by the authority of medical dogma conveyed to her by a fully recognized member of that profession. As a professional, the doctor's credentials have been "certified" by a medical school, hospital, and licensing agency. The authority to speak knowledgeably in these matters emerges from the doctor's certification. Generally, society accepts and reinforces the authority pecking order found in the medical profession. Titles such as surgeon, general practitioner, psychologist, registered nurse, licensed practical nurse, and nurse's aide reflect an elaboration of this system.

A more restrictive example of societal norms has to do with craftsmen. Today, they often lack the recognition given to many professionals. For example, the general public may place a machinist in the same category with tool makers, brick layers, and carpenters. Yet, in the tool room of a particular company, the authority of the machinist is very clearly established relative to tool engineer, tool maker, polisher, and apprentice. In the event of a technical problem, the authority for correcting the situation generally rests with the one who has the most technical know-how.

In general, then, the more widely recognized and acknowledged authority is in a society, the more authority relationships will be established by considerations outside of an organization. In such cases, the granting of authority and authority pecking orders are, therefore, largely determined by the professions, trades, and society at large.

The more authority is determined by internal institutional considerations (history and management philosophy, for example) the greater the likelihood of differences in job content and authority assignments, especially between similar jobs performed in different organizations.

Authority and Training: The Ability to Deliver

Authority is reinforced by the ability to deliver requested assistance, information, and the like. The authority of the supervisor is established initially by virtue of position and the importance attached to it by the organization. From that point on, it's "fish or cut bait." The expectations of work-group members regarding supervisory behavior emerge from the responsibilities assigned to the job. The production foreman is expected to provide technical help if an employee calls for assistance. The Nursing Supervisor is expected to have the answers when someone asks, "Where's such and such?" or, "What do I do now?" If the answers are not forthcoming, are slow, or are largely incorrect, authority will be seriously damaged. As a result, the reestablishment of authority becomes exceedingly difficult. Thus it seems rather clear that the acquisition and improvement of abilities through training are central to acquiring and maintaining your full authority.

Five Models of Supervisory Authority: Past and Future

One hundred years ago, the world of supervision was largely industrial in nature and was concerned mostly with production or manufacturing. In the 1960s, employees in service institutions (banks, insurance, education, government) accounted for approximately one-half of the work force and by 1974 this figure had increased to three-fifths. See Figure 7–4 for some projections into 1980.

Figure 7–4
The Relative Numbers of Various Supervisory Types

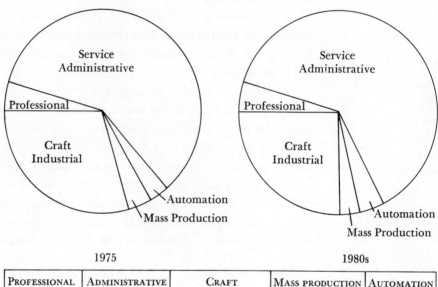

1975   1980s

PROFESSIONAL	ADMINISTRATIVE	CRAFT	MASS PRODUCTION	AUTOMATION
Architecture Accountant Engineer Educator Scientist, nurse	Office supr. Department supervisor	Tool maker Machinist Foreman—open hearth Electrician Maintenance supr.	Line supervisor	Unit supervisor

By around 1980, it is expected that one out of every three members of the workforce in service units will be employed by some level of government. In addition, various professions will show sustained increases. In the industrial sector, it is expected that some important shifts will take place as automated units become relatively more important. Mass production occupations are expected to shrink as meaningless job roles are automated, whether because of human or economic considerations.

Authority: Industrial vs. Service

In general the activities of industrial supervisors center on work technologies. Thus, equipment of all types plays a central role in supervision, and authority issues frequently emerge from the man-machine complex present in all manufacturing organizations. To this extent, matters requiring supervisory attention are similar across many different types of production units. However, the nature of manufacturing systems differs markedly. In craft operations, production is in single units, or small batches, and differs from lot to lot. Technical skills and problem-solving abilities are all important in establishing supervisory authority in such operations.

In mass production, operations combine the human element with machines in a complex fashion. Here, supervisory authority often reflects how well the needs of assembly-line employees are serviced in order to keep the line moving. The line defines work stations, work activities, and the work system, thereby establishing the concerns and limits of supervisory authority. In the automated system, supervisory responsibilities and authority lie largely outside of the system itself. The ability to monitor the performance of the system and the technical expertise to maintain flows are minimal conditions for maintaining supervisory authority in such situations.

The service enterprise frequently presents a vastly different sort of work setting. The technology of work typically assumes a modest or minor role. In these organizations, supervisory authority depends on the responsibilities assigned to a position, how well supervisors meet these responsibilities, and personal qualities of leadership. Person-to-person relationships are vital and represent the central challenge to establishing and maintaining authority in these cases.

In summary, the central differences between the industrial and service areas of supervisory authority are related to the relative importance of work technology in performance. The more performance depends on individual effort, the more supervisory authority must relate to behavioral rather than technical matters. The greater the importance of work technology to performance, the more authority depends on an individual's ability to deliver technical expertise.

Types of Supervision Compared

To clarify the similarities and differences among the five supervisory types described in this section, Figure 7–5 and 7–6 were prepared. The six categories selected for comparison included: (a) Bases for authority or behavior; (b) relative importance of education versus experience;

(c) the role played by technology (work system) in establishing performance requirements, the need for formal knowledge, etc.; (d) aspects of communications and relationships between supervisors and group members; (e) the extent to which the supervisor (and workers) must deal with uncertainty or complexity in their work activities; and (f) other considerations in authority.

If one examines, for example, the bases for authority among the five supervisory types, it becomes more evident that they vary widely and depend greatly on the situation. The greatest differences probably occur between the professional and the mass production supervisors. On the other hand, the craft supervisor is not so far removed from the professional as one might conclude from their work settings. Both enjoy the respect provided by membership in organized bodies—professional societies or organized trade groups. Based on tradition, a pecking order of authority has been established, acknowledged, and reinforced by employers, clients, patients, peers, fellow supervisors, and other organizational members.

Figure 7–5
Five Models of Supervision: The Concept

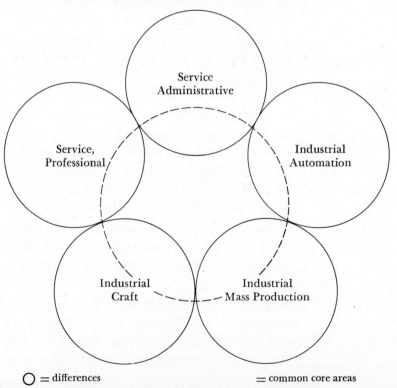

○ = differences　　　　　　　　　　　　　　= common core areas

Figure 7–6
Five Models of Supervisory Authority Compared

Factors in Supervisory Authority

TYPES OF SUPERVISORY AUTHORITY	BASES FOR BEHAVIOR AUTHORITY	EDUCATION VS. EXPERIENCE	ROLE OF TECHNOLOGY
Professional	Certification Societies Professional groups Application of— usually of small importance	Formal education of central importance Builds on structured knowledge Experience serves to enrich knowledge application	Modest role Considered secondary to knowledge of worker Scientific methods/ systematic approaches Application of skills may be subject to technology "limits"
Administrative	Emerges largely from organization Reference to "boss" for resolution Often assumes cross-section of authority activities Ability to apply sanctions often important	Involves both with emphasis dependent on the situation Supervisor or "super worker" may command respect	Tends to be frequently standardized Sophisticated technology (computer) may supplement
Craft	Established through long years of tradition, apprenticeship Master-apprentice concept Pride of workmanship	Experience of central importance— thought to grow for many years	Machine technology of some importance but only as guided by craft art
Mass production	Keeps work moving Services work system and work group members Application of worker sanctions often greatly limited	Work related very important— Peaks out after a few years	Paces work Standardized, high technology control
Automation	Super. usually expert combining both education and experience Comprehensive rules and procedures Authority central challenge; keep it moving; minimum costs	Utilizes mix of both	Central and typically complex

Figure 7–6 (Continued)
Five Models of Supervisory Authority Compared

Factors in Supervisory Authority

TYPES OF SUPERVISORY AUTHORITY	RELATIONSHIPS COMMUNICATIONS	COMPLEXITY UNCERTAINTY	OTHER ITEMS
Professional	Participative, two-way communication Participation valued Peer relations Opinion of peers valued	Path towards end/ goal *not* clearly defined Approaches highly contingent on situation	State of awareness accreditation demands— professional societies
Administration	Defined by situation— impersonal to personal	Seeks standard-ization, low un-certainty, low complexity	Opinion of employees may be valued to be popular or accepted May come from employee group Ability to get "things" for group may be quite valued
Craft	Based on craft activity Individual oriented Specific instructions may be given	Both vary greatly— subject to inroads of experience	
Mass production	Often nominal due to work pace Communications often flows up	Mostly certainty regarding schedules People often source of uncertainty Complex blend of people and work Uncertainty re-garding raw material	Union tends to intervene and standardize Supervisor often comes from employee group
Automation	Built around monitoring of the performance of the work system Face-to-face communications not especially important	Systems tend to be complicated Uncertainty lowered through experience and application of scientific principles	

Guidelines

Our discussion of the five models of supervisory authority makes it clear that the specific content of various jobs, along with different institutional circumstances, prevent a detailed listing of guidelines. Yet, there are certain similarities among supervisory positions, which suggest the following guidelines:

1. Note the types of authority that have started to assume new significance, those that are declining in importance, and those that continue to be important. (These are summarized in Figure 7–7.) In general, flexibility, participation, and delegation are becoming increasingly important in supervisory-subordinate relationships. On the other hand, depending on the authority of one's position is shown as becoming increasingly ineffective.

2. Facilitate the development of newer authority practices by assuring the competent training of work-group members.

3. Lean more on approaches for using authority that recognize what people can contribute, regardless of race or sex.

4. Increase the meaningful participation of work-group members and be prepared to share some of your authority in decision making.

5. Get feedback from members of your work group as to how well things are going and whether they are able to handle new responsibilities and increased authority.

6. Develop a relationship with fellow supervisors which helps to provide needed feedback plus a sounding board for problems or issues you may need to talk out.

7. Discuss authority matters frankly with your boss. Reach an understanding on your responsibilities and the scope of your authority.

The Authority Story or, "What's Left for Me after Everybody Else Slices Up the Authority Pie?"

For years supervisors have been discussed as caught between managers and employees. One of the problems in this area stems from the distribution of authority in organizations from most at the top to least at the bottom. In some organizations, as a practical matter, least has also been taken to mean little, or none. Of course, the president typically has the final word and the broadest (most) authority. In large organizations, a large number of officers, managers, and superintendents slice up the "authority pie," and then the union invites itself in for dessert. Consequently, there may not be too much left for the supervisors. In recognition of these points, which are exaggerated for emphasis, it is necessary to clarify a few central assumptions underlying discussions to follow.

Assumptions

First, supervisors are members of management, fully entitled to whatever privileges accompany their assignments. Second, supervisory jobs still retain sufficient authority and, therefore, higher management can-

Figure 7–7
Sources of Authority: Growth and Decline

RELATIVELY LESSER IMPORTANCE
- Reward/punishment
- Rules and procedure
- Job title, position
- Name
- Physical size of supervisor
- Phone, parking space, office
- Size or type of car
- Age
- Years of experience
- Information withholding
- Rigid use of authority

RELATIVELY GREATER IMPORTANCE
- Participation of group members
- Presenting options
- Gaining acceptance of activities
- Information sharing
- Effective two-way communications
- Information feedback
- Flexible use of authority

CONTINUING IMPORTANCE
- Technical know-how, knowledge
- Training of supervisors and workers
- Authority and responsibility matched
- Clarity in understanding of responsibilities for supervisor, workers, and boss

not be charged with tokenism. Third, where authority has been stripped from supervisory positions, opportunities exist for making these positions more meaningful through various approaches to job design.

Authority: What Should Be and What Is

For many years, it has been assumed, or imagined, that the members of formal organizations could be managed through a careful delegation of authority. Whether in factories, insurance offices, or ancient kingdoms, breaking things down into smaller and smaller clusters of people and groups of activities was precisely the process for making organizations manageable. Thus, it is not surprising that a package of organizational "principles" emerged which implied that tasks and individuals could be tied together in a neat and orderly fashion.

Unfortunately, organizations and people do not always behave as predicted. That which we thought was certain turns out to be not so certain. For example, we assign the Service Supervisor in a food store to the task of dealing with irate customers. The supervisor is "authorized" to handle complaints concerning price, quality, and weight. Unfortunately, no one bothers to clarify other matters regarding fairness in package labeling, situations where the number of available and advertised items differ, or serious questions of honesty regarding a customer's claim. Also, a requirement that "all adjustments be approved by the Store Manager" may lead to impossible demands on the time and availability of that person.

By reviewing the preceding example, it is not surprising that the job descriptions for many positions have become more elaborate as we seek to identify in advance more of the specific instances that limit authority. Or, we may seek to develop more flexible arrangements where the authority to be exercised depends on the factors in a given situation. Returning to our example of the food store Service Supervisor, a simple word such as "quality" could be expanded to include labeling, packaging, contents, and both food and nonfood items. The Service Supervisor would then be authorized to deal fully with problems in these areas. For example, the Service Supervisor could be authorized to deal with any deviations determined to exist between products advertised or available, so long as the retail value of these did not exceed $20.00. Where this value is exceeded, any adjustment would be jointly authorized by the Store Manager.

Clearly, then, many changes continue to affect the job content and authority of supervisory positions. However, it is not always clear that supervisors have kept pace with these changes. Some still operate according to the way things used to be done. Have you changed enough? If you are curious, see the following section on obsolescence.

Supervisory Authority Obsolescence

As a summary to this chapter, it is important to recognize the types of obsolescence that affect supervisory authority. One is technical obsolescence and the other is social or interpersonal obsolescence. Both undercut authority, but in far different ways. Technical obsolescence is the growing loss of problem-solving skills, procedural know-how, or knowledge of modern management methods. Interpersonal obsolescence is shown in the use of outdated behavioral techniques or a lack of awareness of advances in the use of supervisory authority.

Both technical and interpersonal obsolescence undermine supervisory authority. On the one hand, technical obsolescence frequently makes supervisors feel defensive because they do not have the answers. In turn, this forces them to rely more on formal authority, to give orders, to turn off questions, or to hide more and more behind their authority.

Social or interpersonal obsolescence has the same effects on the use of authority, but operates in quite a different way. Young people in organizations, plus numbers of older members, have come to expect far different treatment from supervisors than that which was acceptable in past years. At one time supervisors were told to conduct themselves by giving orders while dealing with subordinates at arm's length. Although successful in the past, this approach is becoming increasingly unsatisfactory in modern organizations, and employees view it as lacking an understanding of interpersonal relationships and human needs. In other words, the "authority tradition" is no longer a reliable guide for meeting either current or future supervisory responsibilities.

Bibliography

Argyris, Chris. *Personality and Organization.* New York: Harper and Row, 1957.

Burack, Elmer H. "Technology and Supervisory Practices: A Preliminary View." *Human Organizations* 26 (Winter 1967): 256–264.

———. *Organization Analysis: Theory and Application.* New York, Dryden Press, 1975.

———. "Industrial Management in Advanced Production Systems: Some Theoretical Concepts and Preliminary Findings." *Administrative Science Quarterly* 12 (December 1967): 479–500.

Burack, Elmer H., and McNichols, Thomas J. *Human Resource Planning: Technology, Policy, Change.* Kent, Ohio: Center for Business and Economic Research, Kent State University, 1973.

Calhoon, Richard P. *Personnel Management and Supervision.* New York: Appleton-Century-Crofts, 1967.

Kirkpatrick, Donald L., and Planty, Earl. "Supervisory Inventory on Human Relations." Brookfield, Wisc.: D. I. Kirkpatrick, 1965.

Maurer, John G. *Work Role Involvement of Industrial Supervisors.* East Lansing, Mich.: Bureau of Business and Economic Research, Michigan State University, 1969.

Sartain, Aaron Q., and Baker, Alton W. *The Supervisor and His Job.* 2d rev. ed. New York: McGraw-Hill, 1972.

Yaney, Joseph P. *Personnel Management: Reaching Organization and Human Goals.* Columbus, Ohio: Charles Merrill Publishing Co., 1975.

Questions for Discussion

1. The expectations of young people coming into organizations are said to pose considerable challenges to supervisory style and "the authority tradition." What are some of the issues emerging and how might you deal with them as a supervisor?

2. Participation by subordinates has been said by some people to undercut a supervisor's authority. Comment.

3. Some organizational consultants and researchers feel that various circumstances call for the use of traditional authority in giving orders, controlling, etc. Comment and be sure to clarify your assumptions.

4. It has been said that the increasing level of education among all sectors of the population is gradually reducing the need for formal authority in organizations. Comment.

5. Many writers on authority indicate that responsibility cannot be delegated. Comment.

6. If a supervisor asks a member of the work group for assistance, he will "lose" authority in the eyes of that individual. Comment and be sure to state your assumptions.

Case Incidents

1. Charlie Smith, General Shift Supervisor, was about ready to blow up. Today, another member of Jack Finley's work group had been in to complain about "the work situation in that department." Quality wasn't holding up, machines were breaking down, and the department was behind in production. Some of the workers claimed, "Jack's on everybody's back."

Most of the trouble seemed to start about six months ago when a new production line was installed in Jack's department. It was the first major change in equipment and procedure in many years. Plant management had been eager to get into production on a new line because they were way behind schedule on orders coming in. Several times when Charlie went out to Jack's department to see how things were coming along, Jack seemed to be having an argument with some members of his group.

a. What type of authority probably existed before the new equipment changes?

b. What new challenges to Jack's authority have arisen as a result of the work changes?

c. What authority problems are indicated by Jack's people going in to see Charlie Smith?

d. What problems or issues might account for the difficulties described here?

e. Propose some ways of dealing with the problems you have identified.

2. A notice was posted on the third floor bulletin board of Single's Department Store: "We are pleased to announce that Mary Blair has been appointed Third Floor Supervisor to replace Tom Jenkins, who is being promoted. We feel sure that you will all give her the fullest cooperation."

Single's was a very large, full-line department store in a Midwestern city. The work force of the store contained almost 50 percent part-time employees; almost two-thirds of the employees were females, although few were in supervisory positions. The third floor of the department store had furniture items, appliances, hardware, and other household items. Most of the third floor departments had been staffed by men in the past, although a few women had been brought in recently. Consequently, it was with considerable surprise that most of the third floor employees read about the appointment of Mary to supervise the floor.

a. What circumstances are likely to influence the response of third floor people to Mary's appointment.

b. What issues may arise regarding Mary's authority?

c. What type of authority approach should Mary use as she assumes her new position? Show the assumptions that support your recommendation.

Leadership

H. Kirk Downey and John W. Slocum, Jr.*

H. Kirk Downey and John W. Slocum, Jr.*

Chapter Objectives

1. *To define leadership and to discuss why individuals want to become leaders.*

2. *To show how leaders obtain their influence.*

3. *To examine the impact of leadership on group effectiveness.*

4. *To analyze different types of leadership and their contributions to group effectiveness.*

5. *To emphasize the changing nature of leadership in modern society.*

What Is Leadership?

ALTHOUGH the terms *leader* and *leadership* are used frequently in our everyday language, the meanings we attach to these terms vary widely. It is, therefore, essential that we spell out the key definitions to be used in this chapter.

A popular definition of leaders refers to them as persons who draw others to themselves. These are the persons others want to follow. They are the ones who command the trust and loyalty of followers. They are the great persons who capture the imagination and admiration of those with whom they deal. They are the heroes others want to copy. For example, the young golfers who admire Jack Nicklaus, Johnny Miller, Carol Mann, or Sandra Palmer might try to copy their swing and dress patterns, or might use clubs named after them. Additionally, they would probably name these athletes as leaders in the sports world. Teachers in the public schools usually point out great people (such as George Washington and Abraham Lincoln) when teaching children about our country's history and often refer to these figures as "born leaders."

*H. Kirk Downey is Assistant Professor of Management, College of Business Administration, Oklahoma State University; John W. Slocum, Jr. is Professor of Organizational Behavior, College of Business Administration, The Pennsylvania State University.

Most of the world's work, however, is done by people like you and us, that is, people who work in hospitals, insurance agencies, universities, steel mills, and federal agencies. Among other things, people in these organizations plan, organize, communicate, and accept the responsibility to reach their organization's goals. For example, Ms. Smith works for a large university and has been elected chairman of the local United Way drive. An important part of her job is to prepare the budget, talk with people, write letters, make phone calls, and perform many other duties that do not directly involve the supervision of others. She is a leader in the sense that she *is a person who is able to communicate ideas to others in such a way as to influence their behavior to reach some goals.* What we are asking Ms. Smith to do is to get others to act in a way that will lead to an accomplishment of the United Way goals.

What, then, do we mean by the term *leadership*? Leadership is something that leaders do, not something they have.[1] *Leadership involves influencing a group's activities toward the accomplishment of certain goals.* It is a process involving the behavior of both a leader and followers.

Even though leadership is something a person does, it should not be confused with activity level. Aggressiveness and the constant direction of others does not necessarily indicate leadership. At times appropriate leadership involves staying in the background so that others may talk, or hesitating before making judgments.

Why Do People Want to Become Leaders?

One of the important features of leadership is that it cannot be studied in a vacuum, but must be studied in group settings. Is anyone following you? If not, you are not influencing the activities of others and are not exercising leadership.

In most instances, you cannot really threaten or force people to behave in specific ways. Leadership is the result of an exchange between followers and a leader, and must carry satisfaction for both parties. In accepting a leader's ways of doing things, followers voluntarily give up some of their freedom to make decisions. In effect, followers permit another person, the leader, to make certain decisions that affect them in specific situations. In return for permitting them-

---

[1]R. M. Stogdill, *Handbook of Leadership: A Survey of Theory and Research* (New York: The Free Press, 1974), pp. 7–16.

selves to be influenced by another person, followers want to receive certain economic and psychic rewards from the leader. For example, Ara Parseghian, former football coach at Notre Dame, demonstrated his coaching abilities by leading Notre Dame to national football championships. The football players at Notre Dame followed his advice on the field and suspended their individual judgments because of Ara's ability to bring psychic and economic rewards to them. Examples of psychic rewards might include a sense of achievement from being Number 1, national attention to the team, or the fulfillment of personal goals. Economic rewards might include a high draft choice by a professional team, well-paying summer jobs provided by alumni, and the like.

Why do people want to become leaders? First, it is important to realize that very few people are forced to assume leadership positions against their will. Those who are not motivated to become leaders generally choose not to run. A substantial number of people are simply not interested in becoming leaders and resist placement in such positions. Thus, it is not rare for an employee to decline a chance to be promoted to a superviser's job or to the executive ranks. Such people are simply not motivated to become leaders in these particular situations.

Even though some persons avoid leadership roles, and we hear that there is a shortage of qualified leaders, many do seek leadership positions. Obviously, then, leadership positions must be viewed by these people as having a great deal to offer. Consequently, if we hope to attract the types of people best able to perform the leadership functions, we should attempt to identify what it is that attracts people to leadership jobs.

There is little doubt that leadership positions can provide important rewards. Among these are economic rewards. Without a successful collegiate coaching career, it is highly unlikely that the Ford Motor Company would have used Coach Parseghian to advertise its cars. Similarly, without a successful career as a professional quarterback, it is highly unlikely that Faberge would have offered Joe Namath approximately $5 million to endorse its men's cologne products. In many organizations, top executives are paid ten to twenty times as much as the lowest-paid employees. The point is not whether you think these people are worth such high salaries, but that somebody thinks they are.

Leadership, however, is often sought when economic rewards are absent. For example, the football team captain, union steward, leader of a church group, and president of a local PTA are not paid for their positions, but people who willingly occupy these positions usually exercise leadership. Why? Leaders also attempt to satisfy psychic needs and those who aspire to leadership positions may seek recognition, esteem, or acceptance.

Followers must make it possible for leaders to satisfy some of these needs. Knowing that one can affect the destiny of others and oneself, or being recognized as the best in a field, can be important psychic rewards for the leader. This is the price followers pay for their leadership. The leader receives rewards from the group just as group members receive rewards from the leader. Therefore, to remain in a leadership position, the leader must help group members gain satisfactions otherwise beyond their reach. In return, the group satisfies the leader's needs for power and prominence while helping reach organizational goals.

How Does a Leader Influence Behavior?

Since not all leaders hold formal organizational positions, there must be additional ways to influence others. One way to examine these is to consider the sources of power or influence available to a leader. These have been identified as: legitimacy, reward, coercion, reference, and expertise.[2]

Legitimacy

This type of power is vested in all management positions and gives each manager the authority to make decisions in specific areas. For example, foremen have specific legitimate power over their subordinates solely because of their formal position and this source of influence is available to any person who might occupy a foreman's position.

Reward

This type of influence stems from the leader's control of rewards valued by subordinates. Subordinates who act as their supervisors wish do so, in part, because they believe their behavior will be rewarded. Consequently, reward power depends on the leader's ability to provide

[2]J. P. French, Jr. and B. Raven, "The Bases of Social Power," in *Studies in Social Power,* ed. D. Cartwright (Ann Arbor, Michigan: Institute for Social Research, 1959), pp. 150–67.

either psychological or economic rewards for subordinates in exchange for their compliance. For example, the supervisor may be able to reward workers through task assignments, vacation schedules, lunch breaks, and pay increases.

Coercion

This type of power is based on fear. If subordinates alter their behavior because they believe that a failure to comply with orders from a superior will lead to punishments, they are responding to coercion. Examples of punishments might include official reprimands for not following orders, poor work assignments, and a strict enforcement of all work rules. The behavior resulting from the use of coercion is highly uncertain. Coercion may stop undesired behavior, but it does not necessarily produce desired behavior. The worker who is reprimanded for shoddy work, for example, may simply stop performing the task completely. Additionally, some workers may seek to avoid being reprimanded by falsifying performance reports rather than actually changing the quality of their performance.

Reference

Reference power is based on the followers' identification with the leader. This identification may be based upon personal admiration and usually includes a desire by the followers to "be like" the leader. In other words, reference power is usually associated with people who possess admirable personal characteristics, charisma, or a good reputation.

Expertise

This power stems from the perceived and demonstrated competencies of leaders to implement, analyze, evaluate, and control the tasks that their groups have been assigned. Street gangs usually assess and assign expert power to those who can fight the best, academicians to those colleagues who write journal articles and books. Expert power is narrow in scope since we tend to be influenced by another person's expertise within specific task areas. For example, a star quarterback with high expert power on the football field may not possess such power in a chemistry class.

In summary, it is worth noting that leaders need not possess the same amounts of each of these types of power. The areas of reward, punishment, and legitimate power are largely specified by the organization. For example, a first-line foreman is at a lower level of authority than a vice president for manufacturing. Consequently, the foreman's legitimate, reward, and punishment power bases are less than those of the vice president. On the other hand, some supervisors may possess personal characteristics that increase their reference or expert power regardless of their position in the organization's hierarchy.

How Do People Get to Be Leaders?

How do you get to be a leader? What special qualities, abilities, and personality traits are needed to be a leader? Can we predict who will rise to the top and who will succeed or fail when they get there?

Questions of this sort have been asked for centuries, and the answers depend on many things. Most people expect leaders to have certain personality or physical traits that set them apart from other group members. However, it is evident that a person can be a leader in one group and a follower in others. Few people are leaders all the time. Therefore, personality and physical factors alone cannot determine who becomes a leader.

Many positions require some specialized training or experience, though being at the right place at the right time certainly helps. Most universities are run by people with educational backgrounds and experience, most hospitals require the chief of the medical staff to have a medical degree, and most Supreme Court Justices have legal backgrounds.

Although many managers would agree that situational requirements are more important than the personal qualities of an individual, people with certain personal traits are still more likely to become leaders than others. Some examples of these personal traits include: An ability to verbalize feelings and concepts; intelligence above the level of the average, but below the level of genius; empathy with group members; a degree of insight into group situations; a high level of technical skill in the task(s) the group will be undertaking in its goal-seeking activities; and flexibility in formulating new concepts and ideas. Although none of these personal attributes is absolutely necessary, they all predispose people toward leadership.

The one necessary personal attribute for those who assume a leadership role is the motivation to be a leader. In general, the stronger a person's motivation to be a leader, the more likely it is that the person will achieve a leadership position. Of course, there are many reasons why an individual might desire to become a leader. Some examples are: (1) An urge to dominate others; (2) devotion to the group and to the group's goals; (3) a high-level aspiration for either self or group; (4) a need for prestige and esteem; and (5) economic rewards.

All of the personal traits mentioned may play a part in influencing the group's choice of a leader. However, situational factors are more important than personal traits. People may become leaders because they are in the right place at the right time. They may have specific knowledge or ability that directly fits into the requirements of a leadership role at the time it is available; they may have the longest seniority among group members; they may be the correct age; or they may have access to important information and the ability to control the flow of this information to other group members.

The means by which people become leaders varies from group to group. Most groups, but not all, have formally designated leaders. In some cases, the leader is selected by people outside the group, for example when management assigns a person to a supervisory position. In other groups, existing leaders may choose their own successors, as is done by some dictators. In still other groups, the members elect their leaders. This is especially true in societies with a democratic tradition, such as the United States. The election process is easy to observe in political settings, but it can also be seen in fraternities, bowling teams, and tree-house clubs composed of eight year olds. Finally, in juvenile gangs or primitive cultures, some kind of fitness test may be used to designate leaders. These fitness tests may seek to determine who is the fastest, the best fighter, or simply who owns the football.

So far, we have been discussing leaders who are somehow formally recognized as such. This is not always the case. Many people are leaders without the titles that go with such activity. These people are called informal leaders. Groups without formal leaders still need leadership if the members are to work toward common goals. In these types of groups the persons providing leadership may not even be aware that they are acting as leaders. Nonetheless, if they are influencing group members' behavior, they are exerting leadership. Informal leaders are also found in groups with formally designated leaders. This is especially true when the formal leaders are not helping the groups to reach their goals or when they are not providing their followers with the satisfactions they desire.

When groups have formal leaders, the informal leaders usually do not officially replace the formal leaders. This is especially true when the formal leaders were officially appointed to their positions. Instead, an informal leader usually arises because some group member displays abilities that are lacking, or only partially present, in the formal leader. Informal leaders may have more expertise than formal leaders, and therefore group members turn to them rather than to the formal leader for advice. Or, informal leaders may be sympathetic to other group members while the formal leaders are abrupt or intolerant of their feelings. The result is that group members recognize the informal leader's ability and respond to it. Consequently, informal leaders are able to influence group member behavior in the direction of their intentions—our definition of leadership.

What Does Leadership Contribute to Group Effectiveness?

The popular belief that good leadership will cause a group to be effective is comforting, but unfortunately it is also naive. The belief is comforting in that it reduces the problem of group effectiveness to one of searching for "good" leaders. At the same time, it is naive in that it views leaders as the sole and all-powerful influence on group effectiveness. A leader, however, is obviously neither the sole nor the all-powerful influence on group effectiveness. It is, therefore, necessary to identify potential leadership contribution to group effectiveness.

Phillip Selznik has identified four basic areas in which leadership can affect group productivity.[3] First, a leader can define the group's mission or task. Second, a leader can establish the means for accomplishing the group's mission or task through policies, plans, and other guidelines. Third, the leader can represent the group to the outside world. Finally a leader can resolve conflict within the group. Although these four areas of potential leadership contribution are obviously interactive, we will discuss them individually.

Group's task

Most leaders are obviously not the sole influence on the definition of a group's task. In industrial or business settings it is more common to find a workgroup's task defined by its place in the total organization. For example, the foreman of a paint shop does not normally define the paint shop's primary task. Instead, its task will most likely be defined by superiors as painting certain parts according to a specified procedure and schedule.

At first glance it may appear that voluntary groups, or those not a

[3]P. Selznik, *Leadership in Administration* (New York: Harper and Row, 1957), pp. 62–64.

part of some larger organization, would provide their leaders with the opportunity to define group tasks or missions. In the latter case—autonomous groups—leaders may be able to influence missions or tasks to the extent that they can provide satisfactory rewards in exchange for member contributions to the task. For example, wages represent an exchange of monetary rewards for employees' efforts. Even in this case, however, leaders are limited in determining tasks by the value employees place on the money offered for their services.

In voluntary groups leaders usually work with members who have been attracted to their groups because of their stated tasks or missions. Thus, leaders most likely are able to influence tasks or missions only within very narrow limits. Moreover, the leaders of voluntary groups are usually selected by group members and, therefore, are likely to lose their leadership positions if they do not adequately embrace their group's tasks or goals. For example, the president of a local service club is expected to further the club's goals, not change them.

We do not want to leave the impression that leaders have little to do with the definitions of group goals. The restrictions discussed here usually concern only primary group goals or tasks. In fact, members do not see their groups as having only a single purpose. Consequently, most groups also serve secondary purposes for the members. An important example of these secondary purposes involves the need for social interaction. It is here that leaders sometimes have their greatest influence on goal formulation. Thus, the foreman of the paint shop referred to earlier may have little influence over when and what painting is to be done, but may have considerable influence in determining whether subordinates look upon their jobs as providing opportunities to develop and maintain meaningful social relationships.

To review, most leaders are usually constrained by factors beyond their control when a group's major missions are being defined. At the same time, leaders can greatly influence their groups' secondary goals. Additionally, there are strong indications that secondary goals are most likely to determine such important outcomes as group solidarity, low job turnover, reduced absenteeism, and commitment to primary group goals.

Finally, it is important to recognize that the overall policies, technologies, or member desires that constrain leaders are not always clear to individual group members. Thus, the leader can influence group effectiveness by clarifying primary goals for members, especially for new group members or during periods of rapid change.

Group's Goals into Action

The second important area of potential leadership contribution to group effectiveness involves the translation of group goals into action, or the establishment of means for accomplishing tasks. This area has traditionally been associated with leadership, especially in business organizations.

Group tasks normally represent efforts toward a common goal. As mentioned before, however, leaders may be more constrained than we normally think. Technological processes, machines, physical or geographical characteristics, the abilities of group members, and other factors combine to limit the means that can be used to accomplish group tasks. For example, the manager who has salesmen scattered throughout fifteen states cannot use daily, face-to-face meetings to insure cooperation and coordination among the salesmen. Similarly, the supervisor of a group of unskilled laborers cannot use work procedures that require high skill-levels from subordinates. Obviously, company policies, union contracts, legislation, and the like further restrict potential leader contribution in this area.

It should be easy to see by now that tasks that allow leaders little potential influence through the establishment of means for their accomplishment are likely to be routine. Thus, at first glance, it may appear that highly nonroutine tasks would provide a great opportunity for leaders to influence group effectiveness. Unfortunately, this is seldom the case. When tasks are highly nonroutine, they usually require that individuals performing the tasks respond to information that is available only at the time the tasks are performed. Thus, tasks that have many constraints as well as those which have very few constraints are both unlikely to allow leaders to influence effectiveness through the specification of procedures, etc.

More specifically, the foreman of an assembly line may have little discretion in establishing specific work procedures because of technological constraints. Likewise, the supervisor of a research and development laboratory may have little discretion in establishing specific work procedures because the procedures must be constantly modified and adjusted to meet changing situations. Consequently, leaders are most likely able to influence group effectiveness through establishing means when group tasks are neither very high nor very low in constraints.

Representative of Group

Representing group members to the outside world implies that leaders may serve as linking pins. This linking function should be recognized as a dual responsibility. First leaders can contribute by seeking, collecting, and screening information that affects the performance of group tasks. To a large extent, the recognition of external pressures and constraints falls into this category. For example, if the organization requires certain outputs from a work group, the leader can make sure that such demands are known and acted upon by the group.

Additionally, leaders can communicate the needs and desires of groups and their individual members to the outside world. This potential contribution to group effectiveness has been recognized for some time in management literature and is seen in references which characterize the supervisor as the man-in-the-middle. This characterization is most often used to describe supervisors as caught between opposing forces, but it also points out their role as a representative of the group. Thus, supervisors are expected to represent management to their subordinates, and at the same time, represent their subordinates to management.

Studies in business organizations show that practicing managers spend large portions, if not a majority, of their time communicating with individuals outside their immediate work groups. When the accomplishment of a group's task is dependent upon work performed by other groups, this function is even more important. Likewise, when work groups require outside resources, the potential for leadership contribution in this area is increased. In some groups, such as voluntary organizations, this function may be so critical that it becomes the acid test that determines whether elected leaders continue in their positions. For example, when shop stewards cease to represent their groups, they will most likely be replaced by the membership.

Conflict Resolver

The last area identified as having potential for leadership contribution involves the resolution of conflict within the group. To the extent that group members agree on both the goals and the means for their attainment, the potential for conflict is reduced. In this case, leaders can, at best, contribute by allocating resources according to the wishes of the group members. This, of course, assumes that the goals and means are within any external constraints.

When there is agreement on the means for accomplishing goals, but disagreement concerning which goals should be sought, leaders can contribute by promoting compromise between group members. In order to promote compromise, leaders may encourage the members to work together so that all might realize partial satisfaction of their individual goals. Or, leaders may encourage the members to work together so that goals can be met in sequence: one person's goal this week, someone else's next week, and so forth.

When members agree on goals, but not on the means for their attainment, leaders can contribute by acting as an expert authority for the group. In other words, when leaders are better qualified than their subordinates to choose among means for goal attainment, they can reduce conflict and improve effectiveness by selecting the most appropriate means. Fortunately, group leaders are usually in a favorable position to influence the group in such situations. They have often received inputs from more group members than any other individual, and are more likely to have less of a personal stake in the selection of a particular course of action.

When group members agree on neither goals nor the means for their accomplishment, leaders are in a position to contribute much to group effectiveness. If the leaders possess skills or knowledge greater than those of group members, they may contribute through their judgments. On the other hand, if the required skills and knowledge are beyond those of the leaders, they may be in a position to contribute to group effectiveness through the use of participative problem-solving techniques.

Although much of this discussion has concerned factors that tend to reduce a leader's potential contributions to group effectiveness, it does not imply that leaders are without opportunity to influence group effectiveness. Rather, it serves to highlight the errors in the everyday assumption that leaders alone cause groups to be effective. More specifically, leaders can contribute to group effectiveness by influencing member behavior within the constraints of their abilities, the tasks to be performed, the abilities of the subordinates, and other situational factors. In short, it is the realization of the potential within a specific setting that should be considered as "good" leadership.

How Do Different Leadership Styles Affect Group Effectiveness?

In real life settings, people obviously do not respond to abstract concepts such as sources of power or areas of potential leadership contributions. Instead they respond to the behavior of leaders. Consequently, the ultimate interest in leadership usually begins with, and almost always returns to, leader behavior. In turn, this behavior is usually discussed in terms of leadership styles.

Leadership Styles

Leadership styles attempt to capture the essential character of a whole range of leader behavior. As a result, the study of leadership has produced a multitude of classifications of leadership styles. For our purposes, however, these classifications can loosely be condensed into two general categories.[4] The first category includes styles that tend to be directed toward the satisfaction of task requirements. Such behavior usually includes close supervision with tight controls, rigidly defined tasks, and limited upward communication from subordinates. The *second* category includes styles that tend to be directed toward satisfying the needs of individual group members. This behavior includes loose, democratic supervision with few controls and limited direction by the supervisor.

In some cases, studies of leadership styles have found that close supervision contributes to workgroup effectiveness. At the same time, other, equally impressive studies have found the opposite relationship between these leadership styles and workgroup effectiveness. Which group of studies is correct? Probably both. Leadership studies have not covered, and may never cover, all possible situations. The types of leaders, followers, tasks, and situations studied vary from basketball teams, bomber crews, and open hearth furnace workers, to scientists. Thus, given our previous comments concerning the various sources of power available to leaders and the various potential leadership contributions, it is likely that no one style is best in all situations. Consequently, an effective leadership style is one that uses the power sources available to leaders to maximize their potential contribution to group effectiveness.

The many possible combinations of power sources and potential leadership contributions make a complete listing of appropriate leadership styles beyond the scope of this chapter. This would be true even if we knew, based upon sound research, the appropriate style for each situation. We do not.

[4]Lee R. Tannenbaum and W. Schmidt, "How to Choose a Leadership Pattern," *Harvard Business Review* 36 (1958), pp. 95–101.

Choosing a Leadership Style

The following example is designed to demonstrate how the concepts presented in this chapter can be used to choose an appropriate leadership style.

The foremen in charge of various assembly line operations in large industrial plants usually have limited power, as specified by the organization. For example, they may have some, but not large amounts, of legitimate, reward, and coercive power. At the same time, their expert power is often limited by the low skill-levels that are required of subordinates in their jobs.

The amount of reference power available to these foremen is, of course, dependent upon their personal characteristics. Given the situation and tasks involved, these formen will have little influence on their workgroup's effectiveness through definitions of primary missions or the means for their accomplishment. In fact, these areas are most likely defined by forces beyond the control of the foremen or their workgroups, namely, other managers in the organization. This means that if the foremen are to contribute to the workgroup's effectiveness, they must do so by defining secondary tasks and the means for their accomplishment, representing the group and its members, and resolving internal conflict.

These areas of potential contribution all involve the personal desires of individual group members. If the foremen possess high reference power because of their personal characteristics, a directive leadership style may be more effective. In these cases, subordinates are likely to allow the foremen to decide upon matters relating to their personal desires because of their strong identification with their foremen. On the other hand, if the foremen have low reference power, they may contribute more to group effectiveness with a considerate, less directive leadership style. Subordinates in such cases are likely to resist their foremen's decisions concerning their personal desires because of their lack of identification with them. However, this less directive leadership style does not mean that the foremen are without influence in such situations. If the foremen can assist the members of their workgroups in identifying secondary goals and means, while assisting them in resolving their own conflicts, they will contribute to job satisfaction and other outcomes such as low turnover and low absenteeism.

While the above example demonstrates the use of this chapter's information in a specific situation, the question remains—How can leaders take the information presented here and choose an effective leadership style? First, leaders must identify and understand the variables associated with their situations. Second, they must resist the temptation to give up when frustrated. Leaders who consciously attempt to analyze their situations may feel overwhelmed and be tempted to simply stay with their past leadership styles. This blind return to past behavior is effective only if their past behavior was appropriate and if their situation does not change. Changes in the leaders' situations may make past leadership styles which were effective become ineffective.

Third, leaders need to approach their leadership styles as scientists approach their experiments. Scientists carefully define the variables with which they are working. Leaders should attempt to identify their sources of power and the areas in which they can contribute to their groups' effectiveness. Scientists then make predictions which they test. Based on an analysis of their situations, leaders should make predictions of their leadership style and test them. Lastly, a scientist is skeptical. Leaders also need to be skeptical when they test their predictions. A leadership style may appear to be effective when it is not. Or, situations may have changed without the leaders' knowledge.

In summary, leaders need to be aware that the selection of a leadership style is also difficult because they must examine their own behavior. When people attempt to examine their own behavior they can never be totally objective. Leaders can all too easily mislead themselves when they define their situations so that their favorite leadership styles are suggested. Similarly, we all have a tendency to ignore changes that might require that we give up old ways. We have invested large amounts of time and usually no small amount of our egos in our behavior patterns and we do not give them up willingly. The task is difficult, but the alternative is to give up and to be at the mercy of change and forces beyond our control.

What is the nature of the changes in our society that affect leadership?

Today, one of the most striking features of change is its rate. Only a few generations ago, the rate of change was such that most people could expect to go through life without experiencing major changes in the world about them. People were able to define their world, find their place in it, and live out their days. Today, however, we live in a rapidly changing world. Many of us will change jobs several times in our careers. Others will remain in a single job only to find it constantly changing. Many of the jobs new college graduates will take this year did not exist when they entered college four years ago.

Faced with this increasing rate of change, today's leaders must constantly study their jobs for signs that might indicate a need for altering their leadership styles. Additionally, the nature of work performed by most groups is changing. In the past, workgroups tended to be relatively free to accomplish their tasks with little consideration of other groups. Today, however, modern technologies and increasing specialization require workgroups to coordinate their activities. In turn, this need to coordinate tends to reduce a leader's ability to define primary tasks and to select the means for their accomplishment, thereby decreasing the potential for leadership contributions to workgroup effectiveness in these areas. At the same time, however, the need to coordinate activities increases the potential for leadership contributions through representing the workgroup and resolving conflict.

It is also evident that changes among followers place new demands upon today's leaders. Employees are less likely to seek only monetary rewards in their work and to seek other satisfaction elsewhere. Even in periods of high unemployment, people have shown a surprising willingness to quit their jobs when they were not seen as "meaningful." Without question, such attitudes are significantly different from those held by employees prior to World War II.

Summary

Leadership is the ability to influence others toward specific goals or objectives. It is behavior that uses and stimulates the efforts of others in certain directions. Although the personal characteristics of leaders can help determine their effectiveness, the followers' personal characteristics, the tasks to be performed, and other situational factors are also important.

Leaders can perform four basic tasks for their groups. First they can define the group's tasks or missions; second, they can establish the means for accomplishing group tasks; third, they can represent group interests to others; and finally, they can resolve conflicts within the group. Leaders accomplish these four basic tasks through leadership styles. On a continuum these styles range from considerate and empathetic leadership to impersonal and autocratic. The particular leadership style that is effective in one situation may not be effective in others because of changes in the group's goals, the situation, and how the leader has defined the group's basic tasks.

1. In general, what is leadership?

2. Why do people want to become leaders?

3. Why do people follow leaders?

4. How do people become leaders?

5. What are the four basic ways in which leaders can affect group effectiveness?

6. Is it usually better to stick with one leadership style throughout your career? Why? Why not?

7. What are the factors to consider in choosing a leadership style?

8. Do leaders have the power to change their leadership style or are their styles dictated by their superiors?

1. Scott Davis has been a middle manager in the production department of Outland Steel Corporation for about eight months. Just prior to joining Outland, Scott retired from the army after serving a tour of duty in Vietnam as a company commander. According to the army, Scott had a distinguished military career, but had elected to retire for personal reasons. Morale in Scott's department has been low since he joined Outland. Some of his subordinates act dissatisfied and the number of grievances filed has been increasing steadily.

At lunch one day, Scott asked Gerald Clark, head of the metallurgical laboratory, if he knew anything about the low morale in the production department and the "real" reason why the number of grievances filed had increased. Clark replied that he had heard through the grapevine that Scott's employees were unhappy with him because he was making all of the decisions for the department. Scott was taken back by Gerry's comment and replied, "In the army I made all of the decisions and we had one of the best records around. Besides, I think the men expected me to."

a. What leadership style had Scott been using in the military? Why might it have been effective?

b. What are the important factors that define Scott's present situation?

c. What might the consequences be if Scott cannot change his leadership style? As his superior, what would you recommend?

2. Ed Ross was one of the best technical minds that ever worked for Texas-Northern Pipeline Company. He graduated with honors from Ohio State's engineering program and just recently completed his master's degree at Oklahoma State. He enjoyed doing research and prefered working alone, seldom coming into contact with other em-

ployees. Because of his outstanding contributions to the company, Ross was promoted to coordinate the work of several young engineers in the lab.

The research team seemed to have problems from the very beginning. Ross appeared to ignore the administrative duties of his job, but was ready to help solve any technical problems that arose. Several of the team members commented to the personnel department that Ross lacked basic human relations skills. Ross's superior was aware of these problems, and called Ross into his office for a chat. Upon entering the office, Ross told his boss that he was in the middle of an experiment and did not have time to chat about unimportant matters.

a. What leadership skills does Ross have? Are they in proper balance?

b. What source (s) of influence is Ross relying on to influence his subordinates?

c. Should Ross have been promoted to coordinate the research team?

d. Assuming that you are Ross's boss, what should you do now?

Communication for Supervisors

Herbert G. Hicks and Karen K. Arnold*

The Importance of Communication

IMAGINE, if you can, a world without communication. Of all the things that you might imagine it to be, it certainly would not nearly resemble our modern world. Without some form of communication, organized and goal-directed activity could not exist. People would find it impossible to accomplish objectives that required anything more than individual effort. And there are few objectives in modern society that can be accomplished without the organized activity of two or more people.

Through the use of language, man has been able to record past history and communicate with the people of other generations. However, communication is not restricted solely to the use of language in its forms of talking, listening, reading, and writing. It also includes body movements, facial expressions, and art forms. Even silence can be a

*Herbert G. Hicks, Professor of Management, College of Business Administration, Louisiana State University, and Karen K. Arnold, Louisiana State University.

form of communication, for example, when you wish a co-worker "Good morning" and hear no reply. In the following pages, however, we will direct our attention to language as the primary means of communication. In doing so, we will define communication as the *process by which we transfer information, understanding, and feeling from one person to another*.

Today's trend toward increased specialization and its resulting interdependencies in all segments of society make good communication imperative. However, unlike the signaling behavior of animals, communication through language and speech is not a natural human activity. It must be learned. In other words, we must be taught how to speak, read, and write. Thus, our learned communication skills can be improved.

We hope that after reading this chapter you will have a greater awareness of the complexity of this seemingly simple task that is often taken for granted. This awareness is especially important among supervisors. Any supervisor is a vital communication link between higher levels of management and workers; and, since over 50 percent of a supervisor's time on the job is spent in some form of communication, the importance of understanding communication activities cannot be overemphasized. In addition, communication is basic to all other managerial functions. For example, planning, organizing, coordinating, motivating, and controlling could not be performed without communication.

Unfortunately, although communication skills can and should be constantly improved, they can never be perfected. To have perfect communication, all persons participating in a particular communication activity would have to derive the same meaning from a particular symbol or word. An easy task you might think—just look up the word in a dictionary. This is much like thinking that you can determine the total size of an iceberg by viewing only the portion that appears above the water. Of course, most of the iceberg lies submerged. Therefore, to determine its size, we must consider the total and not merely that part which is most obvious. This is also the case in communication. Just as the largest part of an iceberg lies below the surface, the largest part of the meaning that we attach to a word lies within us. This meaning is based on our own unique experiences, knowledge, levels of understanding, attitudes, and emotions.

Actually, knowing the definition of a word is only one of the requirements for accurate and meaningful communication. In addition, this situation is complicated by the fact that many words have more than one dictionary meaning, with our five hundred most commonly used words having over fourteen thousand definitions. Also, the meanings of words change over time, and new words are constantly being added. Thus, communication is indeed a very complex activity.

A Model of the Communication Process

Many models have been developed to characterize the communication process. Some date back as far as the time of Aristotle, who viewed communication as consisting of the speaker, the speech, and the audience. Aristotle's model is significant because it recognizes the importance of receivers in the communication process. In other words, there is more to effective communication than just saying something. Instead, it involves saying something to people who, like the speaker, have certain viewpoints, educational backgrounds, levels of understanding, emotional outlooks, and past experiences. Needless to say, all of these factors must be considered as they relate to the communication process.

Interestingly, the communication model upon which many subsequent ones have been based was originally designed to increase the efficiency with which electrical signals were transmitted and received. This model was developed for Bell Telephone in the late 1940s and was later adapted to human communication. In addition, many other models of the communication process have been developed. As a result, there are almost as many models of the process as there are authorities on the subject. However, most of the models do have a number of common elements. Let's take a closer look at each of them, as shown in Figure 9–1.

Source

Every communication requires an origin or source. The communication activity is initiated because the source wants to respond to the environment in some way. In this sense, all communication can be seen as a response to the way people perceive the various situations in which they find themselves. This is true regardless of whether they are making conversation, talking to the boss, or discussing the day's activities with their families at dinner. For example, suppose a guest is at a party in a friend's home and begins to find the room unusually warm. As the situation becomes increasingly uncomfortable, the guest seeks some way to convey an internal response to the environment. Thus, we have the initiation of a communication event.

Figure 9–1
The Communication Process

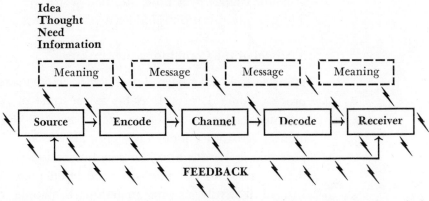

The process of human communication involves the transfer of meaning through the encoding of a message by a source who sends it through a channel to a receiver. The receiver decodes the message and provides feedback for the original source. The small lightning bolts represent noise, which is present at all stages of the communication process.

Encode

In all communication, the source must engage in encoding activities. Encoding occurs when the idea to be transmitted is transformed into a set of symbols by the source. In this process, the most commonly used symbols are words. However, we often search for other ways to symbolically convey the idea, information, need, or thought that initiates communication. In any event, we would not be able to formulate and send a message without the encoding process.

Let's continue with our previous example to demonstrate encoding activities. In response to the increasing unpleasantness of the warm room, our party guest searches for some way to let others know that he is hot.

Message

A message is the end result of encoding activities. It expresses the purpose of the source, and can include gestures, facial expressions, spoken or written words, or drawings. Since most messages follow a predetermined structure or code, our language can be viewed as a code that determines the grammatical arrangement of words in relation to one another.

In encoding we also search for symbols that will convey meaning, since it is important that our messages be understood. If a message is not clear, the probability of a communication malfunction is high.

The message that the uncomfortably warm party guest transmits to the host could be, "I find it very warm in here."

Channel

The channel is the medium used to transmit a message. With most messages, the channels used are those of sight and sound. Any of the five senses, however, can serve as channels for transporting a message from the source to a receiver. For example, a pat on the back given by a supervisor (the sense of touch) can be used to recognize a subordinate for a job well done.

In the case of our party guest, the primary channel used was that of sound. The guest spoke and the host heard the message that was sent.

Receiver—Decode—Meaning

The process of communication functions properly when the receiver decodes the message and derives a meaning from it that is approximately the same as that transmitted by the source. Basically, decoding can be viewed as encoding in reverse, since receivers derive some meaning from the stimulus of the air waves or light waves that have carried the message to them.

As mentioned earlier, it is not sufficient for the receiver to decode a message by merely attaching some meaning to it. Successful communication occurs when the meaning that the receiver derives from a message is similar to that intended by the source. This point cannot be overemphasized, because a failure to understand the intended meaning of a message is probably the greatest source of problems in the communication process.

The root of much misunderstanding lies in the fact that most sources and receivers have differing backgrounds, experiences, viewpoints, knowledge, and emotional make-ups. In turn, these factors determine the meanings we give to certain symbols. Of course, these factors can never be exactly alike for any two people, and therefore, *no two people will ever attach the same meaning to a particular set of symbols.* However, the greater the similarities among these factors, the greater the probability of successful communication.

Getting back to our example, the message, "I find it very warm in here," may be decoded by the party's host to mean that the guest:

1. Has had too much to drink;
2. Has too many heavy clothes on;

3. Finds the room temperature to be high and would like the air-conditioning turned on;

4. Has come down with a fever;

5. Has been engaged in a heated debate about politics with another guest; or,

6. Has some entirely different meaning to convey.

Feedback

How does the source know whether or not the message has been received and decoded correctly? The answer can be found in feedback, another important element of the communication process.

Feedback usually occurs in the form of a response from the receiver. When providing feedback, the receiver encodes and sends a message through some channel to the original source, who is now a receiver. In this way, the original source can tell whether or not the message got through to the receiver. If feedback indicates that the receiver understood the meaning of the message, further communication can take place. If the message was not clear, the source may have to alter the encoding of the message until feedback indicates that the receiver has understood the intended meaning.

Feedback does not always take the form of spoken or written words, however. In a college classroom, for example, a sea of puzzled faces during a lecture should serve as feedback to let the professor know that the message is not getting across.

In our party example, the host's reaction or response to the message, "I find it very warm in here," will let the guest know whether or not the intended meaning was decoded. Let's suppose that the guest did find the room to be too warm and wanted the air-conditioning turned on. If the host says, "I'll turn on the air-conditioning," this acts as feedback to let the guest know that the host derived a similar meaning from the message. On the other hand, if the host's response is, "What's the matter? Is politics getting too hot for you to handle?" the feedback tells the guest that the host did not derive the intended meaning from the message.

Noise

Noise is anything that reduces the accuracy or fidelity of a communication. Thus, it contributes to miscommunication. By being aware of how noise affects the fidelity of communication, we can take steps to reduce it and thereby improve the accuracy of our efforts in this area.

Noise can be present in all of the other elements of the communication process. At the origin of the communication process, noise occurs when the source perceives an object or activity incorrectly. Noise exists in the encoding stage if the symbols chosen do not properly convey the source's mental perception. Here, the ability to reduce noise depends on the source's mental ability and knowledge of language. The greater these two factors are, the lower the noise factor will be.

If the form or code of the message is not understandable to the receiver, noise also exists. This can occur when the sender and receiver speak different languages. In such situations, the noise is so great as to make verbal or written communication impossible without the aid of an interpreter.

In the channel, noise can operate to stop the message from getting through accurately. It is difficult to talk to someone when air hammers are operating in the area, for example. And finally, noise is present if the receiver decodes the message incorrectly.

Continuing with our example of the party guest, if he was too warm and wanted the air-conditioning turned on, he might have chosen the wrong symbols to encode his mental perception. If the party was crowded, the conversations and laughter of the other guests could have prevented the message from being heard clearly by the host. In short, the possibilities for miscommunication are endless. Thus, we should constantly strive to improve ourselves in this important area.

Formal Communication Networks in Organizations

Visualize a section of an organization chart with which you are familiar. It probably resembles the one depicted in Figure 9–2. In addition to showing lines of authority and accountability, it also serves as a diagram of the organization's formal communication network. Through it flows the "lifeblood" of the organization.

Most communication in any organization is either written or oral. Written communication serves as a permanent record that can be referred to again and again. As such, it is usually preferred over oral communication when messages are lengthy or difficult to understand. Common examples of written communication include company policies, rules, reports, memos, manuals, job specifications, bulletins, and contracts.

Oral communication usually occurs on a face-to-face basis. The major exceptions to this include telephone conversations, intercoms, and pub-

Figure 9–2
**The structure of an organization as depicted in its organization
chart determines the formal channels of communication**

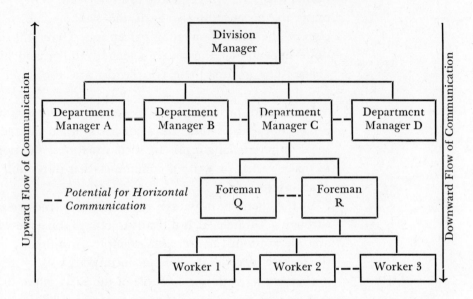

lic-address systems. Regardless of how oral communication is accomplished, however, its directness is unsurpassed. In addition, feedback is immediate and the sender's tone of voice, facial expressions, and personality can be easily perceived. At the same time, the sender can quickly gauge the receiver's level of understanding. Although these factors serve to improve understanding, oral communication has the disadvantage of being subject to perceptual differences. Thus, misunderstandings that are difficult to overcome often result from our attempts to recall oral messages.

Regardless of whether communication is oral or written, it can be further classified according to the direction or flow it takes in an organization. The three directions are upward, downward, and horizontal.

Downward and Upward Flow

In general, policy statements, orders, directions, and decisions flow downward from higher to lower levels of authority in an organization. On the other hand, the information upon which decisions and policies are based must flow upward.

The downward flow of communication is rather easily achieved and composes the bulk of all formal organizational communication. However, because downward communication flows naturally from higher to lower levels of authority, it is often overlooked as a potential source of trouble. Just because two people go through the motions of communicating does not mean that they have actually done so. Thus special care should be taken to ensure that instructions, orders, directions, and other types of downward communication are actually understood by subordinates.

Encouraging upward communication is relatively more difficult than is the case with downward communication. In part, this stems from the fact that upward communication runs contrary to the usual higher-to-lower flow of authority found in most organizations. Yet, it is important that supervisors encourage upward communication since, as was previously stated, the information needed to make decisions and formulate policy must flow upward. In addition, upward communication provides a control function and enables supervisors to judge how accurately their downward communications have been transmitted and carried out.

The surest way to choke the necessary flow of upward communication is to encourage it and then to use its contents against subordinates. Perhaps the fear that the content of upward communication will be used against them is the reason why many subordinates have acquired the habit of emphasizing only those things that make them look good. Information that does not convey a rosy picture may be suppressed or distorted. For example, a subordinate's pay raise may depend in part upon the judgment of the supervisor. In an effort to make themselves look good, employees may tend to communicate only those things that will favorably impress the supervisor. However, the success of any organization depends on communication that provides an accurate picture of all aspects of its operation, not just the favorable ones. Therefore, the responsibility for encouraging accurate upward communication cannot be overlooked.

Horizontal Flow

Horizontal communication takes place between organizational equals. That is, it flows between individuals who are on approximately the same level of authority in an organization. The primary function of horizontal communication is to facilitate the solution of problems arising from a division of labor and specialization. For example, the head of an engineering department and the head of a fabricating department may find that the only way for a production schedule to be met is through a closer coordination of design and fabrication efforts.

One way to achieve this coordination lies in the use of horizontal communication flows. Figure 9–3 summarizes this and the other major communication flows.

Figure 9–3
Major Flows of Formal Organizational Communication

Downward	*Upward*	*Horizontal*
Top management policy	Administrative reports—	Any work flow
Decisions	These include measures	contacts between
Orders	of performance, cost	persons or
Instructions	control reports, planning	positions on
Procedure manuals	and forecasting, and	the same
Bulletins	others of a similar vein.	organizational
House organs	Grievance procedures	level
Performance appraisals	Interviewing	Meetings
Meetings	Suggestion programs	
	Meetings	

The Grapevine

The upward, downward, and horizontal flows of the formal communication network are only part of the total communication picture in organizations. To complete this picture, the communication network of the informal organization must be added.

Informal organizations can be referred to as "shadow" organizations. They exist in every formal organization, but cannot be identified simply by looking at authority relationships on the formal organization chart. This is because informal organizations are composed of all the friendship, occupational, and special-interest groups within an organization. The communication network linking members of informal organizations is known as the grapevine. It carries far more information than the formal communication network, and is often more effective.[1]

One of the major characteristics of the grapevine is its speed in transmitting information. In part, this speed is made possible by the fact that the grapevine does not follow the stated authority relationships shown on an organizational chart. Rather, it follows what has come to be known as a "cluster pattern," where information is passed on to a number of other persons, not just one. These persons, in turn, tell a cluster of others and the process continues until the news value of the information declines.

[1]See Raymond V. Lesikar, *Business Communication: Theory and Application* (Homewood, Illinois: Irwin, 1972), pp. 12–13.

The grapevine can be beneficial as well as detrimental to the performance of the formal organization. Whether the effects are positive or negative depends to a great extent upon the influence that supervisors can exert on informal channels. To turn the grapevine into a constructive tool, one must integrate the interests of informal group members with those of the formal organization. In addition, two other important facts must be considered.

First, the grapevine ultimately develops in any type of organization and is a normal outgrowth of social interaction at all levels of authority. All employees want to know what is going on and how they will be affected. Moreover, they want to know this information as soon as it becomes news. Unfortunately, formal communication systems tend to circulate information rather slowly. Therefore, the grapevine is used to supplement formal communication channels.

Next, it is important to recognize that the grapevine cannot be eliminated. Of course, many supervisors wish that they could do away with the grapevine, and believe it to have only negative effects on workers' attitudes. In part, this feeling probably results from a tendency to equate the grapevine with rumor; however, the two are not the same. Rumors can be described as false informal communication. They arise when people feel that they will be affected by matters over which they have little or no conrtol. Their subject matter can cover such topics as wages, hours, working conditions, supervisory relationships, job security, benefits, and layoffs, to name only a few. Fortunately, rumors represent only a small percentage of the communication carried by the informal network. In fact, most of grapevine information is surprisingly accurate. However, since rumors are misrepresentations and can prove harmful, they should be dealt with as soon as possible.

One way to reduce the occurrence of rumors is to create situations in which people feel relatively secure. This is generally accomplished by keeping formal communication channels open and by transmitting current information. After rumors have started, a supply of facts given to active grapevine communicators in a face-to-face setting is effective in curbing or stopping their spread. These facts should be supplied without specific reference to the rumors, and the person who provides them should have a communication record that is trustworthy.

In summary, it is evident that rumors can have a negative impact on employees' behavior. However, the smart supervisor can use rumors in a positive way to gain additional insights into employees' gripes and misconceptions. Thus, try to determine why and where rumors have started. Then, take steps to prevent similar situations from arising in the future.

Communication Barriers

As mentioned earlier, the accuracy of communication can be improved through a working knowledge of the communication process. In this regard, your communication can be made more effective through an understanding of some of the more important barriers to communication. In general, these barriers act to prevent your communication from conveying a complete or true picture. They include perceptual, abstractional, inferential, and symbolic barriers.

Perceptual Barriers

The world in which we live is constantly changing. An ancient philosopher demonstrated the dynamic nature of the real world when he stated that a person could never step in the same river twice; the person would be different and so would the river. Thus, reality consists of events and processes, not static things. Unfortunately, because of the limitations of our senses, we are unable to perceive all of our constantly changing process world. However, we are able to observe objects that are the perceptible parts of the events in a process.[2] For example, the book you are reading is constantly moving and changing at this very moment. So are you for that matter, as well as everything around you. Thus, we live in a world of constant motion.

More specifically, to view an object as static when it is constantly changing is an incorrect perception that can lead to inaccurate communication. For example, suppose you are asked about the work habits of Joe Smith, a man you worked with five years ago, but have not seen since that time. As you remember, Smith seemed to be lazy and irresponsible. He often came to work a few minutes late and started putting away his tools a few minutes earlier than anyone else in the afternoon. In short, he didn't carry his share of the work load.

Unknown to you, however, Smith has become more responsible in the last five years and is now considered to be a reliable worker.

[2]See Alfred Korzybski, *Science and Sanity: An Introduction to Non-Aristotelian Systems and General Semantics*, 3rd ed. (Lakeville, Conn.: International Non-Aristotelian Library, 1948).

If you had replied to the inquiry about Joe Smith by saying that he was lazy and irresponsible, your communication would have been incorrect. It would not have reflected the reality of the situation, since it would not have described Smith's true characteristics. Thus, a more accurate way to answer an inquiry of this type would be to preface your remarks with, "When I knew him five years ago . . . He may have changed his ways, however. To be sure, why don't you check with someone who has had recent contact with him?"

Abstractional Barriers

Abstraction involves focusing on certain details while leaving out others and occurs anytime we perceive a person, an object, or a symbol. In fact, our constantly changing world and the limitations of our sensory organs cause abstraction to be necessary, since we are able to perceive only a small part of what is actually occurring around us.

Abstraction has both advantages and disadvantages that center on the fact that the process permits classification. On the plus side, classifications are valuable in communication because they permit a great deal of information to be transmitted quickly. In addition, the process of abstraction can be extended to an infinite number of classification levels. A classic example of this is provided by the "abstraction ladder" illustrated in Figure 9–4. Bessie, the cow, is classified on several levels of an abstraction ladder. The cow, Bessie, is uniquely herself and differs from all other objects in the same classification. Because of this quality of uniqueness, any person or object included in a particular classification level will differ from all others. Therefore. accurate communication requires that they not be treated as similar in all respects.

The primary disadvantage of abstraction is that some communication about reality is not the same as reality itself. Problems arise when we confuse the levels of abstraction. As demonstrated by the Bessie example, the more abstract we get, the farther we get from reality. The farther we get from reality, the greater the chances of inaccuracies in communication. This is because abstraction leaves out certain details and characteristics at each level. One way of remedying this situation is to use more words at the bottom of the abstraction ladder. Go directly to the thing or object being discussed. Give concrete examples and illustrations. Express the same thought in more than one

Figure 9–4
Abstraction Ladder: Level 1—World of Events; Level 2—World of Objects; Levels 3 through 8—World of Symbols

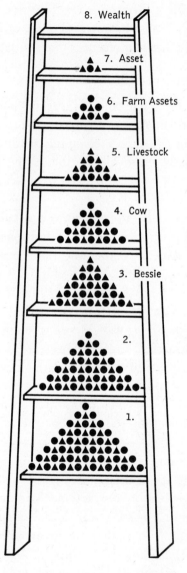

8. Wealth

7. Asset

6. Farm Assets

5. Livestock

4. Cow

3. Bessie

2.

1.

8. The word "wealth" is at an extremely high level of abstraction, omitting *almost* all reference to the characteristics of Bessie.

7. When Bessie is referred to as an "asset," still more of her characteristics are left out.

6. When Bessie is included among "farm assets," reference is made only to what she has in common with all other salable items on the farm.

5. When Bessie is referred to as "livestock," only those characteristics she has in common with pigs, chickens, goats, etc., are referred to.

4. The word "cow" stands for the characteristics we have abstracted as common to cow_1, cow_2, cow_3 . . . cow_n. Characteristics peculiar to specific cows are left out.

3. The word "Bessie" (cow_1) is the *name* we give to the object of perception of level 2. The name *is not* the object: it merely *stands for* the object and omits reference to many of the characteristics of the object.

2. The cow we perceive is not the word, but the object of experience, that which our nervous system abstracts (selects) from the totality that constitutes the process-cow. Many of the characteristics of the process-cow are left out.

1. The cow known to science ultimately consists of atoms, electrons, etc., according to present-day scientific inference. Characteristics (represented by circles [and triangles]) are infinite at this level and ever-changing. This is the *process level*.

way. Again, a very simple way to determine whether or not a listener understands your words is to ask. In other words, seek feedback.

Inferential Barriers

Suppose we have seen the boss, Mr. Smith, leave the office every afternoon for the past week with his attractive secretary, Ms. Jones. As they get into his car again this afternoon, we may think to ourselves, "If only Mrs. Smith knew what was going on between her husband and Ms. Jones!" However, a closer examination of this situation may reveal that we have no evidence to indicate that anything is going on. We only know that Mr. Smith and Ms. Jones have left the office together every afternoon for the last week and have driven away in his car. Anything beyond these observed facts is inference. Thus, we label as inference anything that we do not know to be factual. As such, inference is an additional form of abstraction. There is nothing wrong with making inferences and we do so many times each day. However, inferences become communication barriers when we treat them as facts and, thus, forget that there is some probability that they are incorrect. In our previous example, Ms. Jones may have wrecked her car and Mr. Smith is merely giving her a ride home until she can get a new one. Or, perhaps they are carpooling to save on gasoline. In any event, we must realize that inferences can be incorrect before we can hope to improve the effectiveness of our communication.

Symbolic Barriers

The last of the communication barriers to be discussed focuses on words as symbols. Words are not the same as the objects, persons, or events that they represent. In fact, as explained in the section on abstraction, words are several levels removed from the reality which they seek to represent. They are only symbols that represent our mental perceptions and have no meaning in themselves. Thus, the meanings attached to a particular word will vary because of differences in perception. When significant differences in meaning exist, a barrier to communication arises. Thus, try to determine whether your communication has a similar meaning for both you and the receiver. Again, feedback is helpful here.

Improving Organizational Communication

Probably the biggest and most important step in improving organizational communication is an awareness of the complexity of the communication process. It is not an activity to be taken for granted and, as the basis for all organized activity, it must be performed as accurately as possible.

Greater accuracy in communication can be gained through a knowledge of the workings of the communication process. By being aware of how barriers can enter the process, we can take steps to minimize them. Perceptual, abstractional, inferential, and symbolic barriers demonstrate that we can never communicate reality as it actually exists. However, with an understanding of these barriers, we can work to use those symbols which give the best description of reality as we perceive it.

Finally, being a good communicator involves more than just sending messages. As has been discussed, it also means receiving them. "The Commandments for Good Listening" which follow are practical guides for developing better listening habits.[3]

1. Stop talking. You cannot listen if you are talking.

2. Put speakers at ease. Help them feel that they are free to talk.

3. Show speakers that you want to listen. Look and act interested. Do not read your mail while they talk. Listen to understand, rather than to oppose.

4. Remove distractions. Don't doodle, tap, or shuffle papers. It might be quieter if you would shut the door.

5. Empathize with speakers. Try to put yourself in their place so that you can see their point of view.

6. Be patient. Allow plenty of time. Do not interrupt. Don't start for the door or walk away.

7. Hold your temper. An angry person gets the wrong meaning from words.

8. Go easy on argument and criticism, which will put speakers on the defensive. They may clam up or get angry. Don't argue; even if you win, you lose.

9. Ask questions. This encourages others and shows you are listening. It helps to develop points further.

10. Stop talking. This is first and last, because all other commandments depend on it. You just cannot do a good listening job while you are talking.

Summary

Communication is the process by which we transfer information, understanding, and feeling from one person to another. It is the basis for

---

[3]Source unknown.

all organized activity. Communication, however, is not a natural human activity. It must be learned. The importance of this fact is that we can improve our communication skills.

Many models have been developed to characterize the communication process. These models have a number of common elements, which include source, encoding, message, channel, decoding, receiver, meaning, feedback, and noise. Each of these elements can contribute to communication breakdowns, but decoding activities provide numerous opportunities for barriers to arise. Therefore, feedback is vital in judging whether or not successful communication has taken place.

The formal communication network in organizations can include downward, upward, or horizontal flows. In general, objectives, policies, directions, and decisions flow downward through the hierarchy of authority. However, the information upon which these things are based must flow upward, while horizontal communication facilitates the solution of problems arising from a division of labor.

The communication network of the informal organization is known as the grapevine. It supplements the formal network. The occurrence of rumor in the grapevine can be minimized by creating situations where people feel more secure and, therefore, more willing to trust the communication flowing through formal channels.

Communication barriers demonstrate how our communication efforts are impeded. Some barriers are created by an individual's perceptual ability, or lack of it. Other barriers are caused by abstraction, in which we focus on certain details while leaving out others. Finally, words and inferences lead to other communication barriers.

Unfortunately, no set of formulas can be given to increase the effectiveness of organizational communication. The process is much too complex. However, communication can be improved through a greater understanding of the communication process and the difficulties inherent in it. We hope that this chapter has contributed to your understanding of these factors.

Questions for Discussion

1. Define communication. Why is it so important to organizational effectiveness?

2. Explain the role of each of the elements in the communication process model.

3. What is abstraction? How can we prevent the abstraction process from contributing to inaccuracies in communication?

4. Evaluate the statement, "Meaning lies in the mind, not in the symbols used."

5. What is the grapevine? Does it serve any useful purpose?

6. What steps can be taken by management to minimize the creation and spread of rumors?

7. As a supervisor, what do you consider your number one communication problem? What can you do to solve it?

Case
Incidents

1. Carl Swindle is the machine shop foreman in the Blazer Manufacturing Company. Late one afternoon, he walked into the shop and said, "You men had better clean up here."

Joe Smith immediately started sweeping up the metal shavings from around his lathe. Bob Jones went to the employee locker room, washed his hands, and prepared to go home. Phil Stevens thought that the foreman was tired of hearing the cursing that frequently went on in the shop.

a. What do you think the foreman really wanted to say?

b. Was he effective in communicating his message?

c. If he was not effective, what could he do to improve his communication?

2. You are a department supervisor in the Wood Products Division of Trees, Inc. One of your employees who was very upset came to you this morning and said, "I heard that a number of layoffs are being planned for our department. Is it true?"

a. What type of communication does this illustrate?

b. If no layoffs were actually being planned, how would you handle the situation? Why?

c. Why do communications of this nature arise?

d. Is there anything you can do to minimize the occurrence of this type of communication? If so, what?

Motivation and Productivity

*Fred Luthans**

*Fred Luthans is Professor of Management, College of Business Administration, The University of Nebraska-Lincoln.

Chapter Objectives	1. *To develop an understanding and appreciation of motivation.*
	2. *To indicate how motivation affects employee performance.*
	3. *To discuss the role that motivation plays in understanding today's employees.*
	4. *To provide specific guidelines for effectively motivating employees.*

The What and Why of Motivation

IF SUPERVISORS are asked to name their biggest "people problems," motivation invariably falls at or near the top of the list. There seems little doubt that motivating employees is one of the most important jobs facing the modern supervisor. Many of the other functions and duties of supervisors have been gradually stripped away from them over the years, but motivating the human resources under their control has emerged as a major responsibility. Yet, despite its importance, very few supervisors have a real understanding of what motivation is all about and, even more important, why it is so essential to employee performance.

What Is Motivation?

Words mean different things to different people and even the psychologists cannot agree on exactly what is involved in motivation. Words like *needs*, *drives*, *desires*, *goals*, and *incentives* are typically used to describe motivation. It actually involves all of these descriptive terms and more.

A Motivational Cycle. Perhaps the simplest way to understand motivation is to think of it as a sequence or cycle. In order for the motivation cycle to be initiated, there must be a need. A need is simply a deficiency. There are many types of needs that humans have. Some of these needs the person is born with (needs for food, water, sex, and sleep), and some are learned (needs for power, achievement, affiliation, status, and security). The learned needs, of course, are much more relevant to the motivation of employees.

Once a need develops, it will set up a drive. A drive is simply the behavioral outcome of a need; it is a deficiency with direction. The drive is aimed at a goal which will alleviate the deficiency. Thus, a goal in the motivational cycle can be simply defined as anything that fulfills a need. The motivational cycle can be depicted as follows:

NEEDS ⟶ DRIVES ⟶ GOALS

| Inborn or learned deficiencies | Behavioral outcomes of needs | Objects which fulfill the needs |

Therefore, motivation should be thought of as involving needs, drives, and goals. All three are important to the supervisor in understanding the motivation of employees.

The Nature of Motivation. Supervisors should first of all understand that employees have a wide variety of needs. Some of these needs employees have from birth. More important, however, are the needs that employees learn while growing up, and those that are developed while working in organizations. The middle part of this chapter will give specific attention to these important needs.

Supervisors should also understand that all they can see in motivation are the drives. A supervisor can only observe the behavioral outcome of a need. Supervisors can observe one of their subordinates moving slowly or briskly between tasks or making many or few mistakes. They can try to guess the reasons for the observed behavior. But it would only be a guess. All that can be observed is the slow or fast, accurate or inaccurate behaviors. Supervisors commonly guess that the reason for the slow or inaccurate behaviors is that the worker is not motivated; or, in the case of the fast or accurate behaviors, that the worker is motivated. The motivational cycle would indicate that such guessing is not entirely justified. The slow or inaccurate observable behaviors may be very "motivated" but are aimed at goals that are counter-productive. Employees are generally motivated all of the time. Unfortunately, this motivated behavior is not always aimed at goals compatible with the organizational goals.

The job of the supervisor is to direct motivated behavior toward, rather than away from, organizational goals. Thus, supervisors have to understand the needs of their people, understand that what they observe are the behavioral outcomes of these needs, and understand that the goals which the behavior is aimed at may or may not be compatible with the goals of the organization. In this respect, the *what* of motivation is largely understanding the need-drive-goal cycle and its implications for employee productivity.

Why Is Motivation Important?

Some supervisors may question the importance of motivation. Even though motivation may be the biggest "people problem" they have, does it really make any difference in the performance of their departments? The answer is a definite yes! In practical terms alone, by far the largest percentage of a supervisor's operating budget is devoted to people. For example, in manufacturing, labor costs constitute the largest single cost item, and in the emerging service industries such as in health and education, people costs range anywhere from 50 to 90 percent of the operating budget.

Besides being costly, human problems far outweigh the physical or technical aspects of most supervisory responsibilities. Machinery, materials, procedures, and information flows are not nearly as big a problem for most supervisors as absenteeism, tardiness, quality and quantity of work, and getting more out of employees than just eight hours a day. Today's employees are generally not giving anywhere near their full potential. For example, a recent Gallup poll asked wage earners if they could accomplish more each day. Half of those polled said they could, and three in five of this group said they could increase their performance by as much as 20 percent or more.

The importance of motivation should be clear. If human resources are clearly the biggest costs and are operating way below capacity, then the most significant impact on performance will come from more effective management of people. It also follows that since motivation is the biggest people problem facing supervisors, the importance of understanding and applying motivational concepts and techniques becomes obvious.

Can Supervisors Do Anything About Motivation?

Okay, so motivation is important; the next question is whether supervisors can do anything about it. After all, wage and salary administration has been largely taken away from supervisors and isn't that what motivates people? The answer is yes and no. Money is certainly important to motivation, but the old approach of equating money and motivation is entirely inadequate. As will be shown in the rest of the chapter, motivation involves much more than money.

The old human relations approach of paying people enough money to make them happy and the assumption that happy employees are productive employees can no longer be accepted either. Both research and practice have shown that well-paid employees are not necessarily happy, satisfied employees. In addition, the assumption that happy, satisfied employees are productive employees is also open to question. There is an academic controversy over whether satisfaction leads to performance or the reverse, that performance leads to satisfaction. In other words, are satisfied employees productive employees; or, as many organizational behavior experts believe, does an employee who performs well become satisfied? Probably, there are too many complicating factors that prevent making either assertion. In any event, the simplistic assumptions of the past are no longer valid. Coming to grips with the satisfaction-performance controversy has important implications for motivating employees.

If money is not the end-all of motivation, and organizational behavior experts are not even sure if satisfaction leads to performance or performance leads to satisfaction, what can individual supervisors be expected to do to motivate their employees? The best answer in this difficult area is first to gain an overall basic understanding of employees and then to begin implementing some of the new motivational techniques that are beginning to emerge.

Understanding Employees

Everyone is an expert on human nature. After all, everybody has dealt with people all of their lives. Why should not some understanding of the ways to get the most out of people come naturally with all of this experience? The truth is that most people really do not understand others and do a poor job of getting the most out of people. This group, unfortunately, includes many supervisors in today's organizations. Most supervisors think they understand their people and how to motivate them, but the record speaks for itself. As the last section pointed out, there are many challenges remaining in the management of human resources.

What Are Employees Like Today?

The starting point for a better understanding of employees is to realize that there have been some definite changes in the meaning of work and employee expectations in the last few years. A recently published comprehensive report, *Work in America*, conducted by a special task force for the Department of Health, Education, and Welfare, documents some of these changes. In general, the report substantiates the meaning behind the increasingly popular descriptive terms of "Blue Collar Blues" and "White Collar Woes." Today's employees attach a different meaning to work and have changed their expectations concerning what they want out of a job.

One survey of one thousand supervisors from different types of organizations across the country consistently noted certain changes that were taking place in their employees over the last several years. In rank-order, the supervisors mentioned the following:

1. Less pride in workmanship.
2. Menial work is "not in."
3. Less loyalty to the organization.
4. Those with long seniority are not motivated and you can't touch them.
5. They are less dependent on the employer and look to government to meet their needs.
6. More independent because of other wage earners in the family.
7. Less concern for quality, waste, housekeeping.
8. More awareness of the job, company, community, and society.
9. More mature, sophisticated, and educated.
10. Don't want overtime.
11. More grievances about work environment.
12. Work is not as great a part of their life as it once was.
13. Less responsive to authority.
14. Unionization has leveled out performance between and among grades.
15. Want more control over their destiny.[1]

[1]Reprinted by special permission from *A Guide to Effective Management—Practical Applications From Behavioral Science* by Leslie E. This, Addison-Wesley Publishing Co., Reading, Massachusetts. Copyright ©1974.

Obviously, not all employees are like the above. In fact, one of the most important points in understanding employees is to realize that they are all different. There are individual differences among all employees. In addition, the above survey results substantiate something that all supervisors generally acknowledge: Employees are also different than they used to be. It logically follows that the old ways are no longer appropriate for managing today's employees.

New Assumptions About People

Can any generalized assumptions be made about people? Douglas McGregor summarized two sets of assumptions that supervisors can and do make about people. The first set of assumptions was labeled Theory X and can be summarized as: (1) People are born lazy and will avoid work if they can; (2) because people dislike work so much, they must be coerced, controlled, directed, and threatened with punishment to get them to do any work; and (3) the average person actually prefers this type of treatment, wishes to avoid responsibility, has relatively little ambition, and wants security above all. The experience of many supervisors has led them to make Theory X assumptions. All supervisors have some employees who seem to fit the Theory X assumptions perfectly.

McGregor felt that Theory X assumptions, although containing much surface logic, did not accurately portray employees. Instead, he felt that much of Theory X-oriented employee behavior was the consequence of the way they were treated rather than the way they really were. He proposed a contrasting set of assumptions that he labeled Theory Y. This latter theory is based on a sounder theoretical and research base. Theory Y proposes that: (1) The expenditure of effort at work is as natural as play or rest; (2) external control and threat of punishment are not the only ways to get people to work; people will exercise self-direction and self-control if they are committed to the goals; (3) commitment to goals is a function of the rewards associated with their achievement; (4) the average person can learn not only to accept but to seek responsibility; (5) most, not a few, people have the capacity for a high degree of imagination, ingenuity, and creativity on the job; and (6) under present conditions, the capabilities of people are only being partially utilized.

Theory Y points out that there is nothing inborn in people to make them either want to work or not want to work. Instead, people will react in the workplace according to their past experiences and present conditions. Theory Y gives a lot more credit to people and emphasizes their complexity. McGregor feels that supervisors are largely responsible for whether their employees exhibit Theory X or Theory Y characteristics. For example, he notes that a supervisor's methods of organization and control may very well lead to Theory X or Theory Y characteristics of employees.

As in a court of law, supervisors should probably make Theory Y assumptions about their people until proven otherwise. Merely making Theory Y assumptions could lead to Theory Y characteristics in their people. In any event, Theory Y seems to be much more compatible with the new style of worker depicted in the last section and can serve as a foundation and point of departure for the better understanding of employees.

A Hierarchy of Needs

As has been pointed out, humans have a variety of needs. Abraham Maslow felt that these diverse needs could best be depicted as hierarchical levels. He carefully pointed out that once a given level of need was satisfied, it no longer served to motivate. He felt that the most basic level of needs was physiological—the needs for food, water, sex, and sleep. These were followed, in order, by the levels of needs for safety or security, love or belongingness, esteem (both self-esteem and from others), and, finally, self-actualization. Figure 10–1 summarizes this hierarchy of needs.

Figure 10–1
Maslow's Hierarchy of Needs

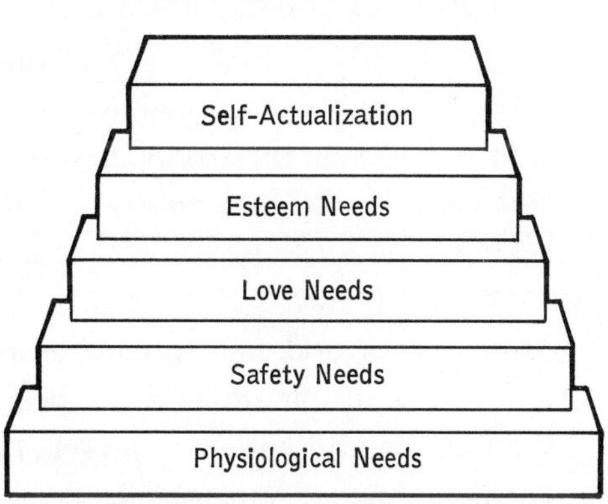

The contribution of Maslow's hierarchy of needs is not the number of levels or what he calls the levels. Instead, the important point is that once a level of needs is satisfied, whatever they are called, they no longer motivate. For example, if a carrot is dangled in front of a very hungry man (his cells are deficient in food), he will run after the carrot (hunger drive) and stuff the carrot (goal) into his mouth. In other words, he is very motivated by carrots. However, if this process is repeated a few times, the man soon becomes full of carrots (there is no longer a deficiency) and he refuses even to walk over to take the carrot (the drive is gone). In order to motivate this man, another level of motives must come into play.

In most organizations today, supervisors are holding up the same carrots and expecting their people to be motivated. Workers, on the other hand, are in essence saying, "We are full of carrots; if you want us to be motivated, you have to give us something better." A few more cents an hour, another day off, pastel colored walls, and a better insurance plan, are the carrots that are continually being held up to employees as motivators. Yet, for the most part, employees are full of these. This does not imply, of course, that the current wage rates, working conditions, and fringe benefits will make employees permanently full. There simply are no carrots that will make people permanently full. They will always want and expect better wages, conditions, and benefits. But, because these are fairly well taken care of in most modern organizations, they will not necessarily motivate employees. Most of today's employees are motivated by things other than the traditional carrots.

The Important Motives

The introductory comments said that the learned needs are more important to the understanding of employee motivation than are the unlearned, physiological needs. In particular, the needs for power, achievement, affiliation, status, and security are relevant to the motivation of today's employees. Psychologists have done considerable study and research on these motives. The following briefly summarizes what is known about these important motives.

Power Motive.   The need for power is the desire for control, to be in charge of and manipulate others. Anyone in an elected office, for example a union steward, or position of authority, like a supervisor, normally would have a relatively high need for power or he/she would not be in such a position. Rank and file employees, on the other hand, would normally have a relatively low need for power.

Achievement Motive.   More is known about achievement than any other motive. High achievers take moderate risks, want immediate feedback on how they are performing, find doing a task intrinsically satisfying, do not depend on others, and are preoccupied with the task at hand. The person with this type of motivation is often considered to be the ideal employee. However, the supervisor should be warned that for certain types of jobs the high achiever would be frustrated, and the last couple of characteristics mentioned above tend to make the high achiever a loner. In jobs requiring empathy for others or close personal ties, the high achiever may perform very poorly.

Affiliation Motive. The need to be with others, to belong to a group, is very intense in most people. Going as far back as the Hawthorne studies fifty years ago, it has been repeatedly shown that group membership and social relationships are extremely important to people in organizations. Whereas managers and supervisors generally have relatively higher power and achievement motives than rank and file employees, the reverse is true with the need for affiliation. Supervisors should realize that their employees generally have different motives than they do. For example, employees may be more concerned with being part of and accepted by a group of co-workers than they are about power and achievement.

Status Motive. Status can best be defined as the relative rank or position one has in a group, organization, or society. Because it is relative, everyone has a status. In an organization there are many widely recognized symbols of status. Formal status symbols include location, title, and privileges. Informal status symbols include dress, function performed, and socio-cultural background. Status and its accompanying symbols are extremely important to most employees, but supervisors often fail to give them proper recognition and attention.

Security Motive. When asked what they want out of a job, most employees rank security at or near the top of the list. There is the conscious need to protect one's livelihood and family from the uncertainties of everyday living, and there is the more subtle, unconscious security need that has deeper psychological implications. Most organizations and unions have taken care of employees' conscious security needs through a wide variety of benefits. On the other hand, supervisors can do a better job of eliminating the more unconscious security needs and fears that most employees possess. The rapid changes that are taking place in today's organizations are a real threat to most employees. Information, understanding, and assurances from supervisors can be very helpful to their employees' security needs.

The five motives discussed above are not the only motives people have, but they are most relevant to understanding the motivation of today's employees.

The Frustration of Employees

If there were a nice smooth progression between needs, drives, and goals, then motivation would be no problem. Unfortunately, there are many barriers in life and in organizations that prevent motivated drives from reaching goal attainment. When drives are blocked, frustration results. People have many reactions to frustration but these can be categorized into four general areas: Aggression, withdrawal, fixation, and compromise. The following model depicts the frustration process:

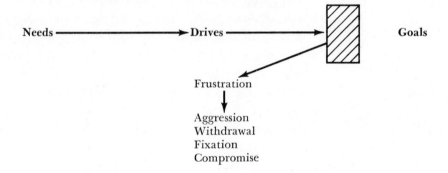

An aggressive reaction occurs when the frustrated individual attempts, physically or symbolically, to injure or do damage to the barrier. Withdrawal occurs when the person backs away from the barrier; in severe cases he may even regress (return to a childhood state). Under fixation the person pretends the barrier does not exist and continually tries to reach the goal but is buffeted by the barrier. A compromise reaction may take two forms. The frustrated person will either strive for a substitute goal (usually less desirable than the one he or she is prevented from attaining) or attempt to circumvent the barrier by taking another, more difficult, route to the goal.

An example can help clarify and demonstrate the frustration model. Suppose that an employee grew up in a neighborhood where he was the fastest and toughest kid on the block. Because he was so successful in sandlot games and because everyone looked up to him, he developed intense needs for power and achievement. Unfortunately, his skills on the sandlot did not help him in school, and he dropped out of high school during his senior year. (The school prevented him from expressing his needs for achievement and power, so he reacted to the frustration by withdrawing.) He then took an unskilled, menial job in the biggest company in town. He still, of course, had intense needs for power and achievement. The job, however, was designed with high degrees of specialization, offered no feedback on performance, and no chance to move up. In other words, the job became a barrier to the goals that would lead to need fulfillment. The employee became frustrated. Since he grew up in a tough neighborhood, aggression could be an acceptable reaction to frustration. He could relieve his frustration by continually getting into fights with his co-workers or boss. He could have reacted by withdrawing, which is more socially acceptable for most mature adults. In this latter case, the employee may start to daydream, become apathetic, or continually whine and complain (regress). Most supervisors expect frustrated employees to fixate. The employee in the example could have pretended that the barrier did not exist while he kept knocking his head against the wall. Finally, he could have compromised. Instead of getting need fulfillment from his job, he could have searched for a substitute goal, such as leadership in the union or a major role in other activities outside the job.

The above example helps explain why some employees are always fighting or sabotaging (aggression), daydreaming and apathetic (withdrawal), blindly plodding along (fixation), or union "rabble-rousers" (compromise). They may be frustrated by their job! To prevent such frustrated behavior, the supervisor must attempt to remove as many of the barriers as possible. This, of course, is easier said than done. Many of the barriers that are frustrating today's employees are beyond the control of the supervisor. On the other hand, some of the barriers can be affected by the supervisor. The next section will describe some specific ways that supervisors can help prevent frustration and effectively motivate their employees.

How To Motivate Employees

The "how to" part of motivation has no simple solutions. As was pointed out, the early human relations movement made the mistake of oversimplifying a very complex and difficult area. Nevertheless, in recent years, behavioral science research and on-the-job experiences have begun to yield some meaningful guidelines on how to motivate today's employees. Money, working conditions, and security remain as extremely important variables in motivating employees. But, although important, they are largely taken care of in most modern organizations and are generally beyond the control of an individual supervisor. What supervisors can do something about is enriching the jobs of their employees and systematically modifying their behaviors through contingent applications of reward and punishment. These (job enrichment and organizational behavior modification) are two of the most important and effective recent developments in the "how to" aspect of employee motivation.

Job Enrichment

Job enlargement has been around for a long time. The theory behind job enlargement is that by decreasing specialization and giving more and varied tasks to do, the worker would not be bored, and performance would increase. This approach did seem to work in some situations with some employees. On the whole, however, this horizontal loading of the job did not live up to its expectations mainly because workers saw it as another attempt to get more work out of them, a new form of job speed-up.

Job enrichment, on the other hand, attempts to redesign jobs by incorporating the opportunities to fulfill higher level needs, not just expand the number of things that the worker performs. Job enrichment is mainly based on the work of Frederick Herzberg. He believes that there are two factors in motivation: The hygiene factors (policies, supervision, pay, and working conditions); and the motivators (achievement, recognition, responsibility, and advancement). The hygiene factors prevent dissatisfaction; they do not lead to satisfaction. Only the motivators lead to job satisfaction. What job enrichment tries to do is incorporate the motivators into the job design. There is vertical loading of the job, not just horizontal loading as found in job enlargement.

One of the major ways to enrich a job is to make the person performing the job responsible for his or her own work. For example, in one situation a group of assemblers performed highly specialized tasks at a work table. Each of the assemblers did his task in assembly line fashion, and at the end an inspector examined the product for any defects. After this process, it was packed and shipped out to the customer. Many customers were shipping these products right back because of poor quality. To improve the situation, job enrichment was implemented. Each worker now assembled the product from beginning to end. This, of course, was job enlargement. But, in addition to assembling the product by themselves, each worker also put his identification number on the assembled product. The inspector was eliminated and assemblers were now responsible for their own work. In this case, the number of units produced remained about the same. Significant, however, was the fact that when high degrees of specialization were eliminated, productivity did not suffer. More important, when the job was enriched, there were virtually no more defects. The workers in this case were given a sense of accomplishment and responsibility to do the job well.

Besides giving employees responsibility, the supervisor can also give employees job freedom. More precisely, a good rule of thumb to follow is to give employees freedom within established limits. In most cases the employees should be allowed to participate in defining what the limits and expectations of their jobs are, and then be allowed to operate freely within those established limits. Another way that a supervisor can enrich a job is to be oriented to ends, not means. The supervisor should clearly spell out, ideally in conjunction with the employee, what results are expected. The supervisor should not give the detailed means for accomplishing the results. Instead, the means for attaining desired results should be left up to the individual employee. This does not imply, of course, that the supervisor cannot give help and serve in a coaching role. It does mean that by allowing subordinates to come up with their own ideas and ways of accomplishing a job, the supervisor is giving recognition and opportunities for achievement and growth on the job.

Organizational Behavior Modification

So far the chapter has been devoted to the concepts and techniques of motivation. As the introductory comments point out, one cannot observe motivation. All that one can see are the behavioral outcomes of motivation. The supervisor can only guess what needs led to a certain observable behavior. Motivation deals with the inner states of people; it is an internal perspective.

A newer, external perspective is to deal with the environmental antecedents and consequences (called the contingencies) of employee behavior. This new approach is called organizational behavior modification, or simply O.B. Mod. It is based on operant learning theory instead of motivation theory and has the significant premise that organizational behavior is a function of its contingent consequences. Under O.B. Mod., the supervisor is more concerned with managing the contingent environment of employees than with managing the internal motivations of employees.

Fred Luthans and Robert Kreitner suggest a systematic O.B. Mod. model that supervisors can use to manage employee behavior systematically. Figure 10–2 shows this model. In step 1 the supervisor identifies a behavior or pattern of behaviors that, if changed, will lead to significant improvement in performance. Next, the frequency of the behavior identified in step 1 is obtained and placed on a chart. The chart shows how frequently the behavior is occurring under existing conditions and is called a baseline measure. The third step in the O.B. Mod. approach is to analyze functionally the antecedents and the consequences of the behavior that has been identified and measured. What things happen before and what things happen as a consequence of the behavior? For example, in one case, a supervisor using O.B. Mod identified unscheduled breaks of his people as being a problem behavior that was affecting the performance of his department. The baseline measure indicated that this was happening quite frequently. When the functional analysis was performed by the supervisor, he noted that the unscheduled breaks were occurring almost exactly at 9A.M., 11A.M., and 3P.M. These represented the times between start-up (8A.M.) and the first scheduled break (10A.M.), between the scheduled break and lunch (noon), and between the afternoon break (2P.M.) and quitting time (4P.M.). In other words, the antecedent cue for these workers to take an unscheduled break was the clock. Importantly, however, the clock did not cause this behavior to occur. It merely served as the cue for the behavior to be emitted. The consequence of the unscheduled break behavior was a social gathering with friends at the restroom. Here they talked about the ball games and had a cigarette. They also, of course, escaped their boring jobs for a few minutes. These consequences were maintaining the behavior; behavior is a function of its consequences.

The fourth step of O.B. Mod. is the action step, where the supervisor can make a planned intervention based on the previous three steps. The supervisor can use a reinforcement or punishment intervention strategy. Reinforcement will strengthen and increase the targeted behavior, and punishment will weaken and decrease the targeted behavior. If at all possible, supervisors should use a reinforcement strategy, because punishment may only temporarily suppress the behavior and has many undesirable side effects. The contingent application of reinforcers will accelerate desirable employee behaviors and eventually replace the undesirable behaviors. If possible, the supervisor should ignore (not reinforce) undesirable behaviors rather than punish them.

Supervisors should not automatically assume what is reinforcing or punishing to their employees. For example, a supervisor may think he is punishing an employee by calling him in for a good "chewing out."

Figure 10–2
Steps In Organizational Behavior Modification (O.B. Mod.)

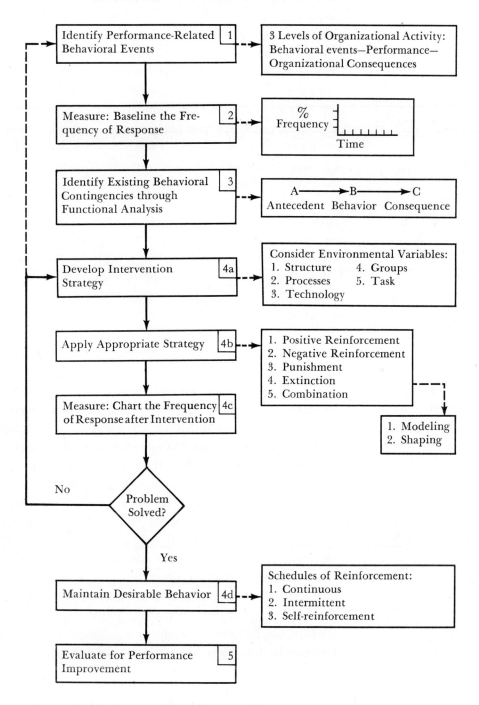

Source: Fred Luthans and Robert Kreitner, "The Management of Behavioral Contingencies," Personnel, July/August, 1974, p. 13. Reproduced with permission of the publisher.

In reality, this may be the only time the supervisor gives this employee any attention and the employee finds this very reinforcing. No wonder supervisors have a hard time figuring why "every time I chew that guy out he goes right back and makes the same mistake over again." It would be nice if supervisors could carry a roll of bills around with them and peel off some dollars when they want to reinforce an employee for desirable behavior, or have the power to give an employee the rest of the day off when they complete a task or attain a standard, or be able to give on-the-spot promotions, but unfortunately these are not under supervisors' control. Potential reinforcers that are available to any supervisor are social reinforcers (praise, recognition, and attention) and feedback about individual performance. Both of these can be very powerful reinforcers when contingently applied.

At first the supervisor should reinforce the desirable behavior as much as possible. However, once the behavior has clearly begun to change in the desired direction, reinforcement would only need to be administered on an intermittent basis. In fact, this will tend to strengthen the behavior. The ultimate goal of this intervention strategy is to obtain a self-reinforcing employee in the pursuit of organizational goals.

The supervisor should remember that all employee behavior, good or bad, is being controlled by the environment. Much of the existing environment in organizations leads to negative control. Workers come to work and on time, not because they are reinforced for doing so, but because they will be punished if they do not. Employees will work on a task, at least in the presence of their supervisors, not because they find it reinforcing, but because they will be punished if they do not. O.B. Mod. attempts to turn this negative, depressive, and all too common situation around. O.B. Mod. attempts to have supervisors positively control employee behavior by the contingent application of rewards for desirable behaviors and withholding (not punishing) rewards for undesirable behavior. In this way a positively reinforcing climate can be created in today's workplace.

The fifth and final step of O.B. Mod. is to evaluate to make sure that performance is in fact improving. Measurement is continued to assure that the intervention strategies are having their desired effect. To date, O.B. Mod. has been successfully used by supervisors in a variety of organizations.[2] Along with other techniques such as job enrichment,

---

[2]See Fred Luthans and Robert Kreitner, *Organizational Behavior Modification* (Glenview, Ill.: Scott, Foresman, 1975). This book is specifically devoted to all aspects of O.B. Mod. and reports some of the successful applications.

O.B. Mod. seems to hold a great deal of promise for more effectively managing human resources—the key to successful supervision.

Questions for
Discussion

1. What is motivation? How do needs differ from drives?

2. Comment on the statement that motivation cannot be seen.

3. Do you think motivation is important? Explain why you think it is or it is not.

4. Do your observations of what employees are like today agree or disagree with the fifteen items listed in the chapter? Explain your answer.

5. Do you support Theory X or Theory Y assumptions about people?

6. If you observe employees who are very apathetic in their work, how could you explain this by the frustration model?

7. What are some ways you could enrich jobs?

8. What are the five steps of O.B. Mod.? Make a case for the use of reinforcement or punishment in changing or controlling your employees' behavior.

Case
Incidents

1. You have a young male employee who is a "motivation problem." He doesn't care about the quality of his work and is chronically absent. You have complained to the personnel department about his behavior, and they say the only thing they can do is start to dock his pay every time he is absent. This does not seem to affect the quality of his work at all, and he is still gone about one day a week. Finally, you call the young man into your office and you say, "What is the problem with you? You are doing very low quality work and, even more important, why do you only come to work four days a week?" The young man looks you straight in the eyes and says, "Because I can't make enough bread in three days."

a. What are some possible reasons for this employee's behavior?

b. What do you think motivates him?

c. How would you attempt to motivate this young man?

2. One of the employees in your department seems to finish her work very early in the afternoon and spends the rest of the day going around complaining to her co-workers that she is overworked and underpaid. You have tried to send her back to her task and have given her additional work to do, but this approach has just not worked out. She com-

plains even more and the union steward has politely informed you that she is working at standard and should not be harassed. Yet, you feel that she is disrupting the rest of the workers in your department and you are going to have to do something.

a. How would you explain this employee's behavior? What do you think some of her major motives are?

b. What would you do if you were the supervisor in this situation?

c. Briefly describe the five steps of the O.B. Mod. model and show how they might be applied in this situation.

Developing Subordinates

*Thomas R. Tirney**

*Thomas R. Tirney, Management Development Consultant, J. C. Penney Company, New York, New York.

Chapter Objectives	1. *To discuss the responsibility of all supervisors for developing their subordinates.*

1. *To discuss the responsibility of all supervisors for developing their subordinates.*

2. *To emphasize that the development of subordinates begins with one's own development.*

3. *To outline a systematic method that will assist supervisors in the development of subordinates.*

WHERE DO you want to be next year? Do you want to remain where you are today? Or, would you like to move ahead and achieve some particular objectives that will advance your future career opportunities? Please don't tell me you are too old, that you don't have enough education, or give other excuses that one can use to cop out. Instead, use these questions to stimulate your thinking about where you stand now and where you want to go. Do you have objectives or goals that you are shooting for?

When you finish this chapter you will not only have an answer to the last question, but also a program and schedule of activities that will help you achieve your objectives. This plan for development will involve yourself, your associates[1], friends with whom you work, and your boss. The completion of your plan will not be easy. In fact, it may be the toughest assignment you ever had. In addition, it is an assignment that only you can do, and one that is entirely up to you. No one will care if you do not do it. The decision is up to you. If

[1]In this chapter, the term *associate* refers to one who reports directly to you in an organizational structure.

you do not wish to commit yourself to achieving career growth, let me save you some time. STOP NOW!

Your Role

If you are still with me, state in the space below where you want to be at this time next year. Be as specific as you can.

This is the first step in a job that is never ending. You will be taking on a life-time job that has always been one of the most important functions of a manager, leader, or parent. This function is the development of yourself and others. Parents are developers of children, leaders develop followers, and managers develop organizational members.

People in the roles of parent, leader, or manager have a direct responsibility for the development of others. And, in addition to these roles where we can influence others directly, there are other opportunities for us to influence individuals indirectly in our work or social environments. However, we will focus only on the work environment in this chapter. In this respect, think of development as a four-way process:

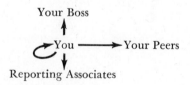

First and foremost is you. If you are not on a developmental track, how can you influence anyone else? The old saying, "You can influence more people by actions than by words," really applies to the development of others.

The next view concerns the development of people reporting to you. As such, it is the traditional view of development. But this view can also aid in your personal development, since it helps you identify your strengths and weaknesses as perceived by reporting associates. Third, the peers with whom you work are viewed as providing lateral opportunities for development. Finally, upward development is the influence that you can exert to help your boss strengthen certain weaknesses that affect relationships between the two of you. Now, before you tell me that it is impossible to develop your boss, let's talk a little more about development.

Development is the growth of individuals in their jobs, in their careers, and in their personal lives. When people stop growing, they are dead. When they think they can no longer grow, they are on their death bed. Consequently, the desire to grow is a personal decision of each individual and NO ONE ELSE. But, people cannot grow by themselves. They need help, all the help they can get. They need it from friends (encouragement and a sounding board), from associates (they can identify weaknesses and strengths faster than anyone else, except maybe wives[2]), and from their boss (he or she knows what you need in order to climb higher, and, in turn, needs your help to move upward).

Does this sound practical? Think for a minute. If you want to achieve the objective you identified earlier in the chapter, you need to know your strengths and weaknesses. You can use your strengths, while attempting to overcome weaknesses, in order to accomplish your present responsibilities more effectively. Keep in mind that this is a difficult role that focuses first on you. People differ in their strengths and weaknesses. Yet, the common thread that ties people together in development is a need to know how others see them. They need to know what weaknesses affect their present performance and how they may block future career opportunities.

When you look at yourself through someone else's eyes, remember that everyone has strengths and weaknesses. It is very hard to sit and listen to someone list your weaknesses. However, when you want to say something in response, bite your tongue and seek a way to overcome the weakness being discussed. Don't fight the other person when something is said with which you do not agree. Let it go and remember it is how that person actually sees you. These points will help you understand how others feel when their weaknesses are being discussed. In addition, a standing rule you should follow is: "Before applying any concept or instrument in this chapter, try it on yourself."

---

[2]If you are single, don't ask your girlfriend or fiancee. Remember the saying, "Love is blind."

Your Associates

Tap your current knowledge

Where does one begin? A starting point is to analyze your associates. You already have a lot of information that you can use to accomplish this analysis. Use it to focus on three areas:

- Job knowledge
- Management knowledge
- The common sense needed in getting along with people (some people refer to this as interpersonal skills)

Make three horizontal rows on a piece of paper as shown in Figure 11–1. Label these rows job knowledge, management knowledge, and interpersonal skills. Now, write the name of an associate who reports to you at the top of the page. To minimize the human tendency to take the best associate, write all of their names on a piece of paper and give each one a number. Now take any book of over a hundred pages. Open it to the middle of the book. The last digit of the right hand page will give you the name of the first person to be analyzed.

Job Knowledge   I cannot get too specific in this example because each job is different. Therefore, instead of specifics, let me raise some points that will get you to think about the selected associate in his or her current situation.

- List the responsibilities of the person as you see them. Do not refer to the job description or seek help from the personnel department.
- This is your associate and you are the leader. What activities do you expect from this person? What results do you look for from this person? (See Figure 11–1 [1]).
- Was that easy? The next question is more of a challenge. You have indicated the person's responsibilities. Now write down the authority you have given this person to accomplish the responsibilities you have listed. (See Figure 11–1 [2]).

The preceding points are critical. Take your time. Write down your thoughts. Think about them tonight and review them tomorrow. You may find some conflicts or gaps between responsibilities and authority. These conflicts must be resolved before continuing this analysis. One way of resolving conflicts is to indicate changes that you will make to eliminate them. During your discussions with the person you can communicate these changes.

In any position there are unique skills or special knowledge that people must have to accomplish their responsibilities effectively. For example, a person in a secretarial position would need the skills of

Figure 11–1
Sample Assessment Form

NAME: _____

MAJOR AREAS	RESPONSIBILITIES	AUTHORITY	CURRENT STATUS	HOW CAN I HELP?
JOB KNOWLEDGE	[1] Write down the responsibilities of this person.	[2] Write down the authority this person has to accomplish the responsibilities identified in step [1].	[3] Operating Skills [4] Reason for each ranking 2 typing 3 shorthand 5 use of dictating equipment 1 phone manners 4 grammar 6 construction of letters (ranked by strength)	[5] Look at lowest two [#5 and #6] items. Indicate ways to strengthen these areas. Include how you will help.
MANAGEMENT KNOWLEDGE	[6] Activities needed to accomplish responsibilities in [1] above. Adequate Level: Find out merchandise in low supply Pull merchandise from stock Price merchandise Put stock on shelf Next Responsibility: (Activities)	[7] List management elements needed to accomplish responsibilities. Adequate Level: Self organizing Inventory control Decision making Next Responsibility: Management elements	[8] Summary Summary list Rank by strength [4] Reason for each ranking	[9] Look at lowest two items. Indicate ways to strengthen these elements. Include how you will help.
INTERPERSONAL SKILLS	[10] Using too many words to get a point across a. People turn him off; the message is never received; people feel they are being talked down to. b. No one may want to work for this person; people are confused and cannot contribute; people tend to get defensive; this person may be rejected by group. Next Weakness	[11] Listening to others a. Ability to listen without interrupting; understands the full message; ability to summarize the content of a message. b. Keeps everyone going in the same direction; clarifies points that others may have missed; people look to this person for help in understanding complex messages. Next Strength	[12] Too many words Slow down when talking; think of what to say; organize your thoughts logically; watch for nonverbal signals that may tell you if you are turning off someone; don't repeat things unless asked.	[13] Too many words I'll give you feedback from my observations of your behavior; we can discuss some nonverbal signals which may say, "You lost me"; I'll register you for a workshop in communication skills.

typing, shorthand, use of dictating equipment, and phone manners. She would also need knowledge of spelling, punctuation, grammar, and construction of letters, to name a few. All of the above are needed to do what she was hired to do, which can be referred to as her operating responsibilities (sometimes referred to as operating work).

Now list in the Job Knowledge row the operating skills that the associate needs to accomplish his or her operating work. Again, the secretary in our example would need knowledge of:

- Typing
- Shorthand
- Use of dictating equipment
- Phone manners
- Others that you can add

Look at each item. Rank them in priority according to the strengths of this person in each area. Do not compare this person to others. Instead, look at each item in relation only to him or her. (See Figure 11–1 [3].) Now explain in writing, with examples where possible, the reasons for your ranking. (See Figure 11–1 [4].) Finish this row by answering the following question as it relates to items that are ranked low.

"How can I help this person strengthen the weak areas?" Do not try to overdevelop this section by stating elaborate plans. Just indicate key words or ideas that will help you later in formulating a development plan with the associate. It is suggested that you look only at the two items ranked the lowest. (See Figure 11-1 [5].)

Management Knowledge Everyone does management work. A housewife is planning when she compiles her shopping list. A college-bound student sets a long-term objective (a degree in a particular field) and a short-term objective (to achieve a B+ average during the first semester). You are doing management work (analyzing your associates) in your role as developer.

Management work is that which a person does in the areas of planning, organizing, and controlling to accomplish organizational or position objectives. The leadership function is then used in working with other people to accomplish stated operating responsibilities.

The secretary in doing her operating work more effectively, would need to use some elements of management. Assume the boss gives the secretary his in-basket. He has placed brief comments on items of correspondence and has outlined a list of activities to be accomplished. In this situation, the secretary could go through the correspondence one item at a time until all were completed. She could start at either the top or the bottom of the pile. She could then do the activities on the list provided by the boss in the same manner. But, to be more effective, she could sort the correspondence into A, B, and C priorities. The activity list could be handled in the same way. By determining what items are most pressing and starting with these, she is organizing her operating work. The work she can give to someone else involves the management element of delegation.

Your associates may not need to use all of the elements of the management process in their present positions.[3] Consequently, your role is to look at their responsibilities and authority in order to identify those elements that they need to best accomplish their present job. In Figure 11–1, use the column headed "Responsibilities" in the "Management Knowledge" row to indicate the activities needed to accomplish the person's responsibilities. For example, the activities needed to fulfill the responsibility for maintaining adequate levels of shelved merchandise in a retail store would be

- find out the merchandise in low supply
- pull the merchandise from stock
- price merchandise
- stock merchandise on shelf

Now determine what management elements this person would use in carrying out the assigned responsibilities. List the elements under the column labeled "Authority" in Figure 11–1 [7]. For example, the activities cited above would involve the management elements of

organizing yourself (make a list of the merchandise needed according to some logical sequence such as the order of merchandise on the shelves).

controlling inventory (when pulling merchandise, compare standards [needs], measure against remaining inventory, and evaluate the results [need more merchandise for inventory?]. If necessary, *take action* [make note to order more merchandise]).

I am sure you could expand the list of management elements. My point is to give you one approach for identifying the management elements in the job of this particular associate. Now, repeat the process identified

---

[3]So that we can remain on the same wave-length, let me indicate one approach for identifying the management process and the elements involved in each function. Planning has the following elements: Objectives, forecasting, programs/schedules, policies/procedures/practices/rules, and budgets. The organizing function has the organization of groups/units/departments/yourself, responsibilities/authority/accountability/delegation, and the use of line/staff as its elements. Under control the elements are standards, measures, and the evaluation of action. The elements of leadership are motivation, communication, selection, and development.

above (see steps [6] and [7] in Figure 11–1) until you have covered all of the responsibilities that you have listed.

You are now ready to summarize the management elements you have identified in the "Current Status" column (see Figure 11–1 [8]). Rank the elements in terms of their priority as related to the strengths of this person. Continue by explaining in writing (give examples if possible) the reasons for your ranking. Finally, in step [9], look at the two items that are ranked lowest. Ask yourself the question, "How can I help this person to strengthen these weak areas?"

Interpersonal Skills   Interpersonal skills are those used in getting along with other people and in getting work accomplished. Weak skills in this area produce roadblocks that usually lead to problems, conflicts, and confrontations.

At this point you may think it unnecessary (the person does not interact with other people on the job) or feel that you are not qualified to evaluate an associate's interpersonal skills. Well, such skills are always necessary and you are not only qualified but are the only person who can provide insight and feedback to the associate in this area. You are qualified because you know what this associate is paid to do (operating work). You receive feedback (positive and negative) from other associates based on their perception of this associate (the group view of interpersonal skills). You have your own perception of the associate's work and how this person relates to you and other people. And, finally, you are in a position to influence the associate since you are his or her boss.

We are now ready to analyze the associate's relationship to other people in the organization. Think for a few minutes of all the data you have gathered from observation, by interacting with this person, and through feedback from members of the work group and other employees. In the process, focus on the associate's weaknesses.

In the "Interpersonal Skills" row under the column labeled "Responsibilities" in Figure 11–1, list those weaknesses that *you* perceive in the associate. As you list a weakness, answer the following questions:

a. How do you see this weakness interfering with the associate's ability to achieve job objectives?

b. What effects do you see this weakness having on others who are interacting with this associate?

Each weakness that you list must be related to the job and must be (a) a barrier in achieving the associate's job objectives and (b) related to specific "people" problems. For an example, see step [10] in Figure 11–1.

When you have completed your analysis of the associate's weaknesses, do an analysis of his or her strengths. Take a few minutes to think about your data on this associate and focus your thinking on the person's strengths. Then, under the column labeled "Authority" in Figure 11–1, list interpersonal skills possessed by the associate that *you* perceive as strengths. As you list a strength, answer the following questions:

a. How do you see this strength as helping the associate achieve job objectives?

b. What effects do you see this strength having on others who are interacting with this associate?

Each strength that you list must be related to the job and must be identified as an asset in achieving the associate's job objectives. In addition, show the positive effects that the strengths have in helping other associates to achieve their job objectives. For an example, see step [11] in Figure 11–1.

The questions cited above may be expanded to consider other areas you believe to be important. For example, you may want to look at behavior not specifically related to the associate's job objectives, although it still takes place in the work environment. In this respect, a weakness may be that the associate drops in on other members of the work group just to "chew the fat." Or, a strength may be that the associate shares information with group members, which, in turn, may help them in doing their jobs. The point is that you must think about how the associate interacts with other people. In short, your analysis should focus on how this person relates to people, gets along with them, and accomplishes required management and operating work with and through people.

At this point, return to the weaknesses you identified in step [10]. Determine the most serious weakness in relation to (a) getting the job accomplished and (b) a future liability to the associate. In the "Current Status" column of Figure 11–1, indicate this weakness. Write down suggestions that may help to overcome the weakness. Your suggestions should be *action statements* of what to do. They should not be platitudes or theory. Your purpose is to give advice based upon your experience and knowledge. For an example, see step [12] in Figure 11–1. Finally, in the "How Can I Help" column of Figure 11–1, write down what you will do to assist the associate in overcoming weaknesses in the area of interpersonal skills. See step [13] in Figure 11–1 for an example.

At this point, it should be evident that you possess the knowledge to analyze your associates. The areas to examine are: (1) Job knowledge and skills; (2) management knowledge and skills; and (3) interpersonal skills. Your analysis must be written and a form similar to Figure 11–1 can be very helpful. Make sure you list both strengths and weaknesses. The initial analysis will take time to complete. For later analyses, however, you need only update the original. Also, the better your analysis, the more successful you will be in performing your management role of developer.

A Plan of Attack
Setting the Stage

Your written analyses completed, you must discuss individual results with each associate. This is the most critical aspect of your role as developer. However, before the actual discussion session, you must prepare your associates. You could discuss with them (either one-on-one or in a group) how you see your role as developer. Get feedback from them as to their thoughts on this role. Discuss the material in this chapter. Even better, let them read this chapter first and then get their reaction. In any event, the interaction between you and your associates should be on an informal basis and one of the points to focus on concerns the benefits that development holds for them, for you, and for the organization.

The Associate's Personal Analysis

Development is a two-way street, involving the helper and the helped. Your associates must want to participate and must be personally involved in all aspects of their development. Consequently, their personal analysis of their weaknesses and strengths is very important, and the information will serve to identify what they see as the most important element of their jobs.

In conducting their personal analysis, have associates follow the same approach you used. This will provide a common basis for discussing the various components of the total analysis. Check with them occasionally to see if they have questions on the techniques. Do not answer questions on content. Do not answer questions on their responsibilities. Let them identify their responsibilities as they see them. Differences often focus on misconceptions that can be clarified in subsequent discussions. Above all, associates must feel that you are sincere and open-minded before they will be honest in their personal analysis. Finally, make sure that you set a specific date and time for a meeting to discuss each associate's development.

The Meeting

The actual meeting to discuss the associate's development is the first "win or lose" situation. It will prove too much for many supervisors, because they will forget that it is not a "you will do this" session, but a discussion between two human beings. The primary objective of the meeting is to find out how the parties can help each other achieve their own career objectives. As the leader, you must express the major objective to be accomplished. Set down a possible agenda, but remember that it is only a rough outline that can change based upon the needs of each associate. The following is a suggested outline:

- State the objective of the meeting. It should include what you intend to cover, why you think it is important, and what you hope to achieve. The entire analysis need not be covered in a single meeting. For example, the first meeting might focus on only job knowledge or interpersonal skills. The final decision will be based upon the time available and the most critical area (s) for each associate.
- Let the associate discuss his or her personal analysis. You listen and make notes, but do not take over the discussion. Ask questions only if some of the associate's comments are not clear.
- At the appropriate time, summarize what the associate has said.
- Show the associate your analysis. Indicate areas of similarities and differences. Do not get into a debate over any differences. The purpose of the comparison is to identify a major weakness that can be strengthened. You can aid in the selection by playing the devil's advocate, but do not select the area for improvement. If you view the selected area as unimportant, try to influence the choice by a logical and practical questioning approach. If this fails, let the associate stay with his or her choice. It may prove to be the right one.
- Share your thoughts on how the associate can overcome the weakness and how you can help. Also, be sure to let the associate offer suggestions.

- Ask the associate to create a program/schedule (activities to be done, time schedule, and people who may help) during the next week to achieve the objective of overcoming the weakness under discussion.
- Close by scheduling a follow-up meeting to discuss the associate's proposed plan for development.

The initial meeting should be scheduled for one hour and the climate should be very informal. Try to schedule the meeting early in the morning, to allow you and the associate to review materials the night before. In addition, it will assure that you are both fresh and will tend to minimize any influence from daily job pressures. Make sure that you select a place where you have room to lay out both analysis sheets, some privacy, and no interruptions. It is a good idea to get away from the office. If you cannot, stop all incoming phone calls and instruct your secretary not to allow anyone to interrupt. If you do not have a secretary, indicate to anyone who comes in that you have an important meeting and that you will call back as soon as you are finished.

Follow-up Meeting

The objective of the follow-up meeting is to discuss the associate's plan to strengthen a weakness that has high priority in his or her present position. Give advice and find out how you can help. Look at the plan from a realistic and operating point of view. Make sure the associate can accomplish the plan. Seek out areas that can cause the associate problems. Make sure the activities relate to the associate's position. For example, going to college for a course in a specific area may not be the best use of the associate's time. Instead, an assignment to work with another associate, or as part of a project team, may be more applicable to the development objective. Questions and challenges by you are important if you are going to succeed in your role as developer. Conclude the meeting when you are satisfied that the two of you have outlined the best plan to accomplish the development objective.

As the associate's manager, you must follow up on development plans. This follow-up should be done informally (ask about progress occasionally and give feedback showing how you see the progress) and formally (a meeting half-way through the timetable). In all cases, your success as a developer depends on an honest evaluation of the strengths and weaknesses of associates in a non-threatening environment. All discussions must allow for differences of opinion. The ultimate objective is a plan of action to strengthen high priority weaknesses. Your commitment to help and give feedback to the associate must be communicated in words and in action. The overall emphasis should be on the accomplishment of objectives through a team effort.

Development—Upward and Across
Your Manager

Remember, development means the improvement of skills, knowledge, and attitudes to satisfy the needs of associates and to accomplish the objectives of the organization. No one will deny that there is always room for improvement. However, the strategy of developing upward must be implemented with finesse.

Often, you can influence upward by example. The initiation of a planned approach for the development of your associates may rub off on your manager. Get your manager involved by asking for advice or by using him or her as a sounding board. The use of planning tools to accomplish your departmental objectives may cause your manager to use them. Still other ways to influence upwards are:

- By discussing department objectives with your manager. This may identify conflicts among objectives that can be clarified.
- By keeping him or her informed of progress toward objectives. This may result in a more realistic two-way communication system.

The major point is that you can affect the development of your manager. In the process, your tactics should focus on how your manager can help you to meet your responsibilities on the road to accomplishing overall organizational objectives.

Your Peers

The development of peers does not mean that you seek out your fellow workers for this sole purpose. During the work day, however, you do interact with other people in carrying out your responsibilities. You may work with them in solving a common problem. You may be involved in a meeting with them. Or, you may be part of a team to accomplish some common objective. These are the times when you may be able to aid in their development. How? There are many ways. For example, you can pass on information that may be of use in their jobs. Share "tools" that have helped you in your job. Show them articles that relate to their areas of responsibility. Or, ask them for help in solving a common problem. These are offered to get you thinking. Take some time to add more to the list.

The Next Step Is Yours

Earlier, you stated where you want to be at this time next year. If you have followed all instructions, you have now identified your strengths and weaknesses and have developed a plan for overcoming your major weaknesses. In addition, you have completed a development program for each of your associates. Together, these programs focus attention on what you and your group need to do to achieve your organizational objectives this year. Continually update your program (and encourage associates to do the same) to meet new situations. When you have strengthened one weakness to a certain level, select another. This will move you closer to your future objective. It is not an easy task, but the rewards are large in return for pursuing self-development while performing your role as a developer of people.

Questions for Discussion

1. Summarize the development process presented in this chapter.

2. What are the major advantages of using some form of written analysis with your associates?

3. Indicate areas of the development process that might present problems to you. How will you minimize these problems?

4. Indicate areas of the development process that might present problems to your associates. How will you help to eliminate these problems?

5. If the management development effort fails, who is to blame? Why?

6. Identify key interpersonal skills needed for the following associates to accomplish their major responsibilities:

a. A salesperson in a large department store.

b. An accountant in a government position.

c. A foreman in a production facility.

d. A salesperson for a drug company.

e. A production worker.

Case Incidents

1. Shirley C. has just been appointed to a supervisory position in the Midwest regional office of Jordan Products, Incorporated. During her ten years with the company she has received no assistance to prepare her for the new position. Thus she says, "I made it on my own and my associates can do the same thing. I'm not going to waste my time developing others. Let them work at it like I had to do."

a. Do you see anything wrong with Shirley's views? Why or why not?

b. If you feel that developing associates is an important supervisory responsibility, how would you proceed to meet this responsibility in an effective manner?

2. Tom was quite upset as the two of you went to lunch yesterday. One of Tom's associates had been in his office most of the morning discussing a request for more training in mathematics and statistical techniques. Tom had suggested that the employee go to see someone in the training section of the personnel department, but the employee persisted in discussing it with him.

"Who does he think he is?" said Tom. "It's getting so bad that I'm listening to every associate who wants a promotion, a salary increase, training, or a day off. From now on, I'm going to show those characters the exit as soon as they come into my office."

a. Do you agree with Tom's views? Why or why not?

b. Associates sometimes want to see you when your schedule is full. How do you handle such situations? Could you handle them in a better manner?

c. Are formal and informal discussions with associates an important part of the supervisor's job? Why? How can formal discussions be planned to maximize their effectiveness?

Labor Relations and the Supervisor

*William F. Glueck**

William F. Glueck

Chapter Objectives	1. *To provide an understanding of the nature of labor problems.*
	2. *To show the structure of unions and how they operate.*
	3. *To examine some of the reasons for labor-management conflict.*
	4. *To outline what supervisors can and cannot do legally when a union is organizing.*
	5. *To emphasize the importance of the supervisory role during negotiations, strikes, and day-to-day relations with union representatives.*

AT ONE TIME, this chapter would have applied mostly to supervisors of manufacturing employees in private companies. Today, however, all kinds of employees have joined unions. Thus government supervisors, hospital supervisors, supervisors working for universities, schools, libraries, museums, and many other institutions are concerned with labor relations.

Definition

Labor relations is a continuous relationship between a defined group of employees represented by a union or association and an employer. The relationship includes the negotiation of a written contract concerning wages, hours, and other conditions of employment and the interpretation and administration of this contract over its specified period.

*William F. Glueck is Professor of Management, College of Business and Public Administration, University of Missouri-Columbia.

Why Labor Relations and Why We Are So Emotional about Them

This chapter is important because about one of every four employees belongs to a union. Thus, at least 25 percent of all supervisors deal with unions each day on the job. Unions have had their ups and downs but, if anything, are becoming more important as they organize some critical employees in society, in hospitals, schools, and government. Who knows, the Army may be next. It's legal. Sweden had a strike of its military recently. Canada's post office has shut down several times in recent years. Police are striking, nurses are striking, and doctors in some hospitals are organizing and striking.

I am no fortune teller, so I cannot predict accurately whether a bigger share of employees will be unionized ten years from now. But I am willing to bet that unions will be more powerful in all sectors except manufacturing (where they are already powerful) in 1986 than 1976. So, you as a supervisor had better learn about unions and how to deal with them.

My father once told me, "Never argue about politics or religion with people." He might have added unions. Why does the subject of labor relations get people so excited? The reason is that it goes to the heart of employee relations problems, which is power. Whoever has the power to fire employees has power over whether they and their families can survive. Whoever has the power to discipline an employee has the power to affect human needs negatively. In some countries where employers were too harsh on employees, revolutions have taken place. Or, labor governments were voted in to protect the workers.

In the United States, conditions considered unfair or exploitative led to the development of unions. Employees joined together so that they did not have to stand alone against the power of Ford Motor Company, the New York City School Board, or Barnes Hospital. In summary, then, we get excited about labor relations because it affects some very basic issues: Who will have the power to hire, fire, discipline, promote, and assign people to jobs. These issues get a lot more people excited than others such as socialized medicine or baptism by immersion versus sprinkling.

A Supervisor's Role in Labor Relations

Supervisors play many roles at work. They are trainers of new employees, technical experts on hard-to-solve problems, communicators of the new work rules or budgets, schedulers of vacations, and on and on. In dealing with the union, supervisors probably have to think of themselves as politicians. Why? Politicians deal with issues that involve a struggle for power and a balancing of interests. The politician must negotiate both sides of an issue and come up with a compromise that all parties can live with later on. In this respect, the politician does not control the sides, but tries to mediate between them.

The supervisor is caught between superiors who want one thing and union officials who want another. In addition, some employees want what management wants, some what the unions wants, and some a combination of the two. This situation calls for political skills to reach a compromise and to keep it working so that conflict is reduced and the work gets out. Here, the supervisor has to be a Harry Truman: A politician who tries to get his way, but realizes that on some issues you've got to give to get; on other issues, you don't budge.

If you didn't think of yourself as a politician before maybe you should begin doing so now. Remember: You can't order your bosses around, you can't order the union around, or the steward. So work on sharpening those political or interpersonal skills.

Understanding Labor Relations

To understand labor relations, a supervisor must understand the parties involved, their goals, and how they differ. However, remember that people act, institutions don't! The union doesn't do anything. Union officials do. The company doesn't act. Managers do.

Part of the conflict in labor relations arises because of differences in goals. Unions desire the best wages, working conditions, and security for their members. In addition, they want to continue in business as unions.

Management seeks to reach its ultimate goals efficiently and effectively (for example, survival, profits, market share, market leadership, and others for a business; quality patient care, excellent training and research results, survival for a hospital, etc.). Consequently, management resists the attempts of anyone to reduce their efficiency or increase their costs. They see unions as doing this even though there are some goals common to the two groups. For example, unions often help maintain discipline at work, a goal sought by both union and management groups in the U.S.

Because of some differences in goals, both sides will see a basic issue like seniority rights differently, the union as a security issue, management as an efficiency and cost issue. Now, let's look a little closer at the parties to labor relations and see what makes them tick (and conflict). The parties include the employees who belong to a union, management and labor officials, government officials, and the general public.

Employees Who Belong to a Union

One of the most important things a supervisor should understand is why employees join unions and stay in them. You are not able to work with unionized employees if you do not understand why they support the union, or joined it in the first place. Each of the following reasons is important, but I have arranged them in the order of most important to least important for the majority of employees. Each person is different and so each joins a union for different reasons. But, when we average the reasons out, these seven seem to be the most important.

Job security and self-respect.

The most important reason for people joining unions is that the contract protects them from poor supervision. By this, I mean the unionized employee is protected from arbitrary supervisors who can hire and fire, promote and pay as they please. Policies and procedures are developed to eliminate favoritism and to provide a systematic approach for handling discipline, promotion, wages, and similar matters. These give employees a feeling of security. They know that if a supervisor is arbitrary, the union will back them up. This gives employees self-respect: no one can "push them around."

Social Relations

People join unions for reasons similar to those for joining social groups, to belong to a group that shares experiences and good fellowship.

Required Membership

Many jobs require that employees join the union prior to, or soon after, taking a job. This explains why many people "join" a union.

Wages

Some people join unions to increase their wages. Most supervisors, however, overestimate wages as a reason for joining unions. Certainly, members feel that unions will raise their wages, but reasons 1, 2, and 3 bring more people into unions than this one. Yes, poor supervisory practices encourage more employees to join unions than a 25¢ hourly wage increase.

Benefits

Some people join unions for better benefits. Unions are largely responsible for getting their members pensions, better insurance coverage, paid vacations, and other benefits which have improved the lot of all employees.

Job Conditions

Many unions have been involved in job design to obtain safer and more interesting jobs for their members. Some persons join unions for these reasons.

Unions as Lobbies

A few people join unions because they provide lobbyists for the worker in state legislatures and the Congress. For example, unions have lobbied for social security, unemployment compensation, workman's compensation, national health insurance, and many other issues that interest employees.

These, then, are the reasons for employees belonging to unions. It is probable that most persons join unions as much for protection, security, and self-respect as to improve their economic status. However, there is evidence that noneconomic reasons are more important in some cases. Therefore, if employers view wages as the only reason for unionization, they will fall short in their understanding of labor relations.

Finally, we should recognize that not all employees accept unions. Attitudes towards unions develop out of the experiences of individuals and the experiences of those whom they know. Thus, new workers in heavily unionized areas such as the East, Midwest, and Far West are more likely to understand and accept the rationale and operations of unions than rural workers in the Southeast. Similarly, many of the reasons employees have for joining unions could be eliminated if more employers would try to satisfy certain employee needs in the absence of a union.

Managers and Union Executives

The people most directly involved in labor relations are the parties sitting across the table from each other, union leaders and employers or employers' officials. Their job is to reach an agreement on future conditions of work (at contract time), or to interpret the contract (between contracts). Most agreements require that the two parties assess the data involved in the decision and decide what set of conditions they can live with.

Employers and union officials are people. The facts and opinions considered in labor relations are influenced by the attitudes and motivations of these persons. Often these two groups have developed unflattering stereotypes of each other. Each side may view the other side and the facts it presents suspiciously.

These attitudes have developed from differences in past experiences, education, social position, and so on. After examining perceptual differences between union and employer officials, Stagner and Rosen believe that these differences may precipitate disputes, since the facts look different to each group. Second, the cumulative effect of these differences in perception will operate to exaggerate actual differences between executives and workers. These groups, on the average, differ in socio-economic background, education, social role, and emotional identification. It has become rare indeed that an ordinary worker rises to a high executive level.

Unlike management officials, who are often hired as managers, almost all union leaders rise from the ranks. Very few have professional backgrounds or much education beyond high school. They come from a working-class background. This is less so in smaller or professional unions, but in the main the union leader is a product of a different background than that of the manager.

As important as the socio-economic and educational backgrounds of these two groups are the differences in the nature of their organizations. Most employer organizations are hierarchically organized. The personnel specialists representing employers are responsible to a boss. They enter negotiations knowing how far they can go and what their boss expects. If they achieve these expectations, they will keep their jobs and be rewarded. Stagner's study indicates that employee relations managers are primarily concerned about relationships with their superiors, and he suggests that these officials would have successfully identified with their fathers.

The union organization is quite different, as are union officials. Stagner found them much more oriented toward peers, and suggests that they identified with peer groups and brothers rather than fathers in their past. This is functional because often unions are less hierarchical and follow a more democratic model. Even a brief look at unions would find some more democratic than others, of course. But unlike the officials representing employers, union officials must submit the contract they have negotiated to a vote of the members, who can and do reject contracts. If they are dissatisfied, they can and do remove officials by voting them out.

Thus to a much larger extent than employers' officials, union leaders are politicians. They must persuade their members that they have done a good job in the negotiations, that they obtained the best contract they could, and that the distribution of compensation, work rules, benefits, and other elements of the contract is fair. This is not always easy to do, especially when the union is composed of a varied membership, with younger workers generally desiring higher wages and older workers opting for increased pensions and "welfare" benefits.

To summarize, many of the difficulties that arise in labor relations come from differences in the persons involved in the process. Management officials may be younger and are likely to be better educated. They do not always know the true hopes and desires of employees, do not know union officials socially, and do not understand the union world. Union officials are often older, have come up from the ranks, and are often less educated. They are subject to political pressure from their members and live in a different world from that of their counterparts.

It is easy for these two groups to develop stereotypes of each other that distort the data presented during the collective bargaining process. In business, the typical union official's stereotype of an employee-relations manager is that of a snobbish, country club type who could not find the way to the bathroom without a map, and who never put in a real day's work. The job of these managers is seen as that of cheating honest workers out of a few cents an hour to get a big bonus. The employee-relations manager, on the other hand, stereotypes union officials as loud-mouthed, uncultured, uneducated goons who probably are stealing pension funds and no doubt beat up uncooperative workers. They will ruin the company because they do not understand the dog-eat-dog marketplace in which business must compete.

Similar stereotypes probably exist in government, hospitals, universities, schools, and other sectors. These stereotypes hurt the labor relations process and should be changed, if possible, to a different model. That model is: He or she is the other side. But, he or she is human and just trying to do the job while learning to work cooperatively. It is not always easy to shift to this model, but in most cases, it makes for more efficient labor relations.

Government Officials, Clients, and the Public

Although the crucial forces in collective bargaining are the employees, the employers, and the unions, government officials and others may enter the process. As will be described later, the government at times provides mediators to try to bring the parties of a dispute together. These officials may have some bias, but it is probably minimal. Just as it is alleged that the Supreme Court of 1937 modified its rulings after reading the 1936 election returns, so it is likely that government policy as interpreted by Presidential appointments to the National Labor Relations Board may tilt government officials' interpretation somewhat. In general, however, mediators form a neutral group whose job is to change an impasse into a contract.

Customers and clients may mobilize to move the negotiation process along. Customers who need goods or services may exert direct pressure on the employer to either settle or lose the business. They also do this indirectly by buying elsewhere and letting the home office know it.

The general public tends to be neutral or uninterested in most collective bargaining situations. Both sides try to mobilize support through the media, however, because if the public is denied service it can bring political or other pressures to bear on a settlement. This normally happens when the public is severely affected by the loss of certain goods or services.

This section should have helped you understand the human side of labor relations, or what is sometimes called the psychology of labor relations. Two more factors need to be understood better before we can discuss the supervisor's role in labor relations, the union organization and the legal side of labor relations.

Labor Unions as Organizations

Many of you may have worked for a number of employers. So you probably know a lot about employer organizations. But few, if any, of you have worked for a union. Yet unions are organizations too. How they are organized sometimes influences what happens at your workplace.

Let's get something out on the table first. Many supervisors are anti-union, because they have had trouble with a steward or a business agent. Yet, unions are like other kinds of organizations. There are big ones, small ones, efficient ones and messed up ones, honest ones and crooked ones. Do not stereotype them. Look at them one at a time and deal with each accordingly. You usually read about the bad ones in the papers. Do not assume they are all like that. If you do not know any Armenians, and you see in the paper that an Armenian rug merchant was arrested for fraud, you do not assume that all Armenians are crooks, do you? Similarly, do not assume because Tony Boyle was sent to jail that all United Mine Workers officials are criminals.

Unions as Organizations

Approximately 20,000,000 U.S. citizens belong to unions. This number represents about 25 percent of the nonagricultural labor force. The largest labor union federation is the American Federation of Labor-Congress of Industrial Organizations (AFL-CIO). Of all union members, 83 percent belong to an affiliated AFL-CIO union. The largest AFL-CIO unions are the United Steelworkers of America (1,200,000 members), International Brotherhood of Electrical Workers (920,000), International Association of Machinists (865,000), United Brotherhood of Carpenters and Joiners (820,000) and Hotel and Restaurant Employees and Bartenders International Union (460,000).

Two large unions outside the AFL-CIO also represent large numbers of workers. They are the United Auto Workers (1,500,000) and the International Brotherhood of Teamsters (1,800,000). Independent unions other than these two represent about 400,000 members.

Membership in U.S. trade unions has not been increasing as a percentage of the total labor force. This is true at least partly because unions are strongest in blue-collar jobs, yet white-collar jobs are growing faster as a percentage of the labor force. Only about 10 percent of the estimated 34,000,000 white-collar workers are unionized. Some of the larger white-collar unions are State, County and Municipal Employees, AFL-CIO (445,000 members), Teachers AFL-CIO (175,000), Firefighters (135,000), Federal Employees (300,000), Federal Employee Association, independent (100,000), and the American Postal Workers Union, AFL-CIO (500,000). If unions are to gain members, white-collar workers must be unionized.

One important factor to remember is that unions and managements have a long history of relations in manufacturing. They are both inexperienced in the government, school, and hospital-service sectors.

Wolfbein gives a good description of labor relations in the government, performing arts, agriculture, hospital, and education sectors. Woodworth and Peterson have good articles dealing with engineers, nurses, teachers, state, county and municipal employees, and federal employees, the emerging labor relations sectors.

How Unions Work

Until the early 1930s, unions had a hard time in the United States. In general, people did not like unions or feared them. The Congress and the courts viewed unions as conspiracies with illegal intentions. Employers would seek injunctions against union activities and the law was sent to remove strikers, pickets, or union personnel. These encounters were often accompanied by violence and bloodshed.

The passage of the Norris La Guardia Anti-Injunction Act (1932) and Wagner Act (1935) allowed unions to operate and the National Labor Relations Board was set up to administer labor law. Although the government could have legally ignored unions, President Kennedy issued Executive order 10988 and President Nixon issued Executive order 11491, both requiring government executives to bargain with unions.

Early union organizations were based on skills or crafts. These craft unions eventually joined into the American Federation of Labor. In the 1930s, the CIO started organizing by employer; that is, instead of Ford having to negotiate with an electrical union, machinists union, and others, all Ford workers belonged to one union (in this case, the United Auto Workers). Generally, craft unions and the AFL were more conservative and the CIO more militant. These federations merged in 1955 and the current organization of the AFL-CIO is shown in Figure 12–1.

The chief governing body of the AFL-CIO is the biennial convention, which sets policy. Between conventions, the executive officers, assisted by the executive council and the general board, run the AFL-CIO. Executive officers are the president, who heads the union staff and interprets the constitution between meetings of the executive council, and the secretary-treasurer, who is responsible for financial affairs. The executive council also has thirty-three vice presidents. It meets three times a year and sets policy between conventions. The general board consists of the executive council and the head of each affiliated national union and department.

Figure 12–1
Structural Organization of the AFL-CIO

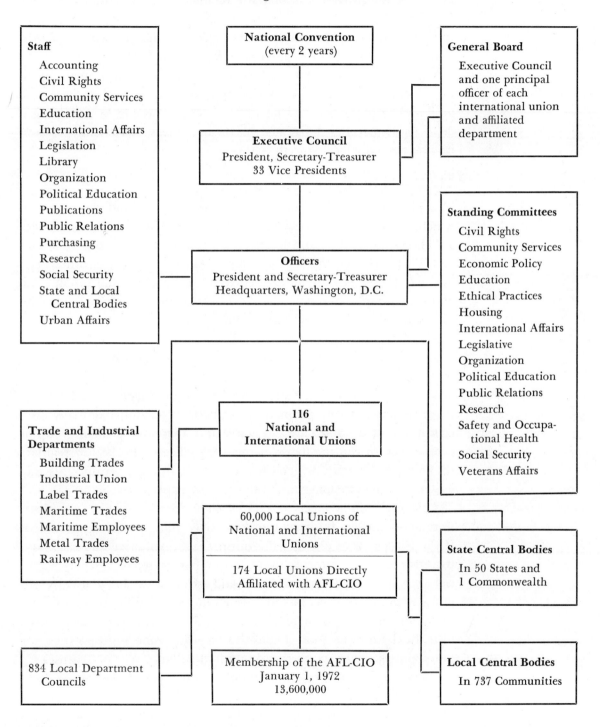

National Convention
(every 2 years)

Staff
Accounting
Civil Rights
Community Services
Education
International Affairs
Legislation
Library
Organization
Political Education
Publications
Public Relations
Purchasing
Research
Social Security
State and Local
Central Bodies
Urban Affairs

General Board
Executive Council
and one principal
officer of each
international union
and affiliated
department

Executive Council
President, Secretary-Treasurer
33 Vice Presidents

Standing Committees
Civil Rights
Community Services
Economic Policy
Education
Ethical Practices
Housing
International Affairs
Legislative
Organization
Political Education
Public Relations
Research
Safety and Occupa-
tional Health
Social Security
Veterans Affairs

Officers
President and Secretary-Treasurer
Headquarters, Washington, D.C.

**Trade and Industrial
Departments**
Building Trades
Industrial Union
Label Trades
Maritime Trades
Maritime Employees
Metal Trades
Railway Employees

116
**National and
International Unions**

60,000 Local Unions of
National and International
Unions

174 Local Unions Directly
Affiliated with AFL-CIO

State Central Bodies
In 50 States and
1 Commonwealth

834 Local Department
Councils

Membership of the AFL-CIO
January 1, 1972
13,600,000

Local Central Bodies
In 737 Communities

National headquarters provides many services to subsidiary union bodies. They provide training for regional and local union leaders, lend organizing help, set up strike funds, and provide locals with data to help them negotiate contracts. Specialists available include lawyers, public relations specialists, and research personnel.

Some national unions have boards of trustees to check financial affairs and audit their books. Larger unions have a level between the local and national called regionals. The regional is run by a vice president who supervises designated locals and serves as a communication link between the locals and the national.

The Local Union

The key building block in the union organization and the one with which a supervisor will become most familiar is the local union. There are about eighty thousand locals in the United States (sixty thousand or so AFL-CIO and the rest in independent unions). Local unions can operate only if they are authorized to do so by a national union. The national issues a charter to the local, which, in turn, must follow the constitution and bylaws of the national.

All officers of a union are elected by the members, usually for one-year terms. The official business of the union is conducted at monthly meetings of the local. Except at contract or troublesome times, these meetings are not well attended. The locals are "democratic"; that is, the members can vote people out, set policy, etc. But, like many associations, most members are not active and, therefore, a small group of people tend to run the locals, namely the officers and the few regulars who attend. This can be good for the union, though, because this way leaders stay in office longer and can get more experience.

The local union elects officials such as president, vice president, secretary-treasurer, business representative, and committee chairmen. If the local is large enough, the business representative and secretary-treasurer are full-time employees. Business representatives play a crucial role in contract negotiations and grievances. They usually administer the local office, including such duties as public relations. The president, vice president and other officials such as committee chairmen, hold full-time jobs. Typically, they get some released time for union duties and are paid several hundred dollars a year in expenses.

The secretary-treasurer is the union's money person, collecting dues, paying bills, and so forth. The business representative (agent) probably has the most strenuous job of the officers. One study of business agents found that they all were energetic and enthusiastic. Their jobs demand lots of time, especially at negotiating time, and place the agent in the middle between members, officers, and the employer.

The shop steward is the union official seen most often by supervisors. Also called shop committeeman, job steward, or chapel chairman, the steward has a position equivalent to that of the supervisor and represents union members at the job site. The steward is normally elected for a one year term by the members and has the major role of handling grievances and interpreting the contract. (See chapter 14, which covers this role in more detail.)

Stewards vary a great deal in ability and attitudes. Most have received limited training for their role. Some are easy-going, others very militant. Some are lazy and uninterested; others are very conscientious. To be reelected, they must represent the members in grievances and assure that supervisors abide by the contract.

Finally, the local union has its committees. Typical of these (which help govern a local's policy) are:

Bargaining Committee
Strike Organization Committee
Grievance Committee
Membership Committee
Shop Stewards Committee

Union leaders, especially at the local level, have much less power than supervisors. They are always subject to reelection, and the contracts they negotiate must be ratified by union members. Union members are typically apathetic about union affairs except when matters affect them personally. This does give some freedom to union leaders during "normal" times, when they can rally the members' support against employers. Effective union leaders realize, however, that the demands made by a union must not put an employer out of business. In addition, good union leaders help employers by policing the contract and keeping maverick members in line.

As in other areas, the personalities of union leaders vary according to the type of work being done. More highly skilled workers choose quiet, competent, senior leaders while semiskilled workers choose those who are aggressive and vocal. In other words, union leaders differ just as much as supervisors. Consequently, some of the difficulties in collective bargaining arise because of personality conflicts between management and union leaders.

Role of the Supervisor in Dealing with the Union

Everyone must get along with someone if a job is to get done. The salesman must get along with the buyer, the school superintendent must get along with the School Board, and the supervisor must get along with the shop steward. This is not always easy.

Ideally, the supervisor and the shop steward develop a good relationship. They respect each other. They keep each other informed on all matters that could lead to problems. The steward warns the supervisor about his relations with certain employees. The supervisor tells the steward about problems with an employee or a new procedure from the home office. They counsel and teach each other, and their relationship is between equals. They are not buddy buddy, nor are they patsies for each other.

If things are not this ideal, supervisors should at least be cooperative and friendly when possible. They must be firm and stand their ground on important issues. But, what is an important issue? Policemen cannot enforce all the laws every day. There are days when they are too busy enforcing laws against murder, theft, and rape to enforce the no-spitting-on-sidewalk laws. Policemen must decide how they will spend the day, and murder is more dangerous than saliva on the sidewalk. Supervisors should realize that some portions of the contract are picky and not crucial to getting the work out. Thus, they can overlook minor violations and save their energy to deal with more important issues.

The Supervisor's Primer on Labor Law

The laws affecting labor relations are complicated, and no one expects the supervisor to be a lawyer. Therefore, most employers and unions have lawyers to advise them on the details, and you can get help when you need it. But certain laws do affect you and what you can and cannot do at work. Let's go over these to protect you and your employer.

The major law affecting collective bargaining in the United States is the National Labor Relations Act (Wagner Act) as amended by the Labor-Management Relations Act of 1947 (Taft-Hartley Act). These acts cover many aspects of collective bargaining, including the procedure by which unions come to represent employees.

Union Organizing Law, or What You Can and Cannot Do at Organizing Time

Union organizing goes through several steps. The first step takes place when employees invite union representatives to come to the place of employment to solicit union membership. Less often, unions seek to unionize employees on their own initiative. The law allows organizers to solicit employees for membership as long as this solicitation does not endanger the safety or performance records of the employees. It can take place at lunch, at break time, and even during working hours if the employer has allowed other groups such as United Appeal to solicit contributions during work time.

Union organizers try to get the employees to sign authorization cards, and 30 percent must sign them before the union can call for a representation election. Although management may observe what is going on in person, it is illegal to interfere physically with, threaten, or do violence to organizers, or to install listening or similar surveillance devices to stop unionization. It is also illegal to discharge employees for pro-union activity, and management must be careful to document discharges for inadequate performance during the organizing period.

It is illegal for either employers or union organizers to threaten employees during the unionization campaign. Unions can picket the organization (1) if the employees are not already unionized; (2) if a petition for election procedures was filed within thirty days to the National Labor Relations Board; and (3) if there has not been a recognition election in the preceding twelve months.

During the organizing period, unions and management pursue campaigns to influence employees' attitudes concerning unionization. Typically the union stresses how it can improve the workers' lot in terms of compensation, benefits, and employee protection. Management stresses how well off the employees are already and cites the costs of union membership in terms of dollars and "loss of freedom." However, it is illegal for either side, in mass meeting, literature, or individual meetings, to threaten employees with either discharge or violence. In addition, it is probably unlawful for management to ask employees individually about their feelings toward unions, but secret polls are allowed.

After the preliminary organizing period, the hearing stage is reached and the National Labor Relations Board (NLRB) gets involved. When the union or employer files NLRB form 502, the regional director of NLRB sends a hearing officer to investigate the situation. The examiner sends the union and management a Notice of Representation Hearing (NLRB form 852), stating place and time of hearing. The situation is examined to decide if there is enough evidence to hold an election (30 percent or more of the employees must sign the authorization cards, for example). The examiner must also decide what the bargaining unit will be, the organization (exclusive of managerial personnel) or a series of subunits.

If there appears to be enough evidence, and if the examiner's decision to schedule an election is approved by superiors at NLRB, the employees are notified of the election and management of its rights (NLRB form 666). Within thirty to sixty days, an election is held by the NLRB, which provides secret ballots and ballot boxes, counts the votes, and certifies the election. The union then becomes the employees' representative, if it wins the election.

Labor Law after Your Shop is Organized

The specific rights of the parties involved in labor relations have been defined by law. The Wagner Act defined employee rights by making it illegal for employers (and their supervisors):

1. To interfere with, restrain, or coerce employees in the exercise of their rights to join unions and bargain collectively.

2. To dominate or interfere with the formation or administration of any labor organization or contribute financial or other support to it.

3. To discriminate in regard to hiring or tenure of employment or any term or condition of employment, to encourage or discourage membership in any labor organization. Section 8 (3), however, included a proviso removing union security agreements from the general prohibition of encouragement or discouragement of labor organizations.

4. To discharge or otherwise discriminate against an employee who filed charges or gave testimony under the act.

5. To refuse to bargain collectively with representatives of the employees.

The Taft-Hartley Act prohibits unions from engaging in six specific unfair labor practices. Thus unions and their stewards cannot:

1. Coerce employees in the exercise of their rights or coerce employers in the selection of their representatives for purposes of collective bargaining or adjustments of grievances.

2. Cause an employer under a union shop agreement to discriminate against employees denied admission to the union or expelled from the unions for reasons other than nonpayment of dues and initiation fees.

3. Refuse to bargain collectively.

4. Engage in a jurisdictional strike or secondary boycott.

5. Charge excessive or discriminatory initiation fees of employees covered by a union shop agreement.

6. Cause an employer "in the nature of an exaction" to pay for services not performed.

The Taft-Hartley Law also includes the controversial Section 14.b, which allows states to pass "right to work laws" prohibiting union shops and other union security agreements, as discussed elsewhere in this chapter.

Although the labor laws discussed thus far apply to the private sector, employees of the federal government also can join unions, by executive orders from two Presidents. Many state and local government employees also can join trade unions. State laws such as New York's Taylor Act prohibit strikes, but they have not prevented mass resignations, mass sick calls, and other mechanisms which can have similar effects. In other cases, public employees like police and firemen in San Francisco have gone out on strike.

The Supervisor's Job When a Union Is Organizing

You now know how a union organizes a workplace and what the union and you can do legally at that time. You also know why people join unions. Now, if you wish to get management's point of view across to employees in order to influence their vote, you ought to know a few facts.

The National Industrial Conference Board studied 140 union attempts to organize white-collar employees with unions winning 67 of these campaigns. Unions were more successful if they already represented the blue-collar workers of a firm, if the salaries of white-collar workers were low, if the workgroups were small, and if the company had no formal grievance procedure. Unions also succeeded more often if employees kept the union activity from management. It was also found that in most cases the employees had asked the union in.

Management counter-campaigns were also studied. Most used group meetings; letters and memoranda were sent by about half of the companies; and about 40 percent held individual meetings with employees. The NICB conclusions were:

> Where there was no *personal* contact with employees (either no verbal or written communication) the unions won 22 of 26 elections. Where there was personal contact (group meetings, individual discussions or both) the unions won 21 elections and lost 20. Where both written communications and personal contact were used, the unions lost by a substantial margin: 49 losses against 24 wins.[1]

[1]See Curtain, Edward. *White Collar Unionization*. Studies in Personnel Policy 220. New York: National Industrial Conference Board, 1970.

You as a supervisor can influence union organizing efforts. By not treating your employees arbitrarily and by providing them with reasonable security, you remove the union's strongest points. If you hear complaints about wages or other factors that may lead to unionization, be sure to alert the personnel department and your superiors so they can take steps before a union comes in. By personally communicating your views and those of management, you also may influence their votes. However, do not get yourself in a corner. Make your position known fairly, honestly, and openly, and the employees will make their choice with both sides clear in their minds.

The Supervisor at Negotiation Time

Once a union is recognized as the bargaining representative for a group of employees, its officials are authorized to negotiate an employment contract. There are usually three phases involved, preparation for negotiations, negotiation, and settlement.

Preparation for Contract Negotiations

Since many persons are involved in contract negotiations and since conditions change, no description can fit each instance exactly. Without question, however, the first contract is crucial. It provides the pattern that later negotiations follow. The union tries to get all it can in wages, benefits, working conditions, and union security arrangements. As will be discussed shortly, it is crucial for supervisors to be involved before the written contract is signed. Then the first contract is signed. If management or the union wishes to make changes in this contract, the other party must be notified in writing of the desire to terminate or modify the contract at least sixty days before the contract expires. This notification also should include an offer to meet the other side to discuss the issue.

During the next period both sides compile a list of issues to be brought up the next time. Management asks its supervisors how they would like the contract modified to avoid or eliminate problem areas. The personnel department studies patterns in grievances to see where problems exist. The contract is examined to identify undesirable sections, especially those which management feels restricts its rights. Management seeks information on economic conditions affecting the organization (wage rates, productivity, etc.) from its staff, industry data, and published sources.

The union, too, is busy. Increasingly, unions are polling their members to find out what they want changed. For example, the Teamsters Union recently polled 400,000 members prior to the development of contract demands. The union processes these responses by computer in order to identify the rank order of members' desires. Its legal and professional staffs examine the contract and prepare economic studies of conditions affecting the employer and its industry or sector.

From their data, both sides prepare lists of preliminary demands (union) and offers (employer). An attempt is made to determine the cost of each demand or offer. Often computer simulation can help here, but this is easier in wage offers than in the elimination of a compulsory overtime rule, for example. Preliminary trade-offs are thought through. The union tends to ask for more than it knows it can get; management tends to offer less.

Both sides begin to muster support. The union holds membership meetings and gets publicity in the press. The employer's position is communicated through the public press and company publications. Both seek employees' support and that of the community as well.

Negotiating a Contract

How the 150,000 or so labor contracts are negotiated yearly in the United States varies a great deal, depending on the size and importance of each agreement. Basically, bargaining can take place in one of two bargaining situations, bargaining with single employers, for one or several locations, or bargaining with multiple employers in a city, a region, or for a whole industry or sector. A majority of agreements are still negotiated between one employer and one union. If the employees have more than one union, the agreement is negotiated with one union at a time. However, there is some trend toward multiple employer and multiple union bargaining. Coalition bargaining takes place when two or more unions coordinate their contract demands and strategies.

Negotiations usually take place between two teams of negotiators. The union team is larger; typically it has about seven members, including local officers, several stewards and committeemen, and a representative from the regional or national union. Management fields a team of three or four from personnel and line management who usually operate within guidelines set by their top management officers.

Contract issues. Any labor contract can have a large number of clauses, and there are numerous issues over which the two parties can baragain. They can be classified into five categories: (1) Compensation and working conditions, (2) employee security, (3) union security, (4) management rights, and (5) contract duration.

All contracts involve compensation and working conditions. This category includes direct compensation rates, benefits, and hours of work. Issues such as whether overtime should be voluntary, cost-of-living adjustments, and newer benefits such as dental care are included here. Unions also bargain not only about who pays for pensions, but also the details of early retirement provisions, for example.

A second issue that frequently comes up is employee security, especially with regard to seniority. Unions feel that seniority should be the determining factor in promotions, layoffs, and recalls. Management contends that it is their right to make these decisions on the basis of job performance; otherwise efficiency will suffer. The clause that many contracts contain usually stipulates that in cases of promotion and lay-off, when efficiency and ability are substantially equal, the most senior employee shall be favored. As such, seniority is continuous service in a work unit, plant, or organization.

The third issue that is usually involved in bargaining is union security. Unions wish to have as much influence over members as possible, so they try to write in a requirement for a union shop. A union shop is an employment location at which all employees must join the union after a brief introductory period. Failing this, the union tries to get a modified union shop, in which all employees except a few exempted groups must join the union. If the union shop clause cannot be won, an agency shop may be acceptable to the union. In this, those who do not join the union must pay the equivalent of union dues to the union.

The fourth issue, which usually presents an especially difficult set of problems, is the management rights issue. Management lists certain areas or decisions as management rights or prerogatives which are thus excluded from bargaining. Management tries to make these lists long, and unions have chipped away at them. Recently the United Auto Workers argued that handling health and safety problems should be a joint union-management area. It also disputes a foreman's right to suspend a worker without pay over issues other than violence, drunkenness, and illegal refusal to work.

The final area of dispute is contract duration. Companies tend to prefer longer contracts so as to have less turmoil. Over 90 percent of U.S. contracts now cover two- or three-year periods.

Bargaining approaches. No two bargaining sessions are exactly alike. But Selekman contends that nine types of bargaining postures can be taken. A few are rather rarely found. These include:

1. Racketeering. Corrupt union leaders have relationships with "co-operating" managements.

2. Ideological. The bargaining process is viewed as part of a class struggle, to reach ends other than just short-run improvement in working conditions.

3. Collusion. Management and labor combine to get an advantage over the public or competitors by illegal or quasi-illegal means.

4. Deal. Management and labor negotiate secretly, with little involvement of employees.[2]

Selekman describes the five more frequent approaches as:

1. Containment-aggression. The union aggressively tries to take over management rights, and management aggressively tries to keep the union down.

2. Conflict. The employer tries hard to get rid of a union and the union resists.

3. Power. Union and management try to get all possible advantages from each other.

4. Accommodation. Both sides "live and let live."

5. Cooperation. Both sides are concerned about the total work environment and try hard to improve bargaining and the work environment.[3]

Over time, the two parties might move from a posture of containment-aggression to one of cooperation. Others may move back and forth, partially as a result of changing leadership and economic conditions. Some sectors have had relatively more labor peace than others.

Bargaining stages. Typically, bargaining follows several stages of development.

Stage 1: Each side presents its demands. Usually the two parties are far apart on some issues.

Stage 2: Reduction of demands. After the postures have been taken, each side trades off some of the demands it was not too serious about.

[2]Selekman, Benjamin. "Varieties of Labor Relations," *Harvard Business Review*, 27 (March, 1949), pp. 177–185.

[3]*Ibid.*

These demands were included for trading purposes. Pressure is received from the public, customers, union members, and others on the bargaining terms.

Stage 3: Subcommittee studies. Getting down to business, the two parties form joint subcommittees that try to work out reasonable alternatives.

Stage 4: Informal settlement. The two sides go back to their reference groups. The management team determines if top management will accept the terms, and union leaders take soundings of the memberships to see their reaction. If management is agreeable, the process develops into the formal settlement stage.

This description of contract negotiations is oriented internally; that is, it describes what takes place between the two parties. As should be obvious, external factors are also very important in the settlement of the contract. If the union is weak and the employer strong, this situation affects the bargaining. If the economy is slack, the union may be under more pressure to settle than in times of full employment. If the employer's business has certain crucial times (for example, new-model time for autos, harvest time for food, Christmas time for the post office), the union may choose this time for negotiation in order to gain an advantage. If the government is committed to few strikes, it may intervene. All of these external factors and more enter the bargaining process.

Settling a contract

To put the contract in final form, the negotiating committee prepares a memorandum of agreement. Both sides sign this memorandum, but the contract does not become official until ratified by the union membership.

Union leadership must now sell the agreement to the membership as the best it could get. At one time ratification was mostly a rubber stamp, but more contracts have been refused ratification in recent years. If the membership refuses ratification, the union negotiating team must try to achieve more concessions from management.

The final agreement or contract restricts some behavior and requires other. Proper wording of the agreement can prevent future difficulties in interpretation. Both sides should thoroughly discuss the meaning of each clause to prevent misunderstanding, if possible. A typical format for the sections normally covered in the contract or agreement is:

Section Number	Subject
1	Purpose of the parties
2	Management rights
3	Union security and dues checkoff
4	Grievance procedures
5	Arbitration of grievances
6	Disciplinary procedures
7	Compensation rates
8	Hours of work and overtime
9	Benefits: Vacations
	Holidays
	Insurance
	Pensions
10	Health and safety provisions
11	Employee security-seniority provisions
12	Contract expiration date

Smart managers use supervisors in the negotiation process. After all, supervisors must live with the contract, so management should use them as part of the negotiating team. The most experienced supervisors can take turns as members of the team. Supervisors can look over each clause and anticipate problems that may develop because the wording is vague, or because management is not alert to certain problem areas. This is especially true in the management rights, grievance, discipline, and security and seniority areas of the contract.

In short, supervisors have a crucial part to play in negotiations. If not involved now, they should encourage their superiors to use them on the negotiating team.

The Supervisor and Labor Impasses

Negotiations sometimes break down. There are three major ways the American system has to smooth them out, conciliation, mediation, and arbitration.

Conciliation and mediation

One of the first steps that management or labor can take to deal with an impasse is to invite an independent third party to help get the process going again. This is called conciliation or mediation. The Federal Mediation and Conciliation Service (FMCS) may have already offered its assistance, or it may be invited in by the parties. Essentially, the mediator meets with both parties, then with each party individually, and tries to serve as a go-between in coming up with a solution. Neither side is bound to accept the solution. But sometimes, especially when the two sides have started to become antagonistic, the mediator can help. Rather than coming from the FMCS, the mediator can be an independent disinterested outsider such as a university professor.

McKelvey[4] found that mediation is likely to work more effectively in smaller communities and rural areas than in large urban centers. She also feels it is more likely to work if the parties must pay for the service and if they freely invite the mediator in, as opposed to mediation that follows automatically at a certain stage of impasse. It is also more likely to work if the parties realize that the alternative to mediation is a strike or binding arbitration.

Arbitration

Arbitration is the process by which management and labor agree in advance of a hearing to abide by the decision of an independent third party called an arbitrator. Arbitration, especially binding arbitration, is the last step in settling disputes, either at contract time or between contracts. As such, it is quicker and cheaper than court action would be in such situations, and the law and the courts have virtually guaranteed that the "loser" cannot win an appeal from an arbitration award.

The first step in arbitration is to select an arbitrator. Some unions and managements have an arbitrator they call on regularly. Others receive lists of the names of arbitrators from the American Arbitration Association or the FMCS. In any event, the arbitrator must be acceptable to both sides. Persons with varying backgrounds serve in these posts, but most arbitrators are lawyers or professors. Typically they are paid $150 to $200 a day plus expenses for their services.

Once the arbitrator, or the board of arbitrators, is chosen, the arbitration hearings are held. The subject of the hearing is spelled out in the submission agreement, which also states that the arbitrator has final authority to settle the issue. The hearings vary in formality from sessions similar to those in court, with the swearing in of witnesses and so forth, to quite informal hearings. The arbitrator seeks to assure a fair hearing to both sides and can admit relevant hearsay evidence,

---

[4]McKelvey, Jean. "Fact Finding in Public Employee Disputes: Promise or Illusion?", *Industrial and Labor Relations Review*, Vol. 22, No. 4 (July, 1969), pp. 528–543.

question witnesses, and ask for more information from one or both parties.

In arbitrating contracts, both sides must present their evidence. In arbitrating grievances or deciding disciplinary cases, the arbitrator tries to see if there is guilt beyond a reasonable doubt, something akin to criminal court cases. In grievance cases, the contract and precedents in the case are examined, as well as how long the precedents have been in existence.

Once the arbitrator has heard all the evidence, and the hearing is adjourned, the arbitration award is written and becomes binding on both parties. The award normally reviews the facts within thirty days of the hearing. The arbitrator writes the award in language understandable to all parties concerned, including the employee involved in a grievance. It should attempt to clarify the problem situation so as to prevent future problems from arising. Although arbitrators will usually look over previous arbitration awards in similar cases, they need not be bound by them.

Strikes and Lockouts

If bargaining breaks down, conciliation/mediation fails, and arbitration is not in the contract, a strike or lockout can take place. A strike is a refusal of employees to work. A lockout is a refusal of a management to allow the employees to work. Lockouts are rare today, and most strikes are at contract time; less than 10 percent of strikes take place at other times.

In the United States, most strikes are total, in that all workers walk out. In Europe, a much more destructive type of strike is used in which employees deliberately slow down, or what appears to be random absenteeism and sick calls take place. In Italy recently, the ratchet or rotating type of strike has been used very effectively. Workers 1, 3, 5, 7, 9, etc. on an assembly line call in sick for the morning. Workers 2, 4, 6, 8, etc., become sick that afternoon. This causes havoc for production and cuts the cost to the strikers in loss of pay. This method was apparently used by striking Canadian rail workers in 1973.

The Bureau of Labor Statistics estimates that fewer than 4 percent of contract negotiations result in strikes and less than four-tenths of 1 percent of working time was lost to strikes in the period 1967–72.

However, strikes, or the threat of strikes, do put added pressures on both sides to settle their differences. Most strikes do not seriously affect the public welfare. If it appears that a strike will do so, the Taft-Hartley Act allows the President to appoint a board of inquiry and issue an injunction for an 80-day "cooling off" period. During this period, the employees are polled by secret ballot to see if they will accept the employer's latest offer. Sometimes Congress steps in at the end of the period to lengthen the period of injunction.

Supervisors have an especially difficult time of it during impasses. You need to be especially careful to keep records and protect yourself on disciplinary matters. Many times, some workers are "looking for trouble" and tact must be used. You must be firm on key issues, however.

Dealing with the Union the Rest of the Time

Most of the time, you are not confronted with negotiations, or union organizing. You are dealing with the shop steward on a day-to-day basis. Some aspects of these daily relationships were discussed earlier. Chapters 8, 9, and 10 should also give you some help on how to do this. In addition, one of your major responsibilities is the processing of grievances. This is so important that all of chapter 14 is devoted to it.

Perhaps the most crucial thing to remember is that supervisory actions on a day-to-day basis help or hinder labor relations. By being inconsistent when interpreting or administering the contract, you lay yourself and your employer open to a loss of authority and create precedents that the union may later use in arbitration to justify what it wants. Where an item is not clearly spelled out in the contract, precedents indicated by your actions can be cited against you later.

Summary

This chapter was developed to acquaint you with some crucial aspects of labor relations, its psychology and law. It was also designed to help you understand how unions are organized, how employers and unions negotiate contracts, and how they deal with each other at other times.

Remember that you have your boss to advise you on labor relations. The personnel department is also there to advise you on organizational policies and ways to deal with labor. But in the final analysis, you the supervisor make or break labor relations at your workplace. I hope this chapter helped a little to make the relations more efficient and effective for you, your employer, and your employees.

Bibliography

Bureau of National Affairs. *Basic Patterns in Union Contracts*. Yearly updated series.

Curtain, Edward. *White Collar Unionization*. Studies in Personnel Policy 220. New York: National Industrial Conference Board, 1970.

Glueck, William F. *Personnel: A Diagnostic Approach*. Dallas: Business Publications, Inc., 1974.

McKelvey, Jean. "Fact Finding in Public Employee Disputes: Promise or Illusion?", *Industrial and Labor Relations Review*, Vol. 22, No. 4 (July, 1969).

Selekman, Benjamin. "Varieties of Labor Relations," *Harvard Business Review*, 27 (March, 1949).

Stagner, Ross and Rosen, Hjalmer. *The Psychology of Union Management Relations*. Belmont, Calif.: Wadsworth, 1965.

Wolfbein, Seymour, ed. *Emerging Sectors of Collective Bargaining*. Braintree, Mass.: D. H. Mark, 1970.

Woodworth, Robert and Peterson, Richard. *Collective Negotiation for Public and Professional Employees*. Chicago: Scott Foresman, 1969.

See also Prentice Hall or Commerce Clearinghouse series of up-to-date information on labor relations.

Questions for Discussion

1. Why is labor relations such an emotionally charged area?

2. Why do people join unions? How can a supervisor prevent a union at work?

3. Why do company and union officials often have differing perceptions of matters involved in labor relations?

4. What can supervisors do if a union is trying to organize? What can't they do?

5. How should supervisors be involved in contract negotiations?

6. What does a local union's business agent do? What are the functions of a union steward? How much power do local union officials have?

7. What are the major laws affecting collective bargaining in the United States?

8. What can supervisors and stewards do to improve their day-to-day relationships?

Case Incidents

1. You are a supervisor in the claims department of RJK Insurance Company. RJK is a new, smaller firm located in San Francisco. Recently, you overheard several claims processors talking about the union business agent who had visited with them in the parking lot after work. RJK is not unionized, pays average wages for the area, and offers standard benefits and working conditions.

a. Do you report this conversation to your supervisors?

b. Do you try to discuss this with the claims processors concerned? Other claims processors?

c. Should you try to talk these people out of joining the union?

d. Should you forbid them to discuss this issue on work time?

2. You are Jerry Symington, a supervisor of maintenance personnel at a small Eastern college. Your employees joined the Teamsters Union two years ago.

You have had a lot of trouble dealing with the steward, so recently you asked him to join you for a beer after work. After buying the steward five beers, this conversation took place.

Jerry: Look Bob, why are you giving me such a hard time over contract wording, discipline, etc.?

Bob: I don't give you a hard time. You're just anti-union, so I gotta be careful and watch you.

Jerry: I'm not anti-union. Where'd you get that idea?

Bob: Yes, you are. I went bowling with Tom (Jerry's predecessor as supervisor), and he always bought the beer and paid for the bowling. I was real cooperative with him cause he wasn't anti-union like you.

a. Should Jerry have taken Bob out for a few beers?

b. Should Jerry get more friendly with Bob? More beer nights?

c. Should Jerry take up bowling with Bob? Pick up the bowling tabs like Tom?

d. What other steps would you recommend to Jerry?

The Supervisor
and
Affirmative Action

*W. Clay Hamner**

<table>
<tr>
<td>Chapter
Objectives</td>
<td>1. To help supervisors understand how the federal government has stepped in to monitor the movement of minorities and women in organizations.

2. To show supervisors how their help is crucial to the establishment and implementation of an affirmative action program.

3. To explain how the frustrations of government intervention in personnel decisions can be overcome and managed.</td>
</tr>
</table>

AFFIRMATIVE ACTION means different things to different people. This chapter will try to explain what affirmative action is, why it is required by law, and how supervisors can comply with the law and still maintain their authority to make decisions affecting the people they supervise. Before this discussion takes place, let's establish two things. First, affirmative action does not necessarily mean that an organization is faced with a quota system. In a quota system an employer is forced (by agreement or court order) to hire a certain number of minorities or women over a stated period of time. Or, an employer is given guidelines, by a local Equal Employment Opportunity Commission (EEOC) Office or by a State Human Rights Office, stating that the composition of the workforce should reflect the makeup of the population around the place of work. For example, in 1972 the Household Finance Corporation entered into agreement with the EEOC to hire 20 percent

*W. Clay Hamner is Associate Professor of Organizational Behavior, Graduate School of Management, Northwestern University.

females for branch representative openings (subject to availability) until such representation was 20 percent female, and to hire 20 percent from specified minority groups for clerical, credit, and branch representative jobs until the total of such employees reached 65 percent of their population in the labor force.[1]

Generally, quota systems such as the one agreed to by Household Finance result from a charge of discrimination and are temporary remedies to overcome the lack of fair treatment, which is the law of the land. A second point to note is that affirmative action does not require a supervisor to hire an unqualified applicant. Instead, it requires that (1) all selection devices (tests, interviews, etc.) be related to actual job performance (i.e., be shown to be valid) and be applied equally to all applicants regardless of race, sex, religion, age, or national origin; (2) qualified minority and female candidates be sought for job openings; and (3) all unfair barriers be recognized and removed by identifying persons unfairly excluded or held back, thereby encouraging and enabling them to compete for jobs on an equal basis. For example, in the Household Finance Case cited above, HFC agreed to train female and minority employees to help them qualify for better jobs where they were underrepresented.

Legal Requirements
1791–1900

Before we discuss how to set up an affirmative action plan, let's trace the history of federal law in the area of personnel practice. As we are all aware, equal employment opportunity is the law of the land. It is required by federal, state, and local legislation, presidential executive orders, and definitive court decisions. As such, the current status of the affirmative action requirement can be traced back to the beginning of this country.

In 1791, the 5th Amendment specified that "No [free] person shall be deprived of life, liberty, or property without the process of law." The 13th Amendment to the Constitution abolished slavery and charged Congress with the establishment of laws to give blacks equal treatment. As part of this charge, Congress passed the Civil Rights Act of 1866, which said that all people, regardless of race, had the right to enter into a contract. In 1868, the 14th Amendment to the Constitution gave equal protection of state laws to all persons. And, the Civil

---

[1]U. S. v. Household Finance Corporation, 4 EPO para. 7680 (N. D. ILL., 1972) (Consent decree).

Rights Act of 1871 provided that state laws must grant equal rights to all persons regardless of race, national origin, or sex.

1900–1960

State and federal laws mandated discrimination as illegal in 1866, but labor statistics show that from 1900 to 1965, little progress was made in the advancement of minorities and females in employment situations. Many reasons for this lack of progress can be given. The industrial revolution had reduced the need for highly skilled workers. Blacks and women were generally less educated than white males. Many companies were family owned and only family members became managers. The depression and two major wars diverted our attention. Congress was busy enacting laws to guarantee minimum wages, maximum hours, and the right to unionize—all three of these were more pressing issues of the day. In the early 1950s, the emphasis began to shift. The military dropped the separate but equal argument and enforced the integration of the military. In 1954, the Supreme Court (Brown vs. Board of Education) ruled that the separation of school children was illegal. Following this decision, the major shift in minority benefits from 1954 to 1964 took place in the schools and colleges in this country.

1960–1976

Because of the pressure brought to bear by several special interest groups (e.g., the NAACP), the President and Congress began to focus on the employment rights (selection, promotion, termination, and training) of previously denied groups of employees. In 1961, President Kennedy established the Commission on the Status of Women to draw up recommendations for improving the progress of women in employment and other areas. As a result of this Commission's work, Congress passed the Equal Pay Act of 1963. This act was an amendment to the Fair Labor Standards Act of 1938, which established minimum wages and maximum hours, and protected women and children from certain physical abuses in the work setting. Under the Equal Pay Act, Congress guaranteed equal pay for equal work on jobs requiring equal skills, efforts, responsibility, and performance levels. In other words, supervisors could no longer pay women a wage different from that paid to men for approximately equal jobs. Today, this act applies to all employees covered by the minimum wage law plus executive, administrative, professional employees, academic employees, and outside salespersons.

From 1964 through 1972, 129,000 employees (mostly women) received more than 55 million dollars stemming from violations of the Equal Pay Act. In 1970, for example, Wheaton Glass Company paid more than $900,000 in back wages and interest to 2000 female employees.[2] Other companies have also paid money to women as a result of this law (for example, AT&T, $68 million; Pittsburgh Plate and Glass, $1 million; Delta Airlines, $700,000; and Corning Glass, $600,000.)[3]

Even though the Equal Pay Act was passed in 1963 and many companies have since paid significant amounts of money to equalize pay between the sexes, the Womens' Bureau of the U. S. Department of Labor noted in 1972 that women who work at full-time jobs the year round earn, on the average, only $3 for every $5 earned by similarly employed men. Ironically, this is the same ratio as seen in 1939 wage figure comparisons.

Based on statistical comparisons of men to women and other employment figures, it was evident to Congress and the President that original federal and state laws had not achieved equal employment opportunity, even though our American heritage encouraged the right of all persons to work and to advance on the basis of merit, ability, and potential. Therefore, Congress provided federal legal enforcement for equal employment in Title VII of the Civil Rights Act of 1964 with strengthening amendments in 1967 and 1972.

Title VII, the Courts, Executive Order 11246, and Affirmative Action

Title VII of the Civil Rights Act prohibits discrimination on the basis of race, color, religion, sex, national origin, or age (40–65 age range, 1967 amendment) in all employment practices, including hiring, firing, promotion, compensation, and other terms, privileges, and conditions of employment.[4] The U. S. Equal Employment Opportunity Commission (EEOC) was created to administer Title VII and to assure equal treatment for all in employment.

Discrimination or job bias under Title VII can be of two types. First, discrimination can take place through conscious, overt action against individuals. The courts have begun to realize that few firms

---

[2]Schultz v. Wheaton Glass Company, 421 F. 2d 259 (1970).

[3]For an excellent discussion of such payments, see "The Job-Bias Juggernaut," *Newsweek,* June 17, 1974, pp. 75–76.

[4]See *Affirmative Action and Equal Employment: A Guidebook for Employers,* Vol. I (Washington, D.C.: U.S. Government Printing Office, 1974).

are guilty of overt, willful discrimination and have redefined discrimination to include "systemic" or practical discrimination. In 1971, U. S. Supreme Court Justice Warren Burger stated, "What is required by Congress is the removal of artificial, arbitrary, and unnecessary barriers to employment when the barriers operate invidiously to discriminate on the basis of racial or other impermissible classification . . . . [Title VII of the Civil Rights Act] proscribes not only overt discrimination, but also practices that are fair in form, but discriminatory in operation."[5]

More specifically, business and other employers are required not only to cease overt discrimination, but also to "make up for past sins" by removing "systemic" discrimination that has resulted from prior acts of discrimination by taking specific remedial actions. Systemic discrimination is said to occur when there is an adverse effect toward one or more protected groups. For example, if an organization has no female supervisors, then there is discrimination in fact (statistically shown systemic discrimination) even though the organization may be an equal employment opportunity employer.

When discrimination can be confirmed by the statistics of underemployment, nonemployment, unemployment, and incomes of minorities and women when compared to those of other employees in an organization, Title VII provides that a court may "order such affirmative action as may be appropriate" to eliminate it. Later, we will describe in detail how an affirmative action program is administered. First, however, we need to examine how a charge of discrimination is investigated and who is required to establish an affirmative action plan.

Title VII of the Civil Rights Act of 1964 (as amended in 1972) covers all employers with fifteen or more employees and includes private and public employers, unions, educational institutions, state and local governments, joint labor and management committees, and employment agencies. Thus, as you can see, almost all supervisors are faced with the enforcement restrictions of Equal Employment Opportunity (EEO) personnel practices.

To ensure that people, regardless of group affiliation, are hired based on merit, Title VII established the EEOC and empowered this body to investigate charges of discrimination, to attempt to persuade employers to restore the rights of parties discriminated against, and, if necessary, to bring civil actions directly into federal courts in order to enforce the provisions of Title VII and to remedy instances of their

[5]Griggs v. Duke Power Company, 401, U. S. 424 (1971).

violation. The EEOC bases its decisions for bringing charges of discrimination on two things. First, do the records kept by supervisors indicate discrimination or adverse effect? Second, are the reasons for the adverse effect (differential numbers of blacks than whites, for example) based on artificial or factual (valid) barriers?

In both cases, then, the EEOC uses statistics to prove discrimination. If charged with discrimination, it is up to employers to prove that discrimination did not take place. They can do this by following the same principle used by the EEOC. First, they can show that there is no disproportionate treatment of people (i.e., no adverse effect). Second, failing the ability to show no adverse effect, they can show that their decisions were based on valid criteria as established by the EEOC guidelines. Although a complete discussion of these guidelines is beyond the scope of this chapter, it should be noted that the guidelines require an employer to show that information gathered and used for making personnel decisions must be statistically related to levels of job performance. If employers cannot show that one of these two principles has been followed, they will probably be forced to make restoration in dollars/or positions, or both, and by setting up an affirmative action program to avoid these same problems in the future.

It should be noted, however, that Title VII does not explicitly require affirmative action, except in those cases where there is a finding of discrimination. In such cases, the courts generally require affirmative action, including numerical hiring and promotion goals where necessary, to compensate for the effects of past discrimination.

At present, some organizations are beginning to work with local EEOC offices to establish voluntary affirmative action programs as a protective measure to avoid being guilty of discrimination. Still others are required to have a written and approved affirmative action plan under the requirements of Executive Order 11246 (as amended by Executive Order 11375). Issued by President Johnson in 1965, this order requires affirmative action programs of all federal contractors and subcontractors and requires that such firms with contracts over $50,000 and fifty or more employees develop and implement written programs that are monitored by an assigned federal compliance agency. Firms that are not in compliance may face termination or cancellation of contracts, or be barred from future contracts.

Setting up an Affirmative Action Program

As you can tell, setting up a written affirmative action plan is practically a business necessity. As a part of the management team, supervisors are charged with helping to establish and, more importantly, implement affirmative action plans in order to ensure that their organizations do not face charges of discrimination. The U. S. Equal Employment Opportunity Commission recommends that eight basic steps be followed in order to establish a nondiscriminatory affirmative action plan.[6]

1. *Issue written equal employment policy and affirmative action commitment.*   The Chief Executive Officer (CEO) should issue a firm statement of personal commitment, legal obligation, and the importance of EEO as an organizational goal. This statement should indicate that the CEO is committed to making his or her organization an equal employment opportunity organization for all persons, regardless of race, creed, color, sex, national origin, or age. In order for this policy statement to have meaning, it must specify a new goal-setting program with measurement and evaluation factors similar to those of other major organizational programs. In addition, management (including first-line supervisors) performance in carrying out this program should be evaluated as is performance toward other company goals.

2. *A top official with the responsibility and authority to implement the program should be appointed.*   The affirmative action program is probably doomed unless the person charged with implementing it has the status and authority to accomplish the task. This person should be charged with developing policy statements, a written affirmative action program, and internal and external communication procedures. In addition, he or she should work closely with the legal staff and the personnel research staff to insure that all governmental requirements are being met.

The Affirmative Action Officer should assist line managers and supervisors in collecting and analyzing employment data, identifying problem areas, setting goals and timetables, and developing programs to achieve stated goals. He or she should look over current personnel records to make sure that the information being gathered is adequate, is nondiscriminatory, and is being used correctly in making personnel decisions.

In many organizations the Affirmative Action Officer has established an advisory council composed of all affected persons, including first-line supervisors, so that full participation and suggestions for overcoming potential problems can be received.

[6]See: *Affirmative Action and Equal Employment: A Guidebook for Employers*, Vol. I, pp. 14–24.

3. *The organization should publicize and promote its affirmative action program.* All managers and supervisors should be told that their performance related to affirmative action goals will be evaluated along with other criteria in making decisions concerning raises and promotions. All employees should be informed of the affirmative action program by posters, written statements, company newspapers, and other media. Union officials should be invited to cooperate in the development and implementation of the program since they, too, can face discrimination charges (see U. S. vs. Ironworkers Local 86, 1969). Recruiters should be trained and charged with nondiscriminatory practices. Employment agencies should not be used unless it is evident that they are nondiscriminatory. Newspapers should be informed that want ads can only be placed under a "Help Wanted" category. Finally, be sure that subcontractors, vendors and suppliers are complying.

4. *Survey and analyze minority and female employment by department and job classification.* This is a place where supervisors can aid in the implementation of an affirmative action program. This step combines both record keeping (the statistical procedure necessary to prove that discrimination did not take place) and goal setting. A sample of the form recommended for use by the EEOC[7] is shown in Figure 13–1. A record similar to the one shown in Figure 13–1 will allow each departmental supervisor to identify the number and percentage of minority and female employees currently employed by job classification. In turn, this will help the Affirmative Action Officer to work with each supervisor in setting goals and objectives for those units where underutilization (fewer minorities and women than expected in view of their presence in the relevant labor market) or concentration (overutilization) is taking place.

5. *Develop goals and timetables and identify causes of underutilization.* After short-term (immediate to one year) and long-term (five year) goals are set, the Affirmative Action Officer should work with each supervisor to make sure that negative internal or departmental factors are not responsible for any underutilization. This may involve more training by the supervisor for minority employees, a review of union contract provisions, evaluations of selection criteria, or other similar actions.

6. *Develop and implement specific programs to eliminate discrimina-*

[7]*Affirmative Action and Equal Employment: A Guidebook for Employers,* Vol. II, Appendices, January, 1974, pp. A24–A25.

SAMPLE

Figure 13–1
Affirmative Action Program
Goals and Timetable Analysis

*N=Nation; R=Regional; S=State; A=SMSA; C=County; L=City.

SAMPLE

Figure 13–1 (Continued)

Location _____

Organizational Unit _____

Name of Person filling out form _____

Date _____

5 YEAR GOAL (NET CHANGE)

	Non-Minority	Negro	SSA	Oriental	American Indian
FEMALE	37	38	39	40	41
MALE	42	43	44	45	46

Projected Total Employees Next 12 Months	Projected Turnover Next 12 Months	Net Job Openings
47	48	49

PROJECTED EQUAL OPPORTUNITY STATUS — PROMOTABLES NEXT 12 MONTHS

MINORITY				NM	FEMALE			
N	SSA	O	AI		N	SSA	O	AI
50	51	52	53	54	55	56	57	58

GOAL NEXT 12 MONTHS — PERIOD COVERED

	Non-Minority	Negro	SSA	Oriental	American Indian
FEMALES (NET CHANGE)	59	60	61	62	63
MALES (NET CHANGE)	64	65	66	67	68

Column 37 … 68

tory barriers and achieve goals. Basically, this involves reviewing the recruitment and training activities of the organization. Since supervisors are involved in both processes, they should make every effort to be unbiased. Remember the overall goal is to maintain the most qualified work force. This does not mean that a supervisor should have to accept any job applicant who happens to "fill a quota." Instead, it means that every effort should be made to select the best qualified/or most trainable applicant, many of whom will be minority members or women. For example, it might be successfully argued that men are better machinists, on the average, than women. It does not follow, however, that all women should be excluded from the job search because they are inferior. Indeed, many women may be superior to some male applicants even though, on the average, there will be fewer superior women than superior men. Graphically this can be shown as follows:

Skill Level (women)   **Skill Level (men)**

(75)

	→ ←			→	
Low	Mean = 56 on Test	High	Low	Mean = 75	High

In this case, men score an average of 75 on a skill test and women score 56. On the average, this means that men are superior to women on this job. However, approximately 33 percent of the women (see shaded area) scored higher than 50 percent of the men (i.e., 33 percent of the women scored greater than 75, the mean score of the men). If 75 is the "cut off" or least acceptable score, then the supervisor should attempt to look for the qualified women and not (a) exclude all women applicants or (b) select women at random (insuring at best an average of 56) while selecting men based on their qualifications above 75. This latter strategy will insure that the women fail.

7. *Establish a continual record-keeping system to monitor and evaluate progress in each aspect of the program.* Remember your best defense against a finding of discrimination is first, a plan of action and second, statistics showing that the employment of minorities and females is increasing in those areas where they have been excluded or underutilized.

8. *Develop supportive company and community programs.* The training of supervisors in their legal responsibility and company commitment is a first step. This will allow each supervisor to express his or her fears and to understand more fully what affirmative action does or does not involve. In addition, companies can set up career development offices to help train and make all employees more mobile so that supervisors can select and promote those women and minorities who are qualified and interested in mobility. Third, managers at all levels can be encouraged to work with local chapters of the Chamber of Commerce, Urban League, National Alliance of Businessmen, and similar organizations in developing community-based educational programs on affirmative action.

In summary, by following the foregoing guidelines in the establishment of an affirmative action program, any organization should be able to meet the requirements of equal employment as specified by the Civil Rights Act of 1964. However, there still is a chance that an organization can be found guilty of discrimination. Or, a supervisor may act in ways that are said to show prejudice, with such actions resulting in a finding in favor of the employee if a suit is filed. Thus we need to examine the ways by which supervisors can avoid discrimination.

Things Supervisors Should Watch For in Order to Avoid Being Charged With Discrimination

Before we explore points to avoid, look at Figure 13–2 and answer each question according to what you believe to be your rights as a supervisor. If you get seven or more answers right, you are doing a good job. But, remember, one mistake can cause you trouble.

Race and National Origin Discrimination

Policies determined[8] to be unlawfully discriminatory because of their effect or impact on minority groups and because they could not be shown to be related (valid) to job performance include:

1. Refusal to hire because of an arrest record.[9]
2. Using conviction record to refuse to hire.[10]
3. Discharge because of garnishment.[11]

[8]See: *Equal Employment Opportunity Commission,* 7th Annual Report, (Washington, D. C.: U. S. Government Printing Office, 1972).

[9]EEOC Opinion No. 72-0996.

[10]EEOC Opinion No. 72-1497.

[11]EEOC Opinion No. 72-0642.

Figure 13–2

Could you be practicing illegal job discrimination— and not even know it?

Answer: True. Due to outdated policies or failure to understand the law, many employers do discriminate in the way they hire, fire, promote or pay.

Take this 30-second test and see where you stand.[12]

An employer . . .	True	False
1. can refuse to hire women who have small children at home.	____	____
2. can generally obtain and use an applicant's arrest record as the basis for non-employment.	____	____
3. can prohibit employees from conversing in their native language on the job.	____	____
4. whose employees are mostly white or male, can rely solely upon word-of-mouth to recruit new employees.	____	____
5. can refuse to hire women to work at night, because it wishes to protect them.	____	____
6. may require all pregnant employees to take leave of absence at a specified time before delivery date.	____	____
7. may establish different benefits—pension, retirement, insurance and health plans—for male employees than for female employees.	____	____
8. may hire only males for a job if state law forbids employment of women for that capacity.	____	____
9. need not attempt to adjust work schedules to permit an employee time off for a religious observance.	____	____
10. only disobeys the Equal Employment Opportunity laws when it is acting intentionally or with ill motive.	____	____

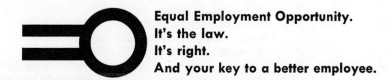

**Equal Employment Opportunity.
It's the law.
It's right.
And your key to a better employee.**

The Equal Employment Opportunity Commission
Washington, D.C. 20506

GPO 870-033

[12]Answers to Figure 13-2: 1. (F), 2. (F), 3. (F), 4. (F), 5. (F), 6. (F), 7. (F), 8. (F), 9. (F), 10. (F).

4. Refusal to hire persons with poor credit ratings.[13]

5. Hiring through unions whose admission preference is to friends and relatives.[14]

6. Using word-of-mouth recruiting by present employees as the primary source of new applicants.[15]

7. Refusal to hire persons wearing beards, goatees or moustaches.[16]

8. Using a transfer rule (change of jobs) which does not allow carryover so as to perpetuate discrimination.[17]

9. Using a high school diploma requirement which cannot be shown to be job related.[18]

10. Inquiring about charge accounts, house or car ownership (unless required for job use).[19]

These are a few of the areas that supervisors should avoid in a job interview, or in forming an opinion about a prospective employee. The area of sex discrimination is also an area where supervisors can avoid problems. The following policies and practices by supervisors have been held illegal because of their impact on women and because they could not be shown to be job related:

1. One cannot ask a job candidate about number and age of children.[20]

2. It is a violation of the law for employers to require pre-employment information on child-care arrangements from female applicants only.[21]

3. Height and weight requirements violate the law when they screen out a disproportionate number of Spanish-surnamed persons, Asian-American, or women, and when the supervisor cannot show these standards to be job related.[22]

4. It may be illegal to refuse to hire, or to discharge, males with long hair where similar restrictions are not imposed on females.[23]

5. State "protective" laws limiting the occupation, hours, and weight that can be lifted by women should be ignored when they deny jobs to women.[24]

[13]EEOC Opinion No. 72-0427.
[14]EEOC Opinion No. 72-1146.
[15]EEOC Opinion No. 72-0599.
[16]EEOC Opinion No. 72-0979.
[17]EEOC Opinion No. 72-1272.
[18]Griggs v. Duke Power Company, *op. cit.*
[19]EEOC Opinion No. 72-0427.
[20]*Affirmative Action and Equal Employment: A Guidebook for Employers*, Vol. I, p. 42.
[21]Phillips v. Martin Marietta Corporation, 400 U. S. 542 (1971).
[22]Castro v. Beecher, 459, F. 2d 725 (1st Cir., 1972).
[23]Donohue v. Shoe Corporation of America, 337 F Supp. 1357 (Consent decree, Calif., 1972).
[24]AT&T Consent Agreement, 1973 EP6, para. 1860.

6. Any written or unwritten policy that excludes applicants or employees from jobs because of pregnancy, or requires pregnant women to stop work at a specified time period is illegal.[25]

7. *EEOC Guidelines*[26] provide that pregnancy, miscarriages, abortion, childbirth, and recovery thereafter, are "temporary disabilities" and should be treated as such for purposes of insurance, sick pay, and job continuation.

8. A supervisor cannot blame his or her failure to take affirmative action on barriers in the union contract.[27]

9. An employer cannot advertise in "male"-"female" ads. Anaconda Aluminum Company was ordered to pay $190,000 in back wages and court costs to 276 women who alleged that the company maintained sex-segregated job classifications.[28]

As you can tell from the preceding items, supervisors are in a very sensitive position, since they come in direct contact with employees and, in many cases, job applicants. Sixty percent of all workers are protected by EEO laws. The EEOC has received 45,000 individual complaints of discrimination and from July 1, 1974 through April, 1975, negotiated settlements granting 44,000 minority workers more than $46 million in back pay.

Two things can help to keep organizations from being charged with discrimination. First, they can develop an affirmative action program as described in this chapter. Second, and equally important, they should expose supervisors to EEOC training in order to help them develop skills in interviewing, rating, and motivating minority and female employees.

Summary: Is There Anything Left?

After reading this chapter, you might be asking yourself if there are any decision-making powers left. Well, the answer is yes. An affirmative action program is designed to bring more qualified applicants into the job pool. It does not mean you cannot discipline a low-producing worker. It only means that you must show that your actions are based on job performance, not on attitudes, speech patterns, dress, mannerisms, age, sex, or color of skin. As a matter of fact, having an effi-

25Green v. Waterford Board of Education, 5 FEP 443 (72-1676, 2nd Cir., 1973).

26Equal Employment Opportunity Commission, *EEOC Guidelines* (Washington: U. S. Government Printing Office, 1970), Section 1604.10.

27Robinson v. Lorillard Corporation, 444 F. 2d 791 (4th Cir., 1971).

28See: *Newsweek, op. cit.,* June 17, 1974, p. 76.

cient affirmative action program should make it easier for supervisors to discharge or discipline any employee without fear of being charged with job bias. Remember also that nothing in the EEOC guidelines requires you to hire or promote unqualified employees. Instead, you are left with the challenge of developing your workforce in such a way that all people are given the chance to become qualified.

Questions for Discussion

1. What does an affirmative action program *not* require you to do?

2. List six ways a supervisor can help in the design and implementation of an affirmative action program.

3. What is the difference between a quota system and an affirmative action plan?

4. What groups does the Civil Rights Act of 1964 protect?

5. What is the EEOC and what are its powers?

6. Define discrimination.

7. How are statistics used when charges of discrimination are made?

8. List the eight steps involved in developing an affirmative action program.

9. List three things a supervisor should avoid asking a job applicant.

Case Incidents

1. Miss Bertha Smith applied for a job with the XYZ Company on May 1, 1975. On July 1, she was called by the supervisor of the night shift and offered a job in quality control. At that time she accepted and began work. She was considered an exceptionally good worker, but two days before her probationary period was up (January 30, 1976) she told Mr. Jones, supervisor of the night shift, that she was pregnant. Because Miss Smith was single, because Mr. Jones felt it would be unsafe under OSHA guidelines, and because the union steward agreed; Mr. Jones fired Miss Smith.

a. Was Mr. Jones legally justified in his actions?

2. Sam Rosen is an Orthodox Jew whose religious practice keeps him from working on Saturday. During the summer months, Sam's supervisor, Ted Smith, is under a lot of pressure to keep production up, which means he must schedule overtime.

The union contract calls for mandatory overtime of up to sixteen hours per month. Smith always schedules the overtime for Saturday, since his wife nags him if he works on Sunday. Most of the men and women under Mr. Smith are indifferent as to which day the overtime is scheduled. Mr. Rosen, however, refuses to work on Saturday and is fired by Mr. Smith.

a. Is Mr. Smith legally justified in his actions?

Constructive Grievance Handling

*J. Brad Chapman**

Chapter Objectives	1. *To identify and explain the four most common areas of employee grievance.*
	2. *To explain the customary steps in a formal grievance procedure.*
	3. *To relate the supervisor's responsibility under each step of the procedure.*
	4. *To classify and illustrate the most common causes of employee grievances.*
	5. *To suggest effective guidelines for constructive grievance handling by the supervisor.*

THE EMPLOYEES of some organizations are represented by a union and contractually guaranteed certain employment rights and procedures. Others are not. In either case, the need for effective and responsible grievance handling is of major importance. Thus, whether established by management, or agreed to in the labor-management contract, the application of grievance procedures is often a major determinant of such critical factors as employee morale and satisfaction, productivity, and labor-management peace. Consequently, it becomes the responsibility of every supervisor to develop specific skills in constructive grievance handling.

*J. Brad Chapman is Associate Professor and Chairman, Management and Organizational Behavior Program, The University of Nebraska at Omaha.

The author would like to thank Dr. Frank S. Forbes, Chairman and Professor, Law and Society Program, The University of Nebraska at Omaha, for his helpful suggestions on an earlier draft of this chapter.

Grievances

The term *grievance* is subject to different interpretations by different individuals. In many instances, the labor contract or the organization's employee handbook will define the term and the formal procedures to be followed in resolving a grievance. For example, some organizations specifically define a formal grievance as "any controversy or dispute arising from the interpretation and application of the provisions in the labor contract." Others define it as "any disagreement between labor (an employee) and management with respect to all conditions of employment," whether the specific area of concern is covered in the labor contract or not. If there is no clause in the contract defining a grievance, a much broader interpretation is usually applied since no restrictions are placed on its meaning.

In light of these various interpretations, some general guidelines to use in differentiating a mere complaint or gripe from a legitimate grievance are suggested:

Violation of Contract

Here, specific provisions in the contract are allegedly violated. For example, a supervisor may assign overtime work to an employee with less seniority than others in the same department when the contract specifically states that all overtime will be offered first to those employees with the most departmental seniority.

Violation of Precedent

Precedents may be based upon an organization's established procedures for handling certain actions in the past, or upon decisions made in resolving previous grievances. Thus, an employee may have a legitimate grievance if given a work assignment based upon a new system of work rotation, when a previous management decision on a similar grievance indicated that work assignments were to be based upon seniority. In addition, it is important to note that precedents may be established by an organization's customary handling of certain actions. For example, if a company has traditionally conducted performance evaluations as a basis for awarding pay increases, employees may have a legitimate grievance if they do not receive a formal evaluation prior to future wage adjustments.

Violation of Law

There is considerable state and federal legislation covering the employer-employee relationship. An employee's perception of a violation of the law by a supervisor or any other member of management is a legitimate cause for filing a formal grievance. Thus, if the supervisor requires an employee to perform work which is considered hazardous and in violation of the Occupational Safety and Health Act, the employee can file a grievance alleging the organization's violation of the act.

Unfair Treatment of Employee

This is perhaps the most difficult area to assess, since it involves the supervisor's and employee's perception of what constitutes unfair or arbitrary treatment. Formal grievance procedures were originally developed to assure employees of some safeguards against arbitrary action. Consequently, it is natural to assume that a legitimate grievance can be initiated because of an employee's judgment that he or she is being treated unfairly. For example, a grievance may be filed charging that the discipline received for being late to work on three different occasions was not fair or justified. In addition, the grievance may charge that the discipline was based on the supervisor's dislike for the employee, rather than the actual offense. In such cases, employees hope that upper management will review the supervisor's disciplinary action and rule in their favor.

In each of the illustrations presented above, it is important to note that the supervisor is usually the focal point of a disagreement. In essence, then, a grievance represents a difference of opinion between employees, or their union representative, and management. How this disagreement is resolved and the supervisor's actions before, during, and after the grievance decision are critical factors affecting the overall labor-management relationship.

Grievance Process

Customary grievance procedures give employees the opportunity to have their grievances reviewed by various levels of management within an organization, and provide them with a system of organizational jurisprudence. In this respect, the emphasis in any grievance procedure is to assure all parties to the contract that complaints will be handled fairly and consistently.

The grievance procedure may be as informal as a statement endorsing an "open door" policy by management, or as formal as a prescribed set of specific steps and time constraints agreed to in the collective bargaining process. As concerns informal or "open door" procedures, the intent is to encourage as much open communication as possible between management and employees in order to establish a friendly, trusting relationship between the two groups. Employees are encouraged to bring differences of opinion to management for resolution; and, although an open door policy emphasizes the resolution of grievances at the first level of supervision, employees are granted the right of appeal to higher levels of management.

Because of a greater need for coordination and consistency between various supervisory units, larger organizations usually find the informal method of resolving grievances inadequate or deficient. Similarly, in unionized organizations, the union's interest in representing its membership in the grievance process requires a more formalized system. These systems vary from organization to organization, but their most typical steps are discussed in the following sections. The supervisor's responsibilities and guidelines for action under each step are presented in subsequent sections of this chapter.

Preliminary Step

Before moving to the first step in the grievance process, the employee discusses the complaint with the supervisor or the union representative. The purpose of this initial dialogue between the supervisor and the employee is to discuss informally the nature of the complaint while attempting to resolve the issue equitably without formally involving other levels of management or the union. If the issue is significant, it is a good idea to keep other supervisors and management informed of the action taken. Clearly, if the complaint is a result of some obvious misunderstanding on the part of either the supervisor or the employee, it can often be resolved through discussion leading to mutual understanding. However, if the employee believes the grievance is legitimate and is not satisfied with the outcome of this informal meeting with the supervisor, the complaint can proceed to the first step in the grievance procedure.

Step One

The first step in most grievance procedures requires that employees, with or without union representation, present complaints to their immediate supervisor. The employee is entitled to union representation at this step and unions typically encourage their membership to involve the steward initially.

The grievance is presented, either orally or in writing, depending upon the contract requirements, and is then discussed between the two parties. After a discussion of the grievance, the supervisor (1) attempts to resolve the issue at that time; (2) indicates a willingness to investigate the issue and report back to the employee within the stipulated time requirements; or (3) states that the grievance does not appear to be justified under the contract or company policy. If not satisfied with the supervisor's decision, the employee can appeal the grievance to the next step in the process.

Step Two

At this step, the issue definitely becomes a formal grievance. It is reduced to writing and involves the union as well as the next higher level of management. The contract will generally specify which union officials and management personnel are to be involved in the hearing. Generally, a chief steward or grievance committee will represent the union and a general foreman or division head will represent the company.

The form and content of the written grievance may vary, but generally it is considered essential to have at least the following information:

1. Grievant identification, including past work record with the company.
2. Management identification, including relationship to the grievant.
3. Other personnel involved and the nature of their involvement.
4. Grievance circumstances, including a complete description of the grievance, when it occurred, how it occurred, where it occurred, and who was involved.
5. Date of filing and subsequent dates for action.
6. Specific contract clause, law, or precedent violated.
7. Statement of customary company procedures or past grievances related to the issue in question.

After an analysis of all data, management is required to submit its decision to the union. If the union or the employee is dissatisfied with the proposed decision, the grievance can be appealed to the third step in the procedure.

Step Three

At this point in the process there is a clear indication of the severity and scope of the issue, and both sides recognize the need for legal counsel and the involvement of higher level officials. Union representation at this step differs between unions, but may include top local union officials and national or international union representatives. The company will generally be represented by the industrial relations department or top management, or both.

After a thorough analysis of the grievance, all background information, related contract provisions, and any other essential material, management makes a final determination. The determination may be to uphold the previous decision made at step two, to offer a compromise decision, or to agree with the union's position. If an impasse occurs at this step, the issue is appealed to the final step in the grievance procedure.

Step Four

The fourth and final step provides for the submission of the grievance to an impartial arbitrator. The function of the arbitrator, who is not bound by precedent but who generally relies on past decisions, is to hear all of the facts surrounding the issue and to make a final decision. Since both parties to the union-management contract have agreed to accept the arbitrator's decision as final and binding, the decision cannot be overruled in most instances and both parties are required to implement the decision.

A few practical points need to be emphasized regarding this discussion of steps in the grievance procedure. First, each step in the procedure must be completed within a prescribed time limit. That is, the supervisor in step one may have only three days to provide the union and the employee with a decision. Any violation of the time limits on the part of the supervisor, without prior consent by both parties, may result in the grievance being settled in favor of the employee regardless of the issue. Second, the burden of proof regarding an alleged infraction by a supervisor rests with the supervisor. Thirdly, the grievance and its appeal should not necessarily be viewed as reflecting supervisory incompetence. From a practical standpoint, the eventual resolution of a grievance may clarify the supervisor's position, build employee confidence in the system, provide employees with an opportunity to ventilate disagreements, and assist other supervisors in resolving similar grievances.

What should be obvious is the critical nature of the supervisor's role in the total grievance procedure. Not only must supervisors determine the merits of a grievance and whether, or how, to resolve the issue before it becomes a formal grievance, but they must also provide a complete and objective summary of the incident for upper management evaluation if it is not resolved at the first step. In short, the supervisor needs to have insight, objective judgment, empathy, knowledge of the contract and work environment, and an analytical mind.

Background Information

To a large extent, the administration of a collective bargaining agreement is the responsibility of first-line supervisors. The critical interface between employees, their elected representatives, and management takes place at the first level of supervision. Consequently, supervisors are extremely influential in creating a favorable work environment, thereby determining, to a great extent, union-management relationships. Hours have been spent at the bargaining table trying to reach agreement on an article proposed by the union or management that was a direct consequence of some inadequate or inappropriate action at the first level of supervision. Some very basic prerequisites for supervisors to consider in their role as management representatives are presented in the following sections.

Know the Contract

Always have a copy of the contract available and have a complete knowledge of those provisions that directly affect the employees' conditions of employment. If the company does not provide formal supervisory training on contract interpretation, be sure to clarify any ambiguities in the contract with the Industrial Relations Department. Step two in the formal grievance procedure is not a good place to learn something about the contract which should have been known earlier.

Know the Grievance Procedure

Be familiar with all steps in the grievance procedure and understand the supervisor's responsibilities under each step. If there is a good possibility that a grievance will be appealed, inform upper levels of management of the nature of the problem. Since the grievance procedure is a part of the total collective bargaining contract, any violation of the procedure itself may result in subsequent union action.

Frequently, a problem arises as to whether supervisors should involve upper management when a question of contract interpretation arises for the first time; or, whether they should merely attempt to be reasonable and fair in their interpretations. It is understandable that some supervisors are fearful of appearing unable to act independently. However, where serious issues are discussed fully with upper management, it has been found that problems involving animosity between the union and management have been avoided, issues have been resolved more rapidly, and supervisors have been viewed as alert, competent, and sensitive to their organization's long-range objectives.

Know Subordinates and Union Representatives

An understanding of the individuals potentially involved in the grievance procedure will assist supervisors in evaluating complaints and discussing possible courses of action. As will be pointed out later, many grievances are caused by interpersonal relationships or personal concerns that do not specifically relate to the contract. Knowing these relationships or anxieties beforehand may save considerable time and energy later.

Know the Job Requirements and Conditions of Employment

Many employees, unions, and courts view the job description as a formal contract between the employer and the employee. Thus any deviation from the job description required by a supervisor may provide the basis for a formal grievance. In this respect, the supervisor is not totally protected by the clause in many job descriptions which states, ". . . and all other work assigned by the supervisor." This clause tends to be interpreted very narrowly, and supervisors who do not know the job descriptions in their units are asking for an embarassing situation that will probably result in an adverse ruling by an independent arbitrator.

Know Past Grievance Decisions and Company Procedures

Although each grievance is unique, the principal issue may have been the subject of previous grievances. An investigation of previous grievances will, therefore, give some insight into how a current issue might be handled. Supervisors must also recognize that deviations from past company practices, no matter how informal, may be cause for a legitimate grievance. In fact, it is not an overstatement to say that there is an element of "contract writing" in the resolution of every grievance.

Similarly, recognize that decisions made now will influence subsequent decisions in related areas.

Potential Causes of Grievances

A grievance generally results from some form of employee dissatisfaction. Certain factors in the work environment may create a feeling of dissatisfaction on the part of the employee that, if not corrected by management, will lead to the filing of a formal grievance. An important distinction to make at this point is that the mere existence of employee dissatisfaction is not a grievance, but the continued existence of such dissatisfaction will more than likely result in an increased number of formal grievances. Consequently, an important function of the supervisor is to identify sources or causes of employees' dissatisfaction, minimize or eliminate such causes, and develop systems that monitor employees' attitudes and encourage open communications.

Few issues have not been used as grounds for some grievance. Thus, no matter how trivial, ridiculous or ill-founded an issue might appear to others, some employee will consider it to have as much merit as a clear violation of the contract. It is possible, however, to identify some of the most common causes of employee grievances. Usually, they are related to one or more of the following broad areas: Organizational factors, supervision, problem employees, and union activism.

Organizational Factors

Among other things, organizational factors include such conditions as highly structured jobs, inadequate or ambiguous job descriptions, inadequate grievance procedures, mismatches between employee qualifications and job requirements, and company policies on promotion, discipline, or other conditions of employment not covered in the contract. Basically, *any factor in the employee's work environment that contributes to frustration or increases an employee's level of anxiety is a potential cause of grievances.* In other words, an employee may be motivated to file a grievance because of some frustration or anxiety experienced on the job. However, the grievance may not be related to the actual cause of the frustration or anxiety.

For example, a supervisor was informed that a formal grievance was being processed regarding the classification of an employee's job. After lengthy discussions with the employee, it was discovered that the complaint was actually not initiated because of the current job classification, but because of the employee's dissatisfaction with the highly routine nature of the job. Provisions were made to rotate the employee between a couple of different jobs, and the major source of the irritant was minimized. In another case, management used the clause in the job description which stated, ". . . and all other duties assigned by the supervisor," to expand job responsibilities without a commensurate change in job classification. A grievance was filed and the ambiguous job description was clarified.

Supervision

Since supervisors represent the primary link between management and employees, a high degree of personal interaction is required in all supervisory positions. Consequently, it is not difficult to visualize the supervisor as a major cause of employee grievances. The nature of the grievance may be directed at a supervisor personally, or may result from the relationship between supervisors and subordinates. Both situations occur with some degree of regularity.

The first situation occurs when some supervisory action is perceived as being unjust by an employee, or when a supervisor violates the contract or a past precedent. Although this situation can result from an honest difference of opinion regarding the interpretation of certain contract provisions or past actions, it can also stem from a lack of familiarity with the rules and regulations governing a supervisor's actions. Differences of opinion can be expected and may actually be beneficial in some instances, but an ignorance of the contract, legal procedures, or company policies is not healthy.

Grievances resulting from negative relationships between supervisors and subordinates eventually involve the issue of "fair" treatment. But why is there a question of fair treatment? In looking at many conflicts between supervisors and subordinates, one can identify major supervisory weaknesses as poor communication, inadequate or inappropriate leadership, a failure to consider employees' viewpoints, or an inequitable handling of employees' problems. In other words, a supervisor's behavior can create an antagonistic environment, which breeds dissatisfaction and eventual grievances.

Whatever the cause, the consequences are the same: Considerable time, effort, and money are spent on situations that could have been avoided through more effective supervision. In addition, many unions have negotiated contract changes as a direct result of poor supervision. Lawyers have a saying, "Hard cases make bad law." This has special application to grievance handling. If a grievance results from great injustice or unfairness, it may cause the union to insist on a clause in the contract that will severely restrict a generally desirable management practice. Consequently, the actions of one supervisor can sometimes result in new contract provisions that limit the management prerogatives of all supervisors.

Problem Employees

Any organization will have individuals who, by their very nature, are negative, antagonistic, or continuously dissatisfied. These employees can file grievances themselves, or can create enough unrest within the work environment to cause others to initiate grievances. How a supervisor reacts to this type of employee is extremely important.

In one grievance, for example, a member of the union's wage and benefit committee, who was known by management to be a "complainer," asked the supervisor for three hours of personal leave. Normally, it is understood that such requests are granted solely at the discretion of the supervisor. In this case, the employee started cleaning up an hour before the three-hour leave was to start. He was confronted by the supervisor who charged him with taking too much time away from the job, indicating that, in essence, the whole afternoon had been "wasted." A verbal exchange followed with the supervisor rescinding the previous approval of the leave and scheduling the employee on a job.

Although the supervisor's actions would appear to have been legitimate under the contract, the employee was able to stir up enough unrest and union support that a grievance was filed. An indirect result of the grievance was that the union proposed, and was successful in negotiating, an article in the contract that severely limited management's discretionary authority in granting personal leaves.

Union Activism

Unions may initiate formal grievances to solicit rank and file support by pointing out ineffective supervision to top management. However, a more common reason for filing formal grievances has been to clarify ambiguous contract clauses. There is sometimes a degree of ambiguity in a particular contract article, especially with respect to the administration of the article. Thus the grievance procedure may prove to be effective in expediting the clarification of an article. This is particularly true if the union believes a favorable ruling will result if the issue goes to arbitration.

By now, it should be obvious that grievances can have either positive or negative consequences, depending upon how they are handled initially by the supervisor and, subsequently, in the grievance process itself. If ineffectively handled, some of the negative consequences can include (1) costly arbitration or even litigation; (2) considerable union-management strife, even if the issue is relatively minor; and (3) various forms of employee aggression. Any of these consequences can adversely affect the labor-management relationship and conceivably result in lower operating efficiency.

Starting with the first line supervisor and moving through the various steps in the process, an effectively administered grievance procedure can yield many positive outcomes for an organization. Some of the more obvious benefits include: (1) Improved communication; (2) an identification of issues to be covered in contract negotiations; (3) the reduction of employees' anxieties; and (4) supervisory development. In short, constructive grievance handling reassures employees that the system indeed works. The final decision on a grievance, whether in the employee's favor or not, at least reinforces the attitude that avenues do exist for constructive problem solving. Similarly, whatever the outcome, mature supervisors should use the experience to improve their own managerial competencies.

Constructive Grievance Handling

As mentioned earlier, most actual or potential causes of employee grievances are related in one way or another to supervisory effectiveness. For example, there may be differences of opinion between supervisors and employees; employees may feel a supervisor has treated them unfairly; or a supervisor may be unable to handle employee dissatisfaction before it leads to a formal grievance. In any event, constructive grievance handling is essential and the following guidelines can help supervisors become more effective in this important area.

Developing the Proper Environment

Constructive grievance handling involves the ability to recognize, diagnose, and correct causes of potential employee dissatisfaction before they become formal grievances. That is, supervisors must be sensitive to issues, working conditions, and attitudes that affect the behavior of employees on the job. This sensitivity can be developed by creating an environment of open communication that stresses the identification and resolution of problems. Creating an environment of this type is no easy task, particularly if past experience indicates that supervisors are unwilling to listen and offer suggestions for resolving employees' problems. Four critical factors can be identified and used in developing a better understanding of employees and in improving the communication process.[1] These factors are timing, listening, evaluating, and acting.

Timing. The time to deal with an employee's problem is when it is initially presented. This does not imply that a problem must be resolved immediately. Instead, the supervisor should spend some time discussing the issue when it is initially presented by an employee. A few minutes spent clarifying the issue immediately may save hours of work later. If the supervisor cannot possibly talk to an employee at the time a problem is presented, a time should be scheduled and a meeting held later in the day.

Listening. Make the employee the center of attention by actively listening to the problem. Do not argue or debate. Provide ample time for hearing the employee's side of the issue. Exercise restraint and attempt to clarify issues without arousing defensiveness on the part of the employee. In short, avoid personalities and stick to the problem at hand. Many times, an initial discussion between the supervisor and the employee will resolve an issue without further action being required. Remember, if the supervisor is unwilling to listen, others will, other employees, the union, or other supervisors.

Evaluating. Each time an employee interacts with the supervisor there is some reason for the interaction and, in the eyes of the employee, the reason is usually important. Therefore, do not prejudge the issue or the employee, but evaluate the problem based upon the facts presented. Such objectivity is critical in reinforcing the employee's belief that open communication does, in fact, exist.

Acting. After a thoughtful evaluation of an issue, the supervisor must initiate some form of action. Either immediate steps should be taken to resolve the issue, or the employee should be told when to expect an answer. The action taken may be quite simple or highly involved. In either case, action lets employees know that their complaints are being honestly considered. On the other hand, inaction by the supervisor not only irritates the existing problem, but can lead to more complaints in the future. *Thus, timely and objective action can be the supervisor's most effective method of communication.*

[1] A. Selden Robinson, "It's a Grievance . . . Or Is It?," *The Personnel Administrator* 19, no. 6, (1974): 28–31.

Beyond the four basic guidelines mentioned above, constructive grievance handling is also affected by such supervisory practices as:

1. Dealing with each employee as an individual.
2. Respecting all employees and treating them in a dignified manner.
3. Recognizing superior performance, and giving credit to any employee who makes a good suggestion.
4. Seeking and understanding the employee's point of view when a problem develops.
5. Being alert to possible sources of employee irritation.
6. Taking prompt and effective action to eliminate the causes of employee irritation.
7. Properly training employees to do their work, especially new employees.
8. Issuing clear orders, giving reasons why they are necessary, and making sure they are understood.
9. Administering the discipline objectively, equitably, and consistently.
10. Enforcing company rules consistently.
11. Avoid favoritism.
12. Cooperating with the shop steward in eliminating causes of grievances.[2]

Admittedly, the factors listed above are incomplete. However, they represent some of the major considerations for preventing employee grievances. In addition, three other supervisory practices deserve special attention.

Knowledge of Contract Articles, Laws, and Precedents. Employer-employee relationships are always influenced by both internal and external constraints. Work assignments, for example, may be influenced by such factors as the union's seniority provision, Equal Employment Opportunity Commission guidelines, and the company's policy on job rotation. Consequently, what may appear to be a fairly straightforward decision must often be preceded by a thorough analysis of the various legal requirements and company policies affecting the action.

One of the major responsibilities of every supervisor is to have a complete working knowledge of the union contract, the various state and federal laws affecting supervisory actions, and any previous company decisions or existing policies that relate to decisions made at the first level of supervision. Some organizations do not have formal training programs designed to cover the union contract and other legal

[2]Maurice S. Trotta and Walter A. Bishop, *Grievance Handling for Foremen.* (Ann Arbor: Bureau of Labor Relations, Graduate School of Business Administration, Univer-

facets of the supervisory job. In such cases, supervisors should make arrangements to meet with members of the industrial relations department or other managers to clarify their rights and responsibilities under the contract and to discuss interpretations of various contract clauses. In any event, supervisors are responsible for knowing the contract, not only to avoid possible grievances, but also to understand the procedures for processing grievances. To meet the minimum requirements for achieving a necessary level of understanding, supervisors should:

1. Study the contract. It is not a mystery novel that can be read rapidly. Spend considerable time studying the total contract, giving special attention to those provisions directly affecting the superior-subordinate relationship.

2. Review company policies. Since some aspects of the employer-employee relationship are not covered by specific contract provisions, review relevant company policies with other members of management.

3. Review past grievance decisions. Meet with other supervisors or check company records regarding past grievances.

4. Be knowledgeable about contract negotiations. Know what issues have been brought up by the union in past negotiations and study the content of those issues.

5. Study special materials prepared by management. Many organizations prepare special handouts on operating procedures covering areas subject to governmental regulations.

Discussions with Other Supervisors. Since one of the major purposes of either labor contracts or formalized company policies is to provide for some degree of equity and consistency in the treatment of employees, supervisors can benefit from sharing common experiences. A complaint by an employee in Department B may be similar to that filed by another employee in a different department. How the supervisor in Department B handles the complaint can often be improved by discussing the issue with the other departmental supervisor. In other words, by sharing common experiences supervisors can develop a better understanding of the contract and the nature of employee relations.

Discussions with Union Officials. A good working relationship between the supervisor and the union steward can be effective in identifying potential grievances as well as in handling grievances once they have been formally initiated by an employee. Most unions encourage their stewards to investigate a member's complaint thoroughly before any action is formally taken. If the steward and the supervisor have maintained a good working relationship, many complaints can be handled informally through an investigation and correction of their causes. Thus the steward is an important communication link between the union, employees, and management.

Handling the Grievance

Once a formal grievance has been presented to the supervisor, a definite course of action must be followed which accomplishes two basic objectives: (1) The grievance is equitably resolved; and (2) the cause of the grievance is determined and corrected. Accomplishing these two objectives requires a process composed of the following basic activities: (1) Investigation; (2) evaluation; (3) implementation; and (4) follow-up.

Investigation.   Once a complaint is formally presented to a supervisor, it represents a significant issue in the eyes of the grievant and cannot be treated lightly. Although the employee initiates the grievance, the burden of proof regarding the specific issue rests with the supervisor. Consequently, the need for objective data gathering and the separation of fact from opinion is critically important in initial discussions between the employee, or the steward and the supervisor.

The following points are important considerations during the initial presentation of a grievance:

- Give the grievant a good hearing. Don't argue.
- Be an active listener by asking questions, giving full and undivided attention, not interrupting, and encouraging a full discussion of the issue by the grievant.
- Take complete notes.
- Repeat your understanding of the issue, as presented.
- Attempt to determine the causes of the grievance as well as the nature of the grievance itself.
- Ask questions to uncover specific details.
- Don't give the appearance of having reached a conclusion on the issue before you have all of the facts.

In discussing the issue with the employee, be sure specific answers are received to the following questions:

- What actually happened?
- Where did it happen?
- What should have happened?
- When did it happen? (Be exact.)
- Who was involved? Any observers?
- Why did the problem develop? What were the circumstances surrounding the incident?

At the end of the meeting with the employee, reinforce a cordial, supportive relationship and indicate when a response to the grievance can be expected. Do not imply agreement or disagreement, but indicate a concern for resolving the issue. Remember, there may be a definite time limit within which the response must be given. Avoid hasty decisions, but make every attempt to get back to the employee as soon as possible.

Once the specific facts of an incident have been determined, investigate other areas that may influence any decision on the incident. This investigation should include a thorough analysis of the contract, past company practices, the employee's work record, and other related job information, previous grievance decisions, and any legal considerations that may have a bearing on the incident. This information can be gathered from company records and through discussions with other supervisors and labor relations personnel.

Without question, the investigative stage of constructive grievance handling is critical. Although it is neither intended nor encouraged, the supervisor should assume that the grievance will be appealed to subsequent steps in the grievance procedure, perhaps all the way to an arbitration hearing. Obviously, the final resolution of the incident will be greatly influenced by the nature and extent of the information gathered by the supervisor.

Evaluation. After all information related to a grievance has been accumulated, the supervisor must evaluate the merits of the case and identify possible alternative actions. It is important at this stage of the process to evaluate both the interpersonal considerations as well as the legalistic considerations. The overriding factor should be the formal contract and its application to the employee-employer relationship; however, there may be a difference between the literal interpretation of the contract and its intent. Therefore, depending upon the nature of the grievance, it is advisable to discuss contract interpretations with other members of management, the union steward, and the company's legal counsel (if appropriate).

In evaluating the issue and possible courses of action, the supervisor should attempt to answer some very basic questions. Is the incident a clear violation of the contract, law, or past practice? What effect will the decision have on other members of management? Will the decision be accepted by the employee as fair and just under the provisions of the contract? What is the cost, feasibility, contribution to objectives, and possible side effect of the decision?

Implementation. After evaluating all pertinent information, a course of action must be selected and communicated to the employee, the union steward, and management. This is normally a sensitive process, and care must be taken to present the decision as objectively and clearly as possible. Anticipate the employee's reaction and develop a strategy that shows empathy with the employee's situation. Explain the reasoning behind, and justification for, the decision, and encourage an appropriate discussion of the issues.

How the decision is presented to the employee or the steward, or both may determine the final outcome of the grievance. At the same time, it may affect subsequent relationships between the supervisor and the employee. If the employee's position is upheld, take immediate action to correct the cause of the grievance and initiate actions to minimize similar grievances in the future. View such decisions as providing opportunities to develop an even better working relationship and, by all means, do not view them as situations where you lost face or respect. If the decision is in favor of management, provide the employee with an opportunity to save face. Remember, the supervisor's working relationship with an employee will continue long after a grievance has been resolved.

Follow-up. Although investigation, evaluation, and implementation are extremely important to the initial grievance, the follow-up process determines the ultimate effectiveness of a decision. The follow-up process is concerned with two main objectives: (1) Implementing and monitoring the original decision; and (2) maintaining employee morale.

Review all of the information collected in the investigation and evaluation stages and initiate positive action to avoid similar occurrences. The formal grievance involves a communication process that may bring to light a number of potential problems not specifically mentioned in the original complaint. Consequently, follow-up strategies should go beyond the original issue and address themselves to the total work environment. In this respect, constructive grievance handling involves not only the resolution of a current problem, but more importantly, the initiation of positive action to eliminate the cause of similar grievance in the future.

Summary

The formal grievance procedure is designed to provide a system for handling problems between labor and management. The emphasis in the procedure is to provide some assurances that problems will be handled fairly and consistently, and that all parties involved will have an opportunity to present their side of an issue. Thus constructive grievance handling involves maintaining equity within the system, developing methods for assessing potential grievances, and initiating positive action before problems become formal grievances.

Complaints brought to the attention of the supervisor will normally emphasize one of the following: (1) Violation of the contract; (2) violation of law; (3) violation of past precedent; or (4) unfair employee treatment. Initially, the supervisor must determine if there is, in fact, a grievance. At the same time it must be recognized that something precipitated the employee's actions. Immediate action on the part of the supervisor involves active communication with the employee in an attempt to understand the total issue. Encouraging and maintaining an atmosphere of open communication requires that the supervisor be particularly attentive to such factors as timing, listening, evaluating, and acting.

Once a formal grievance is filed, the supervisor must become a "problem solver." This involves a distinct process of investigation, evaluation, implementation, and follow-up. The emphasis of the process is two-fold: (1) The grievance must be resolved to the satisfaction of both parties; and (2) positive action must be initiated to correct the cause (s) of the grievance.

Without question, the supervisor occupies one of the most critical positions in management. Consequently, the ability of all supervisors to handle grievances constructively can have a major impact on employee morale and satisfaction, productivity, and labor-management relations. To evaluate your effectiveness in this area, complete the "Checklist for Constructive Grievance Handling" included in Appendix A of this chapter.

Questions for Discussion

1. Identify, explain, and give an example of the four common causes of employee grievances.

2. What is the supervisor's total responsibility in the grievance handling process?

3. If an employee comes to you with an idea, complaint, or suggestion, how should you react to foster a better climate of open communications?

4. Review a labor contract having a formal grievance procedure. What are the supervisor's responsibilities under the procedure? If they are not specifically identified, what do you assume the responsibilities to be?

5. Once a formal grievance has been filed, what steps should the supervisor go through in resolving the dispute? Explain each step and list some of the critical actions involved in each.

6. What is your reaction to the statement "Approach every grievance as though it will be appealed to successive steps in the grievance process and eventually to arbitration?" How does this influence your behavior in the grievance process?

7. What is constructive grievance handling?

8. What essential questions must be answered in order to understand fully the nature of an employee's complaint?

Case Incident

1. After counting his pay and realizing he did not get the increase he had anticipated, Bill Jones went charging into the office of Frank Sims, his supervisor, demanding an explanation, "What's the big idea cheating me out of a five-dollar raise?" Jones hollered. "You know damn well I'm guaranteed that raise automatically. If you don't straighten it out immediately, I'm going to cause a lot of trouble for you with the union."

"When I gave you the third warning for tardiness two weeks ago, I told you that I was disappointed with your poor work attitudes and would not recommend you for any type of wage increase," Sims replied sharply. "Besides, I consider your current behavior to be insubordinate. If you don't straighten up you'll be looking at a 3-day vacation *without* pay."

After a few moments of heated debate, Jones left Sims's office, complained to a number of his colleagues about the company and Sims, and walked straight over to the shop steward. "Well, he's done it again," Jones told the steward. "Sims just discriminated against me and this time I think I've got him right where I want him." Jones explained to the steward what had happened and the two of them read the labor contract and agreed it was a legitimate grievance.

Jones and the steward went up to Sims and the steward stated, "The contract specifically states here on page 24 that after six months of continuous service in a labor grade, employees will receive a progressive pay increase to bring them to the mid-point of that wage grade. Jones has been in grade 0–8 for six months, and he's entitled to an automatic increase. No ifs, ands, or buts about it."

"Wait a minute," replied Sims. "A progressive increase is based upon the employee's progress on the job. Because of Bill's tardiness record and poor work attitudes, I've made the decision that he's not entitled to the increase."

A formal grievance was filed the next day.

a. Is there cause here for a formal grievance?

b. Could the grievance have been avoided?

c. How should Sims prepare for the grievance? Be specific.

Appendix A

CHECKLIST FOR CONSTRUCTIVE GRIEVANCE HANDLING

	Yes	No
I. Background Preparation		
A. Do you have a current copy of the labor contract?	___	___
B. Have you carefully read the contract?	___	___
C. Have you attended supervisory training sessions on contract administration?	___	___
D. Have you clarified ambiguous clauses with upper management?	___	___
E. Do you know the steps in the grievance procedure and your responsibilities under each step?	___	___
F. Are you aware of the interpersonal relations in your area and sensitive to potential grievance issues?	___	___
G. Are you familiar with job responsibilities and job descriptions in your area?	___	___
H. Have you reviewed past grievance decisions and all relevant company policies?	___	___
I. Do you know the union representative in your area?	___	___
II. Initial Interaction with Employees		
A. Do you take time to deal with an employee's problem immediately or within a reasonable time?	___	___
B. Are you an active listener?	___	___
C. Do you let employees express their points of view without interrupting?	___	___
D. Do you remain objective during the dialogue with an employee?	___	___
E. Are you sensitive to the needs of employees as well as the strict rules of the organization?	___	___
F. Do you deal with employees as individuals?	___	___
G. Do you initiate immediate action relative to the issue?	___	___
H. Do you follow through with your decision?	___	___

YES   NO

III. First Step in Grievance Procedure
(Investigation)

A. Do you take complete and accurate notes during discussions
with the employee?

B. Do you ask questions and seek clarification on certain
issues to improve your understanding of the issues?

C. Do you remain objective and not give the appearance of
having prejudged the outcome?

D. Have you attempted to determine the causes of the grievance
as well as the grievance itself?

E. Are specific answers given to questions involving the who, what,
where, when, and why of the grievance?

(Evaluation)

A. Have you discussed the issue with other supervisors
or members of upper management?

B. If the problem involves a major issue, have you consulted
with the industrial relations department or appropriate
legal counsel?

C. Are you aware of the intent of the contract as well
as the literal interpretation?

D. Is the incident a clear violation of contract, law,
or precedent?

E. Have you analyzed the grievance with respect to its effect on
subsequent management decisions and its
effect on the employee?

(Implementation)

A. Are you sensitive in communicating decisions to
employees?

B. Do you use the grievance procedure as an opportunity
to improve your own effectiveness as a supervisor?

C. Do you explain the reasoning behind your decisions and
encourage employees to discuss issues with you?

D. Do you follow through with your decisions and attempt
to prevent subsequent grievances?

E. Do you create an environment of active communications?

*The above items are designed to direct the supervisor in constructive grievance
handling. If you answer "no" to any of the questions, you may be losing the
opportunity to improve your effectiveness in handling employee grievances.*

Personal Management Development

W. A. Meinhart*

Chapter Objectives	1. *To provide the overall framework and basic knowledge necessary to develop a plan for personal management development.*
	2. *To emphasize the challenge of management.*
	3. *To provide an understanding of management development and its technology.*
	4. *To portray the professional nature of management.*
	5. *To examine the importance of career planning in personal management development.*
	6. *To provide guidelines for career planning.*

Do you remember the parable of the talents? The Bible tells us that a wealthy man about to travel to a far country divided up his money for safekeeping among his servants. To one he gave five talents, to another two, and to another one. Then he left. The one who received the five talents invested them and doubled their value. The one who received two talents also was able to double their value through wise investment. But the poor servant who had received one talent had buried the money and could show no increase in value. When the wealthy man returned he asked for an accounting. He was delighted with the two who had invested the money and increased its value. But he was angry with the servant who had buried the money. He took the money from him and sent him away.[1]

*Wayne A. Meinhart is Professor and Head, Department of Administrative Sciences, College of Business Administration, Oklahoma State University.
[1]Matthew 25: 14–30.

There is a lesson here for personal management development as well as the management of an investment portfolio. We must "invest" our individual talents wisely in order to make the best return on our opportunities. A few managers doubtless get ahead by luck or sheer outstanding talent. But this is a poor gamble against the odds. Most of us have to work very hard at developing ourselves to justify our present positions and to qualify for advancement. Even organization-sponsored development programs are not the answer. Management development is basically a "do-it-yourself" project.

The Challenge of Managing

By now the challenge of managing is evident from the materials in preceding chapters. Management is an exciting, dynamic, challenging profession that requires the very best that we have to offer. The rate of change in the managerial environment is accelerating year by year. Yet, the accountability to produce results remains an essential constant for every manager. One way of analyzing the managerial role is to break out functions, such as planning, organizing, coordinating, and controlling. You are already familiar with this approach to the management process. Another way is to view management as involving a mix of certain critical abilities. For example, all management positions involve to some degree the management of people, time, resources, organizational environments, change, and decisions. The extent to which you may need these abilities depends upon the job, the level of management, and the organization.

Key Management Functions

The logical place to begin is with an understanding of what is required of the manager. Briefly, let us examine some of the key management functions.

Managing People

Many people think they know how to manage others, but only a few are really good at it. Managing people is typically the first responsibility of the supervisor. The ability to develop good human relations skills is essential. Terms like *understanding, sensitivity of group and individual differences,* and *awareness* help to define the human relations dimension of management. Space does not permit a detailed examination of these and other "people managing" topics here, though you will find them covered in other chapters. Such topics would include motivation, assessment of subordinates, interviewing and counseling, leadership, delegation of authority, and communication. It is also vital that the manager be skilled at using goals, objectives and priorities as targets for individual and group performance and as keys to performance evaluation. Management systems such as MBO—Management by Objectives—may be extremely helpful in tying it all together.

Managing Resources

Managing financial and other resources is an important part of every manager's job. Knowledge of budgeting, resource allocation strategies and techniques, planning aids, control techniques, and program evaluation is essential. Allocating scarce resources among alternative uses requires both analytical ability and experience. A more extensive treatment of these topics is found elsewhere in the book.

Managing Time

Time is an important resource. It is easy to overlook the need to plan and control the use of time, and to allocate it as a scarce resource. Some useful guidelines in managing time are as follows: Assess time-absorbing (wasting) activities; establish your priorities in the use of time; develop a plan or schedule for allocating time in accordance with your priorities; and try to avoid interruptions and deviations from the plan. Some studies suggest that managers frequently have inaccurate pictures of the way they spend their time. The lesson is obvious: We must spend some time in order to save time. A study of the way we use time is an important step in the development of a plan to help us use time most effectively.

This is an important subject that can easily take more space than we have available. The literature contains some useful sources on managing time effectively. You should consult them. Part of the time problem is similar to that of developing a career plan. Managers need to know themselves and their goals, assess their use of time, build a plan, and develop feedback and control points. They need to use tools, like time logs, to help assess their use of time wisely and to identify time-wasting activities (and people). They need to take action to keep from being overwhelmed by the "too much to do in too little time" syndrome.

In the end, managers must manage themselves effectively before they can be successful at managing others. Managers working far too many hours a week because they "don't have enough time" are, in the long run, creating problems for themselves and their organizations. It also raises questions as to how effective they are as managers. Herman Krannert, then board chairman of Inland Container Corporation, once stated: "When I hear a man talk about how hard he works, and how he hasn't taken a vacation in five years, and how seldom he sees his family, I am almost certain that this man will not succeed in the creative aspects of business...and...most of the important things that have to be done are the result of creative acts."[2]

Managing Change

Rates of change in the managerial and organizational environment are increasing. New products, new problems, new research, government involvement, unions, consumer groups, environmental protection groups, changing economic conditions, and many other factors contribute to the increasing rates of change. Such environmental "turbulence" brings increasing uncertainty and frustration to the managerial job. Many managers are finding that the approach and techniques appropriate to management in the "steady state" are no longer adequate when conditions of rapid change are encountered. It is frequently necessary for managers to develop their ability to manage under conditions of change. In extreme cases we speak of "crisis management" as a necessary adaptation.

To put it briefly, most organizations need innovative, flexible managers. Appropriate study and experience can help us become more effective managers of dynamic as well as steady-state conditions.

Managing Environments

With increasing environmental change, managers must become more sensitive to environmental factors and more capable of managing complex, interdependent constituencies. Many opportunities to manage organizational environments are reserved for executive levels or special management positions, and are not normally considered part of the supervisor's responsibility. Yet supervisors may need to prepare themselves for the day when they do take on an environmental responsibility.

[2]Herman C. Krannert, "The Time Wasters," *The Forum*, Spring, 1969, p. 21. Also cited in R. Alex Mackenzie, *The Time Trap* (New York, 1975), p. 8.

Making Decisions

Managers make decisions about people, time, financial and other resources, change, and environments. Decision making is probably the single most important and pervasive managerial function. Decision making not only involves the ability to analyze decision factors in the light of goals in order to make the most appropriate choice, but it also involves the implementation of the decision in the most effective manner. Nobody becomes a super decision maker just by studying books, but some study and experience will surely help. Assess the decisions you have recently made, and try to evaluate your "batting average." This is a good way to improve decision making and learn a little humility.

What kind of superman does it take to do all these things well? Obviously, many supervisors do not do them all equally well. Some do not have to, for the mix of required management functions varies with different organizations and different levels of organizations. But supervisors should see the range of management functions that may be required of them as they study the problems and the potential of their own management development.

What Is Management Development?

Many of us have had firsthand experience with the managerial manpower shortage. Some organizations have experienced serious bottleneck problems in their ability to expand or improve effectiveness because of a lack of management talent. Many business, government, education, health, social, and service organizations are responding to this shortage of managers by using management development programs. Yet there is confusion over what management development really is.

A typical definition of management development emphasizes improving management performance by enhancing skills, sharing information, or conditioning attitudes. The management literature contains many such definitions. They are representative of traditional thinking about management development. They are useful and appropriate for many purposes, but do not go far enough. They describe mainly the kind of development which is based on traditional behaviorist learning theory. In this concept, man's behavior can be controlled or shaped through the process of reinforcement. But there is another kind of development, a type of psychological maturation described by psychologist Abraham Maslow, where normal psychological maturation provides a growth impulse in individuals, causing them to want to grow and learn.

Given reasonable opportunities for progress toward self-actualization, the manager or potential manager will be motivated to pursue action leading to self-development. Viewed in this way, management development becomes a part of the program by which individuals realize their own potential. It is not something done to us, but a process of individual growth. It is influenced by the total work environment of the supervisor, and what is learned from that environment. It involves the interaction of people, their jobs, and their managers. Individual development, then, results in the acquisition of new knowledge, skills, and attitudes in a planned and orderly manner. It is intended to improve present job performance as well as prepare the person for advancement into more responsible positions.

Personal management development should become a way of life within an organization. Supervisors must seek to make the most of their experience and their opportunities to attain maximum personal development. They must develop enthusiasm for and commitment to their own personal growth. Our view of management development is that of self-development. The organization has responsibilities for management development, of course, but this chapter seeks to emphasize what individual supervisors should do to help themselves.

What Should the Organization Do for the Manager?

Through appraisal, testing, counseling, and performance evaluation, supervisors should seek to develop their strengths and work to eliminate their weaknesses. The organization must be helpful and supportive. Specifically, it should provide the following:

1. A climate from top to bottom of the organization that encourages development. This means more than just lip service. It means actual support, encouragement, and enthusiasm for management development.
2. A stimulating environment.
3. Opportunities that encourage "trying" and forgive "mistakes" (at least understandable mistakes).
4. Clear and frequent feedback about success and failure and development needs.
5. Sufficient freedom of action to promote learning.
6. An appropriate incentive to stimulate peak performance.
7. Communication of objectives.
8. Consultative management.

Many organizations provide these advantages. Some go further and maintain extensive management development programs, including short courses, tuition refund programs for employees who undertake university study, and so on.

The Manager as a Professional

Management development should lead managers to become more effective in their jobs and more professional in their values. There are four key elements in professionalization: Expertise, or the need for specialized knowledge and skills; autonomy, or the right to decide how the duties are to be performed; commitment to the profession; and responsibility to society for maintaining professional standards of work.[3] All managers do not necessarily regard themselves as professionals, or see the importance of becoming a professional. But aspiring managers should consider the advantages of developing themselves as professionals. There is no question that management in most organizations is becoming increasingly professional. This is a process that should be encouraged.

Personal Characteristics in Management Development

What personal qualities are important to future success as a manager? Robert Townsend, in his amusing book *Up The Organization,* states his fundamental requirements for managerial success: Humility; respect for people on the firing line; deep understanding of the nature of the business and the kind of people who can enjoy themselves making it prosper; respect from way down the line; a demonstrated record of industry, loyalty, judgment, fairness, and honesty under pressure.[4] In addition, supervisors with high managerial potential usually demonstrate superior ability to master new assignments and quickly make a contribution to the operation. They initiate and implement improvements within their spheres of influence. They see the big picture and can relate their contribution to the whole. They grow in their ability to handle responsibility.

Certain skills are required of potential managers. These include the ability to withstand pressure, job knowledge, the ability to appraise oneself and others, analytical skills, and communication skills. Robert Katz has developed a three-skill approach to executive selection. Successful managers need three basic skills: Technical, human, and con-

[3]George Strauss, "Professionalism and Occupational Associations," *Industrial Relations* 2 (May, 1963): 8–9.

[4]Robert Townsend, *Up The Organization* (New York: Alfred A. Knopf, 1970), p. 71.

ceptual. Technical skill involves proficiency in a specific kind of activity, particularly one involving methods, processes, procedures, or techniques. Human skill is the manager's ability to work effectively as a group member and to build cooperative effort within the team. Conceptual skill involves the ability to see the enterprise as a whole. It includes recognizing how the various functions of the organization depend on one another, and how changes in any one part affect all the others.[5]

Some of the personal characteristics important to managerial success are skills that may be obtained through training and experience. Others are personal qualities that may have long-run potential for development, but can't be "reached" in some specific training program. Still others are deeply imbedded in the personality of the individual. One example of the latter is self-image. An accurate and objective perception of self is important to every manager. Awareness of self-image, capacity to be a self-starter, and maintenance of self-control are all key elements for the successful manager. These are qualities that individuals can enhance in themselves through self-study and the creative use of feedback.

The Technology of Management Development

Management development requires an "intensive" technology. That is, a variety of techniques may be used in order to achieve change, but the selection, combination, and order of application are determined by feedback from participants. Formal management development programs should be custom-fitted to each person.

Our emphasis is on career planning and self-development, not on company-sponsored management development programs. However, we need to look briefly at such programs in order to understand them and take advantage of them when available. Management development techniques are broadly broken down into two types, group methods and individual methods. Group methods include sensitivity (or other laboratory) training, role playing, case discussions, business "games," and team building. Individual methods include job rotation, coaching, understudy training, lectures, special assignments, self-study (especially through reading, programmed learning, and video-tape replay study), and "autonomy" (do-it-yourself) training. Company management development programs are normally aimed at enhancing technical skills,

[5]Robert L. Katz, "Skills of an Administrator," *Developing Executive Leaders,* ed. Edward C. Bursk (Cambridge, Massachusetts: Harvard University Press, 1971), p. 56.

human skills, and conceptual skills. Supervisors planning their own development programs can find ways to use these methods when appropriate and available.

Personal Management Development—Career Planning

One approach to personal management development is called career planning. Career planning in its simplest form involves setting down your major goals and interim objectives in the form of a chart or graph. It also means setting up a time schedule to let you know whether you are on track and on schedule. A career plan involves thinking and looking ahead. It means studying the advice and examples of those already ahead of you, following a few simple guidelines, and realistically appraising yourself.[6]

Career planning is one approach to personal management development. There are four key steps in personal management development. Let's examine them in turn.

The First Step: Know Yourself

The first, and possibly hardest step is to know yourself. It is hard to be objective about yourself, to clearly assess both strengths and weaknesses. It is so hard you may need help to carry out such an analysis. A growing number of psychological profile and vocational aptitude tests are available. Many personnel departments offer testing and counseling programs, and universities offer such services to students. Some companies use assessment centers, elaborate programs designed to assess management potential and determine development needs. The assessment is frequently done away from the organizational grounds. Managers selected for the program are given various interviews and individual and group tests. They are carefully observed by the professional staff. The results are used by higher management in making personnel decisions. Results are also fed back to the participants to aid them in building their own self-development plans.

At the present time, only a few large companies are using formal assessment centers. For the few supervisors who have such services available, this partially solves the problem of self-assessment. You should explore and use whatever assessment opportunities are available to you. There is no substitute for an accurate understanding of yourself.

Psychological profiles are only a possible beginning. Even more important, and certainly more down-to-earth, is the self-analysis of what

[6]See "Plotting a Route to the Top," *Business Week*, October 12, 1974, pp. 127–138.

you actually do and the results you achieve. How do you spend your time? What goals have you established? What are your priorities? What results have you achieved?

All supervisors can try to answer these questions themselves. It is frequently helpful to devise a special form so that you can record what you do and how long it takes. Such a study should be conducted for at least a week, and will help to answer some of the "what do I do" questions. If you prefer, you can devise a form that requires your analysis of each day in terms of decisions made, meetings attended, time wasted, things not done that should have been done, and so on. You are limited only by your ingenuity in devising reports and data sources to help in self-analysis. We have already reviewed some aids to self-analysis under the heading "Managing Time."

Of course, it is easier to get good feedback from a supportive boss than to generate it yourself. The total relationship between you and your boss is complex. But we are here concerned with those aspects of the relationship that affect learning and development. First, can we learn how to improve ourselves by studying the boss? Frequently, we can learn, even by studying the ways of a poor boss. If you've got a good one, so much the better. You can learn even more.

Second, what does the boss do to try to develop your abilities? Ideally, there should be a demonstrated interest in your growth and development. The boss may consent to serve as a "coach" for you, working closely with you in identifying and improving your weak points. At a minimum, your boss should be clear and helpful to you in your evaluation interviews and should work with you to establish clear goals for the next review period. In addition, this person should be supportive and objective, and provide specific information on what you need to do to improve.

We should mention other aspects of knowing yourself. Maslow has arranged man's needs into hierarchical form—a sequential ladder. He said that the needs that motivate people come in the following priority order (from lowest to highest): (1) Physiological needs; (2) safety and security needs; (3) love and belonging needs; (4) self-esteem needs; and (5) self-actualization. Higher level needs do not motivate us very effectively until lower level needs are met. What motivates you? Where do you stand on the ladder? Does this help you to understand yourself? For additional help, review chapter 10.

Also, we should note that David McClelland has studied basic motivational drives and has categorized them into three groups: (1) The need for achievement (which is an inner drive to be successful); (2) the need for affiliation; and (3) the need for power. People differ in their basic drives, but studies have shown that successful managers typically score higher than most others in tests of need for achievement. Furthermore, McClelland suggests that the need for achievement can be enhanced through proper training and experience. It seems clear that successful managers are highly motivated to achieve success, and are committed to their goals and to the concept of excellence in performance. How do you assess yourself with respect to these factors?

The Second Step: Know Your Goal

Committed managers know their goals and have a clear idea of how to attain them. There is simply no comparison between managers who have only a vague idea of their goals and those who are highly goal oriented. It is the difference between drift or ambiguity and purposive clarity. Frequently, it is the difference between success and failure.

There are many possible reasons why organizational goals are frequently unclear. We are all subject to human frailty. It is normal in organizational life for certain processes to muddy the waters. Sometimes, what was once a clear goal becomes deflected, so that the activity of "getting there" becomes more important than the goal itself. Sometimes we fail to communicate clearly and effectively. In some cases, disagreement arises over organizational goals. Whatever the reason, it is essential that confusion be eliminated and that goal clarity be established.

First, we must achieve clarity and understanding about organizational goals. This is a necessary foundation for both organizational effectiveness and management development. Second, we must establish individual goals with respect to management development. The two go together, but management development goals must necessarily be derived from organizational goals. They are like two sides of the same coin.

The evaluation interview can serve to communicate information and obtain commitment for both types of goals. Every manager should have an individual interview or counseling session with each subordinate at the beginning of the review period. These sessions should focus on goals for the review period, both organizational goals and management development goals. They should lead to an agreement as to the results expected, the forecast of relevant conditions during the review period forthcoming, and the organizational response appropriate if goals are or are not met. The interview should also focus on what the boss can do to help the subordinate achieve both organizational and development goals. At the end of the review period another interview focuses on assessing the results actually achieved, in contrast to the goals established. See chapter 5 for a review of these points.

The Third Step: Have a Plan

Planning is so essential to managerial behavior that it has been called the primary task of management. Planning involves evaluating the future course of events and making provisions for these events (or taking advantage of them). Planning makes things happen, rather than waiting for things to happen to you. It requires that we take an active hand in shaping the future, rather than merely reacting to it. Planning goes beyond forecasting to include choosing goals, charting courses of action, and moving along the chosen path to realizing the goal. Managers who are weak in their ability to plan effectively are not likely to be very successful. As managerial performance depends on planning, so too does personal management development.

Once you have a goal, information on your strengths and weaknesses, and an understanding of available career paths and improvement information, you need a plan. The plan puts it all together. Included in the plan should be:

1. Know your goals as you understand them. You should consider both long- and short-range goals.

2. Know your assumptions or planning premises. Assess the future. Determine controllable and uncontrollable factors. Seek to influence the controllable factors and forecast the uncontrollable ones. Get help from company sources or any other sources. Examine your assumptions very carefully, for you will be making important decisions based upon them.

3. Examine carefully the requirements of the job for which you would like to qualify next. Personnel people or your boss should be of great help here.

4. Make a personal inventory of strengths and limitations, experience, and management development progress and needs. This is an assessment of the resources you have available to meet your goals. Be frank and honest in your inventory.

5. Define your alternatives. What is available to meet your management development needs? What career progression is possible and likely?

6. Set priorities—what training or experience should come first?

7. Have an action program, the selection of alternatives and choice

of a course of action: What you plan to do and how you plan to do it. Develop your action program in a realistic sequence to get the job done.

8. Create timetables and mileposts. Some of these may be "guestimates," but the process will help you to manage your progress over time.

9. Plan for feedback. What kind of information do you need and when do you need it? What are your critical review points?

The Fourth Step: Establish Feedback and Review Points

You must make the most of your opportunities for training and experience. You can help assure this by establishing feedback and review points. Do not leave this to chance. Determine for yourself the time of review and the feedback required to help you decide if you are "on target."

You may find that charting your progress is helpful. Establish a planning path that represents your progress toward professional development and your management goals. You are probably familiar with Gantt charts or PERT charts. Create a similar chart for your development progress. Establish check lists of programs you need to complete (e.g. improve human relations skills or build an improved schedule to allocate your time). Build a plan of study for any formal classwork that may be helpful. Determine the intermediate job experience that will be helpful in developing your ability to handle the job that represents your ultimate goal.

We all know the essential difference between the manager with five years of experience and the manager with one year of experience repeated five times. The question is: How can we get the most from our experience? The answer is: We must learn from it. We must try to understand it. We must examine our decisions and management actions and learn from them. We must seek out challenges and strive to improve ourselves. We must solicit help from any relevant source in improving our understanding of our experience. It is never easy to do these things, especially when the press of new concerns leaves little time for a reexamination of experience. But it will pay dividends. It is worth the effort to make your experience more valuable to you. It is a key element in your personal management development.

Some Guidelines for Career Planning

Let's consider some career planning guidelines. They are just guides to action, and there is no guarantee that following them will lead to success. But see if you do not think they can help you as they have others.

1. Keep ahead of the field. Scan management and business journals for new ideas and trends. Read applied management books.

2. Be an innovator. Try new ideas or those borrowed from other organizations.

3. Prepare yourself for flexibility. Try to be adaptive and flexible in your approach to management problems. Invite suggestions from your subordinates and colleagues.

4. Join a professional management association. Go to at least some meetings, and compare notes and ideas with managers in other organizations.

5. Work constantly on your goals and priorities. Be a goal-directed person.

6. Stick to your plan. Update it as it becomes necessary, but don't toss it out or modify it drastically without an extensive study of the situation. If a drastic reevaluation seems required, get all the help you can. Here again, you should turn to the boss and to the personnel people for help if at all possible.

7. Seek out challenges; be visible. It goes without saying that there is an advantage to being the person who comes to mind when special problems and challenges come up. Many times in our professional lives we face decisions as to whether or not to accept challenges (and risks). When fate hands you the football, run with it as far as you can. Many managers who had initial doubts as to their ability to handle a job have grown to meet the challenge. So can you!

8. Maintain your mobility. The things that will maintain your mobility in the marketplace will also add to your value to your present organization. Attend professional meetings. Keep working on personal management development. Build an impressive list of accomplishments. Be knowledgeable about what is happening in the world of management.

9. Study your organization. Know the problems it faces, the past history, and the management philosophy. Examine what the future holds for this organization. Consider whether this organization is the best place for you to meet your goals, or whether you ought to be alert to other career opportunities.

10. Study your predecessors. Where did your boss come from and where is he or she going in the company? What about your boss's predecessor?

Does the company promote from within? How have others qualified for promotion? You can learn a lot by studying these questions.

Overview

The sports world has given us labels for some important managerial concepts. We have all heard of the importance of "a winning attitude," "paying the price for success," and "desire" (the team that most wants to win will win). A team leader recently inspired his colleagues to a peak effort with the slogan "Yes we can!" This phrase making illuminates some important truths. The lesson is not that confidence and attitude are everything and talent nothing. In sports and in management there is no substitute for ability. But there is also no substitute for desire, a positive attitude, and hard work toward clearly understood goals. This is what personal management development is all about.

This chapter has presented a framework for personal management development. Use it as best you can. It does not have all the answers, but it does show you the way. The principle of individual differences requires that any development program be tailored to your special needs. You must be involved in the process. This is why the concepts of career planning and personal management development are so important. Pay the price to develop your management potential. You can do it!

Questions for Discussion

1. What do we mean when we say that management development is self-development?

2. What are the respective responsibilities of the organization and the individual in management development?

3. Why do we need to understand organizational goals before we establish management development goals?

4. What kinds of technical, human, and conceptual skills does the supervisor need to develop?

5. Does growing management expertise lead automatically to a more "professional" concept of management?

6. How can we get the most from our experience?

7. How should we manage time as a resource?

Case Incidents

1. Bob Meyer has been a supervisor for the XYZ Manufacturing Company for five years. His boss indicates overall satisfaction with his work, but has not discussed Bob's goals with him, his need for development, or what his future might be with the company. As a result,

Bob has recently become somewhat dissatisfied, especially since his raises have been less than he thinks he deserved. What should Bob do now?

2. Steve Young is a supervisor in a large retail store. He has twenty people under him. He tries to schedule their work and his so that things run smoothly, but lately it seems that no matter what he does there is not enough time in the day. His phone rings constantly. His workers come to him with all manner of problems and information. Steve works long extra hours in the evening and on weekends, but he never seems to catch up. Steve mentioned the problem to his boss one time, but the boss did not seem too concerned. He told Steve that he was interested only in results, and that Steve should take whatever action was necessary to produce the expected results. What should Steve do now?

Index